Quantitative Methods

C I *m* A

Published in association
with the Chartered
Institute of Management
Accountants

Other titles in the CIMA series

Quantitative Methods

Stage 1

Kevin Pardoe

Heinemann Professional Publishing

Heinemann Professional Publishing Ltd
Halley Court, Jordon Hill, Oxford OX2 8EJ

OXFORD   LONDON   MELBOURNE   AUCKLAND

First published 1988

British Library Cataloguing in Publication Data
Pardoe, Kevin
  Quantitative methods: stage 1.
  1. Accounting. Quantitative methods
  I. Title
  657
 ISBN 0 434 91512 2

Printed in Great Britain
Redwood Burn Ltd, Trowbridge, Wiltshire

Contents

1 Introduction

There are many situations facing accountants and other management decision-makers in which a knowledge of mathematics and statistics can prove a valuable aid. In this text we explore six areas of quantitative methods which are of particular relevance to those involved in financial decisions and analyses.

We begin by laying the foundations of mathematics which will be necessary throughout the text. In addition, the first part introduces the concepts of a *graph*, a valuable aid in business communication, and of the *solution of equations*. The latter can assist in making many decisions such as:

'What product mix will fully utilize all available machinery?'

In Part Two we begin the study of statistics by considering how to obtain and describe the numerical information needed when solving certain business problems. In particular, further *graphical representations of information* are introduced and we answer commonly occurring questions such as:

'What are the typical weekly sales of this product?'

by looking at *averages* and other *descriptive statistics*.

Many business activities such as budgeting, planning, purchasing, and so on, depend critically on *forecasts* of sales, personnel requirements, or whatever. There are many approaches to the production of the necessary forecasts, some statistical, some otherwise. In Part Three we look at two of the major methods of statistical forecasting in business. In doing so, we shall be addressing typical questions such as:

'If we increase advertising expenditure by 10 per cent next year, what will be the effect on our sales?'
'I have some figures on past monthly overtime expenditures: can we use them to forecast our overtime requirements for the next year?'

1

In Part Four we investigate how statistics can aid in analysing problems involving uncertainty:

'How likely is it that this new product will be profitable?'
'You have budgeted a personnel cost between £600,000 and £700,000 for next year: how sure are you that the upper figure will be met?'

The formalization of the concept of uncertainty involves the study of *probability*. The six chapters of this section develop intuitive notions of 'chance' into a coherent theory of probability with many applications in finance and business decision-making.

Part Five sees a return to the study of mathematics, particularly those parts which concern *optimization*:

'What is the most efficient production level?'
'Which price level would give us most profit?'
'What combination of the available products would cost us least, while satisfying all our requirements?'

These and similar questions all involve making the best of things, by minimizing costs, maximizing profits, or whatever. The topics of *linear programming* and *calculus* are developed here since they are particularly suited to such optimization problems.

The final part concentrates on a number of areas of a more overtly financial nature. Beginning with fundamental calculations of *interest*, the section develops mathematical models and techniques that help solve problems of *investment appraisal, stock control*, and *project management*.

In conclusion, then, this text introduces a variety of mathematical and statistical aids to financial and management decision-making. It should be noted, however, that the methods *are* aids and do not replace the decision itself. As we shall indicate at appropriate points, all such techniques have inherent limitations and drawbacks, and management *judgement* is still required to use quantitative information.

Part One

Basic Business Mathematics

2 Functions, graphs and equations

Introduction

This first section is concerned with the basic mathematics which we shall need to use throughout the text. We begin by introducing a number of fundamental words and concepts.

Variables and functions

Anything which can have more than one value is called a *variable*. Thus the set of positive whole numbers can be considered as a variable. If we denote it by x, then this variable can have many values

$x = 1$
or $x = 2$
or $x = 3$, and so on.

Another example is the set of the major points of a compass. If this variable is denoted by c, then it can have more than one, but only a limited number, of values:

$c =$ north
$c =$ south
$c =$ north-west, and so on.

These examples show that variables can take on non-numerical 'values' as well as numerical ones. In this text we shall concentrate on *numerical variables*, that is, those whose values are numbers, like the first case above.

A mathematical *function* is a rule or method of determining the value of one numerical variable from the values of other numerical variables. Initially, we shall concentrate on the case where one variable is determined by or depends on just *one* other variable. The first variable is

4

called the *dependent* variable, and is usually denoted y, while the second is called the *independent* variable, denoted x. The relationship between them is a *function of one variable*, often referred to as a 'function', for brevity.

A very useful way of stating a function is in terms of an *equation*, which is an expression containing an 'equals' sign. The *equation of a function* will thus take the typical form

$y = $ a mathematical expression containing x.

If we know the value of the independent variable x, then the expression will completely determine the corresponding value of the dependent variable, y. We give some illustrative examples.

Example 2.1:
The following equations represent functions of one variable. Evaluate the dependent variable when the independent variable has the value 2.

(a) $y = 3 + 2x$
(b) $y = x$
(c) $y = 1 + x + 3x^2$

To find the value of y, we write the known value of x (2 in this case) in place of x in the mathematical expression and perform the necessary arithmetical calculations. This is known as the *substitution* of the x–value into the equation.

(a)   Substituting $x = 2$ gives

$$y = 3 + 2 \times 2$$
$$= 3 + 4$$
$$= 7$$

Thus the dependent variable has the value 7 in this case.

(b)   Clearly, this dependent variable has the value 2, the same as x.
(c)   Substituting $x = 2$:

$$y = 1 + 2 + 3 \times 2^2$$
$$= 1 + 2 + 12$$
$$= 15$$

so the dependent variable has the value *15* here.

Graphs of functions. Linear graphs

For each function of one variable, there is an associated *graph*. This is a pictorial representation in which every value of x, with its associated value of y, is shown. In order to do this, pairs of values of x and y are *plotted* on graph paper as follows:

Example 2.2:
Calculate the values of y in the function

$y = 3 + 2x$

corresponding to the values $x = 2$
$$x = 1$$
$$x = 3$$
$$x = 4$$

Plot the four corresponding pairs of values on a graph and hence draw the graph of the function.

This function was introduced in example 2.1(a), where we saw that,

when $x = 2$, $y = 7$.

Substituting $x = 1$ gives

$y = 3 + 2 \times 1$
$= 3 + 2$
$= 5$

In the same way, it can be seen that $x = 3$ gives $y = 9$
$$x = 4 \text{ gives } y = 11.$$

The four pairs of values are shown as the points A, B, C and D respectively in Figure 2.1. Two things should be noted about this figure:

1   Values of x are always measured in a horizontal direction, along the x–axis: positive values to the right, negative to the left. Values of y are measured in a vertical direction, along the y–axis: positive values upwards, negative downwards. Thus the point A is plotted by moving from the point where the axes cross (the *origin*, where both variables have value zero)

    2 to the right (*plus* 2)
    7 upwards   (*plus* 7).

    These values are known as the x– and y– *coordinates* of A, respectively.

2   Note the *scales* on the two axes. These distances are marked off on each axis as an aid to plotting. They need not be the same as each other (indeed, they are not in this case) but they must be consistent. In other words, if you decide that one square on your graph paper equals one unit (or whatever) along the x–axis, you must keep this scale throughout the x–axis.

We can now join the points up, in order to form the graph of the function. It will be noted that, in this case, the points lie *exactly* on a straight line, and so the joining up can be done best with a ruler. This is an example of a *linear graph*.

The next example has a more practical setting.

Example 2.3:
A company sells a product at £10 per unit. If it sells x units daily, then its revenue (£y) is represented by the function

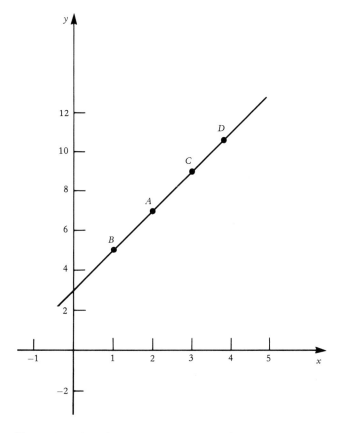

Figure 2.1 *Plot of points and line, example 2.2*

$y = 10x$

The fixed daily costs of producing the product are £100, and the variable costs are £6 per unit. Daily costs (£) are

$y = 100 + 6x$.

Plot the graphs of these two functions for daily production figures (x) from 0 to 60 in steps of 10.

The question advises us to plot just seven points; so we begin by systematically calculating the necessary y–values.

Revenue calculations

x	0	10	20	30	40	50	60
$y = 10x$	0	100	200	300	400	500	600

Cost calculations

x	0	10	20	30	40	50	60
100	100	100	100	100	100	100	100
6x	0	60	120	180	240	300	360
y = 100 + 6x	100	160	220	280	340	400	460

Note how, in the latter, slightly more complicated, case, the calculation of y has been broken into stages, which are then added to get the total value of y.

The calculated points are plotted as crosses in Figure 2.2. This has been done in the same way as before, but the origin has been placed at the bottom left, since there are no negative $x-$ or $y-$ values. In this instance, the scales on the axes have commercial meaning and so have been marked appropriately.

As in the preceding example, we can see that the two sets of points lie *exactly* on straight lines, and so can be joined using a ruler. In fact, you can check that *all* the intermediate points *do* lie on the straight line. For instance,

$x = 15$ gives revenue $= 150$
and cost $\qquad = 190$

and these two values can be seen to lie on the respective lines.

We shall shortly be using such graphs, but the reader may wish to consider now what lessons the company can draw from Figure 2.2.

Functions whose graphs are straight lines are called *linear functions*. Much time could be saved if you could recognize a linear function *before* beginning the calculations necessary to plot its graph: only *three* points need then be found and a ruler used, the third being a check on accuracy of calculation and plotting. By looking at their equations, you will see that the three linear functions seen so far have the form

$y = a + bx$, where a and b are numbers.

In the revenue function of example 2.3:

$y = 10x$, and so $a = 0$, $b = 10$;

and in the cost function:

$y = 100 + 6x$, and so $a = 100$, $b = 6$.

In fact, *all* linear functions have this form and, conversely, *all* functions of this form are linear. It is, therefore, possible to recognize a linear function from its equation in the *general linear form*

$y = a + bx$.

The numbers a and b in this expression are given names: a, called the *intercept*, is the value of y when x is zero, and so is the length 'cut off' or intercepted on the $y-$axis by the line. Also, b is the *gradient* or slope of the line, representing the increase in y per unit increase in x. In the cost graph of Figure 2.2, for example,

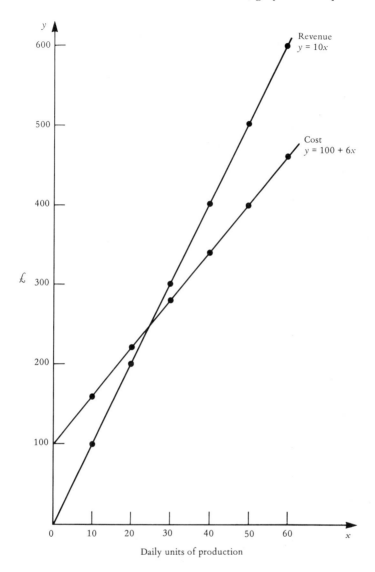

Figure 2.2 *Revenue and cost functions, example 2.3*

the graph cuts the y–axis at the point $y = 100$, and so $a = 100$;
the line rises by £6 for every extra unit of production, and so $b = 6$.

Example 2.4:
A small workshop manufactures just one article. From past experience, it is known that:

if 50 units are produced weekly, the total manufacturing costs are £1800;

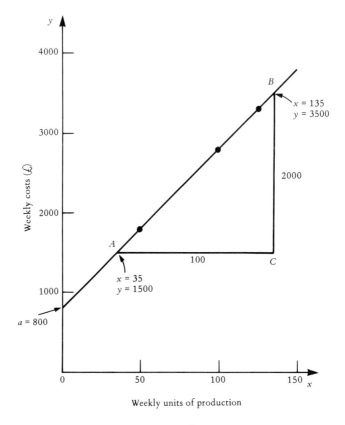

Figure 2.3 *Cost function, example 2.4*

    if 100 units are produced weekly, total costs are £2800;
and if 125 units are produced weekly, total costs are £3300.
(a)   Assuming costs form a linear function, draw a graph and find the
      intercept and gradient of the corresponding line, and hence state
      the equation of the weekly cost function.
(b)   What are the commercial meanings of the gradient and intercept of
      this linear cost function?
The three given points have been plotted in Figure 2.3, with x as the
number of units of production and y as the costs. The variables have
been allocated this way round because costs are the *dependent* variable
(depending on the number of units made) and so are denoted by y. We
are told to assume a linear function, and so a straight line has been
drawn.
(a)   A reading from the graph shows that the intercept (on the y–axis)
      has value
            $a = 800$.

The triangle ABC has been drawn in to enable us to calculate the gradient. It shows that, as we move from A to B, x increases from 35 to 135 while y increases from 1500 to 3500. Thus

b = increase in y per *unit* increase in x

$$= \frac{3500 - 1500}{135 - 35}$$

$$= 20$$

There is nothing special about the triangle we have used: any other choice of A and B on the line would give the same value for b.

The cost function therefore has the linear equation

$y = 800 + 20x.$

(b) The value 800 (£) is the cost (y) incurred if there is no production ($x = 0$). It thus represents the *weekly fixed costs* of production. The value 20 (£) is the increase in costs if the level of production increases by one. Therefore, it is the *variable cost* of one unit's production.

Quadratic functions and graphs

A *quadratic* function is one of the form

$y = a + bx + cx^2,$

where a, b and c are numbers, so called because of the 'squared' or quadratic term in the expression. This quadratic term clearly distinguishes such functions from linear ones, and so we should not expect their graphs to be straight lines. One consequence is that more than three points require plotting to get an accurate graph.

Example 2.5:
In the range 0 to 100 units of production, a factory's daily cost function (£) for a certain item is

$y = 500 + 5x,$

where x is the number of units produced daily.

In the same range, the price (£P) the company can obtain for each unit of the item is related to daily production by

$P = 25 - 0.1x$

(a) Show that the company's daily revenue function (£) for the item is

$y = 25x - 0.1x^2$

(b) Plot these revenue and cost functions.

(a) The company can sell x units at £P each; so the revenue is

£$P.x$

Thus the daily revenue function is

$$y = Px$$
$$y = (25 - 0.1x)x$$
$$y = 25x - 0.1x^2$$

(b)   First of all, we note that the cost function is linear, and so only three points need be plotted. The revenue function is quadratic:

$$y = a + bx + cx^2, \text{ with } a = 0$$
$$b = 25$$
$$c = -0.1$$

Therefore, more than three points will be plotted. Exactly how many is our choice, provided we stay in the given valid range of x, namely 0 to 100. Generally speaking, the more points are plotted, the more accurate is the graph.

Cost calculations

x	0	50	100
500	500	500	500
$5x$	0	250	500
$y = 500 + 5x$	500	750	1000

Revenue calculations

x	0	20	40	60	80	100
$25x$	0	500	1000	1500	2000	2500
$-0.1x^2$	0	-40	-160	-360	-640	-1000
$y = 25x - 0.1x^2$	0	460	840	1140	1360	1500

The graphs are plotted in Figure 2.4. Note that the cost graph is *exact*, as it must be a straight line. The revenue graph, however, is only an *estimate*, as we have had to gauge where the curve goes between the plotted points. It *is* a curve, with no 'sharp points' or straight portions. We could have obtained a better estimate of the graph by plotting at x–intervals of ten, but this would have been more time-consuming.

Summary

A *function* of one variable is a rule, equation or formula for determining one variable (the dependent variable, y) from another (the independent variable, x). The *graph* of a function is (theoretically) obtained by plotting all pairs of coordinates (x, y) associated by the function against a pair of axes. In practice, only a few points are plotted and the graph gauged from these.

A *linear* function is one whose graph is a straight line. Its general form is

$$y = a + bx$$

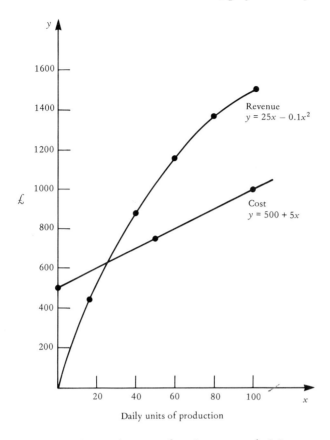

Figure 2.4 *Cost and revenue functions, example 2.5*

where *a* is the *intercept*, or value at which the line cuts the *y*–axis, and *b* is the *gradient*, or increase in *y* per unit increase in *x*.

A *quadratic* function has a parabolic shaped graph and has the general form

$$y = a + bx + cx^2.$$

Exercises on Chapter 2

1 (a) Draw the graph of the linear function which passes through the points $x = 1, y\ \ = -1$
$x = -2, y = -7$
$x = 3, y\ \ = 3.$

Determine the gradient and intercept of this line and hence the function's equation. (Note that the intercept has a *negative* value in this instance.)

(*b*)   Plot on the same graph paper the graphs of the functions

$$y = 1 + x$$
$$\text{and } y = -1 - x + \tfrac{1}{4}x^2$$

for x between -2 and $+3$.

2   A hire car company charges a standard fee of £5 to be called out, then 70p for every mile travelled. The revenue for a journey of x miles is therefore given by the function

$$y = 500 + 70x \text{ (pence)}.$$

In a costing exercise, the company allocates £2.50 as a fixed cost to every journey. The running (variable) cost of the cars is 50p per mile. The total cost (y pence) of a journey of x miles is thus

$$y = 250 + 50x.$$

If the company will not undertake journeys over 50 miles, plot the graph of the revenue and cost functions for a journey undertaken by this company.

3   (*a*)   In a very price-sensitive market, a manufacturer reckons that, for selling prices between £10 and £100 per unit, the number of units which he can sell (u per week) is related to the price (£x) by

$$u = 600 - 2x.$$

Show that the manufacturer's weekly revenue function (in terms of *price, £x*) is

$$y = 600x - 2x^2 \quad \text{(£)}.$$

(*b*)   The weekly fixed costs are £5,000 and the variable manufacturing costs are £20 per unit. The total weekly costs (£) are therefore given by

$$y = 5000 + 20u.$$

Show that this gives a weekly cost function *in terms of x* (selling price)

$$y = 17000 - 40x.$$

(*c*)   Plot the graphs of the weekly revenue and cost functions for values of x (selling price) from £10 to £100. (Note that the cost function slopes *downwards*, due to its *negative* gradient, -40.)

4   (*a*)   The equation of the straight line in Figure 2.5(a) is

A $y = 2x$
B $y = -2x$
C $y = 4 - 2x$
D $2y = 4 - x$
E $y = 4 + \tfrac{1}{2}x$.

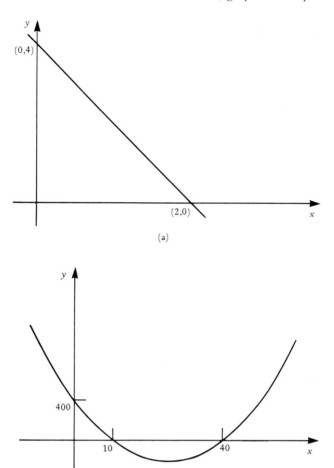

Figure 2.5 *Graphs for exercise 4*

(b) Which of the following best describes the parabola in Figure 2.5(b)?

    A $y = x + 400$
    B $y = x^2 - 50x - 400$
    C $y = x^2 - 50x + 400$
    D $y - 400 = x - 10$
    E $y = x^2 + 30x + 400$

ICMA, November 1985.

5   A manufacturer has fixed costs of £5,000 per week and variable costs of

$$\tfrac{1}{2}x^2 + 10x,$$

where x is the number of tons produced. Research has shown that, within the range of practicable prices, the relationship between price, p, and quantity, x, is approximately

$$p = 160 - \tfrac{1}{2}x.$$

All production can be sold.
Determine the weekly cost function, show that the weekly revenue function is

$$y = 160x - \tfrac{1}{2}x^2,$$

and plot the graphs of these two functions for x–values up to 300.
ICMA, May 1982.

6   Following market research into the price elasticity of demand for one of your products, you have established that there is a linear relationship between sales (x units) and selling price (y, £/unit) over the price range £3.80 to £4.70 per unit. When

$y = $ £3.80/unit, sales are expected to be 10,200 units;
$y = $ £4.70/unit, sales are expected to decline to 7,500 units.

(a)   Determine the equation of the linear function

$$y = a + bx.$$

(b)   The total cost function is

$$\text{total cost} = \text{£15,000} + \text{£1.80}x.$$

Determine the revenue function, in terms of x, and plot the revenue and cost functions.
ICMA, November 1980.

3 Solution of equations

Introduction

We met the term *equation* in Chapter 2, relating to functions. In this chapter we look at the *solution* of equations, which consists of the determination of the unknown values of variables which make the two sides of an equation balance. This will enable us to solve certain types of practical problems.

Linear equations: Graphical solution

As we saw in Chapter 2, a linear function is one with an equation of the form

$$y = a + bx.$$

A *linear equation* is an equation based on such a function and takes the form

$$a + bx = 0,$$

the problem being to find the value(s) of x which *satisfy* this expression, that is, those value(s) of x which make the expression '$a + bx$' precisely equal to zero.

Example 3.1:
If a company produces and sells x units in a day, its profit function (£y) is

$$y = -100 + 4x.$$

(a)   Plot the graph of this function for x–values from 0 to 60.
(b)   At what value of x is

$$y = 0 ?$$

17

(c)   What equation has been solved here? What is the commercial significance of the solution?

(a)   Noting that this is a linear function, we have plotted only three points to arrive at Figure 3.1. (The details of the calculations are left as an exercise for the reader.)

(b)   The point at which y is zero is where the graph crosses the x–axis. This is indicated on the figure, and so can be seen to be

$x = 25$ *units.*

(c)   If we write y as zero in the equation of the function, the equation solved is

$-100 + 4x = 0.$

The solution is

$x = 25.$

The commercial importance is that this is the production level at which the company begins to make a profit. Below 25 units per day, a loss is being made, and above, a profit is made. Such a point is called a *breakeven point.*

Before leaving this example, we note that this linear equation has produced just *one* solution. That is, only one value of x makes the value of '$a + bx$' equal to zero. If you consider a straight line crossing the x–axis, you can see that this is always the case.

Quadratic equations: Graphical solution

Just as the concept of a linear function was extended to that of a linear equation, so can a quadratic function give rise to a *quadratic equation*. A quadratic equation is one of the form

$y = a + bx + cx^2,$

and so a quadratic equation has the form

$a + bx + cx^2 = 0.$

Example 3.2:
In the range 0 to 100 units, the daily profit a company can make from producing and selling x units is given by the function

$y = -500 + 20x - 0.1x^2$ (£)

(a)   Plot the graph of this function.
(b)   Determine the breakeven point(s) in this case.

(a)   In plotting this graph (Figure 3.2), which is *not* linear, more than three points have been used. In fact, steps in x–values of 20 were computed: the details are left to the reader.
(b)   The breakeven point(s) occur where the profit is zero, and so, effectively, we are being asked to solve the equation

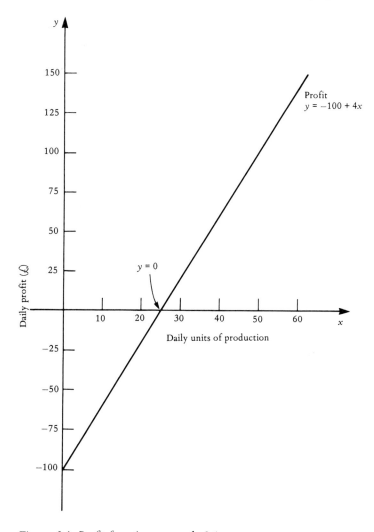

Figure 3.1 *Profit function, example 3.1*

$$-500 + 20x - 0.1x^2 = 0$$

This solution, marked on the figure, occurs at approximately

$x = 29$ units.

It should be emphasized that this value is only *approximate* because the graph is the result of our estimating where the curve passes between the six plotted points.

This example again shows only one breakeven point. As we shall see later, a quadratic equation can have up to (and including) *two* solutions.

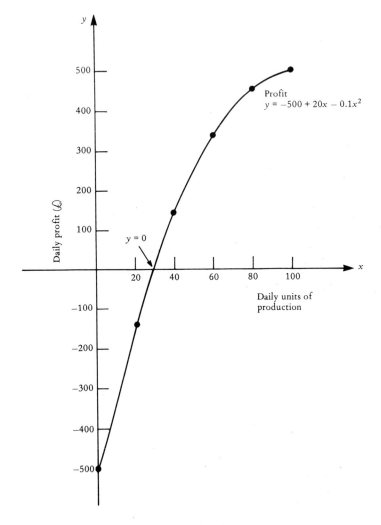

Figure 3.2 *Profit function, example 3.2*

In the example above, the curvature of the graph is such that, beyond the points plotted, the profit curve would decrease to cross the x–axis at a second point, with an x–value of over 100.

Algebraic solution of equations

The graphical method of solving equations, illustrated above, has two major drawbacks. First of all, it is rather time-consuming to plot a graph, particularly in the case of a quadratic, and, secondly, the solutions found may only be approximations, as shown in example 3.2.

Solving equations by a series of mathematical manipulations can, with practice, prove to be both fast and accurate.

There are two basic manipulations used to solve linear equations. A number can be taken to the other side of an equation, provided its sign is changed. Thus, in

$$a + bx = 0$$

the a can be transferred to the right-hand side of the equation to give,

$$bx = -a.$$

Also both sides of an equation can be divided by the same number. Hence, both sides of the equation

$$bx = -a$$

can be divided by b to give

$$\frac{bx}{b} = \frac{-a}{b}$$

that is

$$x = \frac{-a}{b},$$

which is the solution of the equation.

Although the last expression can be regarded as a *formula* for the solution of the general linear equation, the reader is encouraged to master the steps involved, as they will be useful later.

Example 3.3:
Solve the equation of example 3.1 algebraically.

The equation involved here is

$$-100 + 4x = 0.$$

Rather than substitute values in the formula, we shall go through the two steps, as an illustration. First of all, we transfer the '−100' to the right-hand side, changing its sign, to get

$$4x = 100.$$

Now we divide both sides by 4:

$$\frac{4x}{4} = \frac{100}{4}$$
$$x = 25,$$

which gives the same answer as from the graph, but in considerably less time.

We now consider the quadratic equation

$$a + bx + cx^2 = 0$$

The algebraic steps leading up to the formula for solving this are not as generally useful as those for the linear equation above, and so they are omitted here. Readers interested in the algebra involved should consult a standard pure mathematics text. The solutions of the quadratic equation are

$$x = \frac{-b \pm \sqrt{b^2 - 4ac}}{2c}$$

The '±' (plus or minus) symbolism means that we get *two* solutions, one by taking

$$+\sqrt{b^2 - 4ac}$$

and one by taking

$$-\sqrt{b^2 - 4ac}.$$

Example 3.4:
Solve the equation of example 3.2 using this quadratic formula.
   The equation is

$$-500 + 20x - 0.1x^2 = 0$$

Hence

$a = -500$
$b = +20$
$c = -0.1,$

so, substituting these values into the formula, (and taking care not to omit any minus signs):

$$x = \frac{-20 \pm \sqrt{400 - 4(-500)(-0.1)}}{-0.2}$$

$$= \frac{-20 \pm \sqrt{200}}{-0.2}$$

The two solutions are thus

$$x = \frac{-20 + 14.142}{-0.2} = 29.29$$

$$\text{and } x = \frac{-20 - 14.142}{-0.2} = 170.71$$

The first of these is the accurate version of the answer found graphically in example 3.2. If the product concerned was a motor car or a washing machine, it would be practical to round this answer to 29, as it is difficult to produce or sell 0.29 of a car! The second solution, outside the range 0 to 100, is the one referred to at the end of the graphical treatment of this problem.

Problem solving

The ability to solve equations can be very useful when tackling certain practical problems. If a problem involves finding an unknown quantity, you can often denote the unknown by 'x', and set up an equation involving x. Solving the equation by one of the above methods then determines the required value of x.

Example 3.5:
A company has a monopoly on a certain item it produces. The weekly fixed costs of manufacturing the item are £2,000 and the variable costs are £500 per unit. The company finds that, if it charges £P per unit, it can sell x units per week where

$$P = 1000 - 10x.$$

Determine the weekly revenue and cost functions. Hence determine the profit function, the breakeven points and the consequent price range the company should consider charging for the item.

The company can sell x units per week at £P each, and so

$$\text{weekly revenue} = xP$$
$$= x(1000 - 10x)$$
$$= 1000x - 10x^2.$$

If the company produces the x units per week it can sell, these will cost £500 each to make, plus the weekly fixed costs of £2,000. Thus

$$\text{total weekly cost} = 2000 + 500x.$$

Now, profits are the difference between revenue and cost, and so, denoting weekly profits by £y:

$$y = 1000x - 10x^2 - (2000 + 500x)$$
$$= 1000x - 10x^2 - 2000 - 500x,$$

that is:

$$y = -2000 + 500x - 10x^2.$$

The breakeven points occur where profits are zero:

$$0 = -2000 + 500x - 10x^2.$$

The arithmetic in the formula is easier if this equation is first divided through by 10 to give

$$0 = -200 + 50x - x^2.$$

This is a quadratic equation, and so, substituting

$$a = -200$$
$$b = +50$$
$$c = -1$$

into the formula for solving a quadratic equation, we have

$$x = \frac{-50 \pm \sqrt{2500 - 4(-200)(-1)}}{-2}$$
$$= \frac{-50 \pm \sqrt{1700}}{-2}$$

The two solutions are thus

$$x = \frac{-50 + 41.231}{-2} = 4.38, \text{ rounded to } 4,$$

and $x = \frac{-50 - 41.231}{-2} = 45.62, \text{ rounded to } 46.$

The selling prices associated with these weekly sales and production levels are

$$x = \quad 4: P = 1000 - 10 \times 4$$
$$= £960$$
$$x = 46: P = 1000 - 10 \times 46$$
$$= £540$$

Hence the breakeven price levels are £540 *per unit*, at which price *46* units can be sold per week, and *£960*, when *4* units can be sold per week. The company would be advised to fix its prices, and corresponding production levels, between these two figures.

Example 3.6:
A farmer has 1000 metres of fencing to build a rectangular enclosure. Because of the amount of grazing land he wishes to allocate to each animal in the enclosure, he determines that its area should be 50,000 square metres. If all the fencing is to be used up, what should the dimensions of the enclosure be?

We introduce an unknown quantity 'x' as one of the factors we need to find. Suppose the length of one side of the enclosure is x metres, then the opposite side of the rectangle will be the same. What of the other pair of sides?

The perimeter is to be 1000 metres, the first pair of sides has total length $2x$ metres, and so this second pair must add up to

$1000 - 2x$ metres.

Hence each one is

$\dfrac{1000 - 2x}{2}$

or $(500 - x)$ metres long.

Now the area, in terms of x, is simply the area of a rectangle:

$x (500 - x)$ square metres

and this has to be 50,000 square metres. Hence

$x (500 - x) = 50,000$

which gives

$$-50,000 + 500x - x^2 = 0,$$

a quadratic equation in x.
   To solve this, substitute

$$a = -50,000$$
$$b = 500$$
$$c = -1$$

into the formula:

$$x = \frac{-500 \pm \sqrt{250,000 - 4(-50,000)(-1)}}{-2}$$

$$= \frac{-500 \pm \sqrt{50,000}}{-2}$$

The solutions are thus

$$x = \frac{-500 + 223.6}{-2} = 138.2$$

and $x = \dfrac{-500 - 223.6}{-2} = 361.8.$

We note that if one pair of sides is 138.2 metres long, then the other pair is

$$500 - 138.2 = 361.8 \text{ metres long,}$$

and vice versa. The farmer should therefore construct the rectangular enclosure with sides of length 138.2 metres and 361.8 metres.

Summary

A *linear equation* in x is one of the form

$$a + bx = 0$$

and has the solution

$$x = -\frac{a}{b}.$$

A *quadratic equation* in x is of the form

$$a + bx + cx^2 = 0$$

and has solutions

$$x = \frac{-b \pm \sqrt{b^2 - 4ac}}{2c}$$

A *breakeven point* is a level of sales and production, or the corresponding selling price, at which costs and revenue balance, and so profits are zero.

Exercises on Chapter 3

1 Plot the graphs of

   $y = 2 + 3x$
   $y = -1 + 2x - x^2$
   $y = 1 - x + x^2$

   for x-values from -2 to $+3$.
     Use the graphs to solve

$$2 + 3x = 0$$
$$-1 + 2x - x^2 = 0$$
$$1 - x + x^2 = 0$$

   Check your solutions algebraically. In what way do the two quad-ratic examples differ from those earlier in the chapter?

2 For daily production levels up to 80 units per day, the management of a factory know that the total daily costs of producing x units are given by

   $200 + 20x + 0.1x^2$.

   Within this same range, the price (£p) at which the daily produc-tion of x units can be sold is given by

   $p = 80 - x$.

   Determine the daily revenue and hence the daily profit function. Discuss the factory's breakeven points.

3 A customer of a certain company feels that the amount she is charged for a certain article consists of a fixed delivery charge, regardless of the number of units bought, plus so much per unit. The last time she put in an order for 50 items, she was charged £90. If the customer feels that, in view of the distance involved, £15 would be a reasonable delivery charge, what should be the unit price of the article?
   (Hint: call this price £x and set up an equation in x).
     If, in fact, the delivery charge turned out to be £25, what would the unit price of the article be?

4 Last year a company began marketing a new (copyright) board game, Zqkopoly. Experience to date has shown that about 300 games per week can be sold at a selling price of £20 each, but if the price is reduced to £13, about 440 can be sold.

   (a) Assuming a linear relationship between P (price per unit) and X (quantity of units sold per week), show that

   $$P = 35 - \frac{1}{20} X.$$

(b) Write down the equation for the company's revenue in terms of
X.

(c) The company has fixed costs of £2,000 per week and variable
costs of £10X per week. Write down the equation for total cost
in terms of X.

(d) Determine the company's profit function and hence its
breakeven point(s).

ICMA, May 1985.

5 Many of the examples in Chapter 2 can be seen, with the hindsight of
this chapter, to be concerned to some extent with breakeven points.
In each of the following cases determine the profits as a function of x
(units of production) and hence find the breakeven point(s) by solving, *algebraically*, the quadratic equation

profits $= 0$:

example 2.5;
exercise 5;
exercise 6.

In each case, compare the solutions with the graphs already
drawn.

4 Problems in two unknowns

Introduction

All the problems encountered in Chapter 3 had effectively just one unknown quantity and one equation with which to find it. We now extend our attention to problems involving two unknowns, with two equations to solve in order to find them. Because the two equations have to be satisfied together, the topic is often referred to as the solution of *simultaneous equations*.

Simultaneous linear equations

We begin by looking at an alternative form for the equation of a straight line. It may not be obvious that

$$2x + 3y = 13$$

in fact represents a straight line. This can be demonstrated by using some of the techniques from Chapter 3.

First of all, take the '2x' term to the other side of the equation, changing its sign:

$$3y = 13 - 2x.$$

Now divide throughout by 3:

$$y = \frac{13}{3} - \frac{2}{3}x.$$

This is now in the familiar linear form

$$y = a + bx, \text{ with } a = \frac{13}{3} \text{ and } b = -\frac{2}{3}.$$

In this way, any equation

$rx + sy = t$, with r, s, t numbers,

can be shown to be linear.

We now look at examples in which we have two simultaneous equations, both of which are linear.

Example 4.1:
Find the values of x and y from the simultaneous equations

$$x + y = 5 \quad \text{(i)}$$
$$2x + 3y = 13 \quad \text{(ii)}.$$

These two equations are of the alternative linear form shown above. The problem could be solved graphically by plotting the two lines, and seeing where they cross. We do not do this, as it is considerably more time-consuming than an algebraic approach, but if you can picture the graphs of two straight lines, you will appreciate that they will either be parallel, in which case they will not cross and there will be no solution to the problem, or they will cross at *one* point, giving one solution for x and one for y.

The algebraic approach we adopt consists of manipulating one or both equations so that the number of x's or the number of y's in both is the same. Then, by subtracting one equation from the other, one of the variables will be eliminated, leaving a simple equation in just x or y to solve.

Thus, here, we could multiply equation (i) by 2 (to make the number of x's the same), or by 3 (to make the number of y's the same). There is no advantage either way. Adopting the former

$$\text{(i)} \times 2: 2x + 2y = 10 \quad \text{(iii)}$$
$$\text{Repeating (ii): } 2x + 3y = 13 \quad \text{(ii)}.$$

Subtracting (iii)–(ii)
termwise: $0 - y = -3$

The resulting equation is a linear one, giving the value of y as:

$$y = +3.$$

Finally, to determine x, the now known value of y can be substituted into one of the earlier equations: it does not matter which. We choose (i):

$$x + 3 = 5,$$

an ordinary linear equation in x, which gives

$$x = +2.$$

Thus the solution to the two simultaneous equations is $x = 2$, $y = 3$.

Example 4.2:
A shopkeeper wishes to check on the prices she pays for two articles on sale in her shop, but has mislaid the invoices. Her handwritten records, however, show that, in the last order,

6 of item X were bought, 7 of item Y, and the total cost was £34.

In the order prior to that,

5 of item X were bought, 8 of item Y, and the total cost was £37.

What are the unit prices of the two items?

We set up two simultaneous linear equations by denoting the two unknown quantities by x and y. That is, we put

the price of a unit of X equal to £x;
the price of a unit of Y equal to £y.

If we now look at the last order:

6 of item X were bought at £x, cost $= £6x$
7 of item Y were bought at £y, cost $= £7y$
total cost $= £(6x + 7y)$.

As the total cost is known to have been £34, we have

$6x + 7y = 34$ (i).

In the same way, the information on the penultimate order gives

$5x + 8y = 37$ (ii).

Now, to solve these, we could, for example, multiply equation (i) by $\frac{5}{6}$, to equalize the number of x's. However, using such fractions makes the problem more complicated than it need be, as it is possible to use whole numbers if we multiply *each* equation by a suitable factor.

(i) × 5: $30x + 35y = 170$ (iii)
(ii) × 6: $30x + 48y = 222$ (iv)
(iii)–(iv): $0 - 13y = -52$.

Thus

$y = +4$.

(An equally good approach would be to multiply the first equation by 8 and the second by 7, thus making the number of y's equal.)

Now, substituting this y–value into equation (i):

$6x + 28 = 34$
$6x \quad\quad = 6$
$x \quad\quad = 1$

Hence item X costs £1 per unit and item Y costs £4 per unit.

One linear and one quadratic equation

This section is concerned with two simultaneous equations in two unknowns, x and y, in which one equation is linear and one quadratic. In other words,

$rx + sy = t$ (the more general linear form seen earlier)

and $y = a + bx + cx^2$.

As the example following will demonstrate, the easiest way of dealing with such problems is to transform the linear equation into its more familiar form

$y = $ intercept $ + $ gradient. x,

which can then be substituted into the other expression to obtain an ordinary quadratic equation.

Example 4.3:

In the price range £50 to £150 per unit, the price elasticity of a product is such that the daily number of units a manufacturing company can sell (x) is related to the unit selling price (£P) by

$P = 200 - 5x$.

(*a*)   Determine the daily revenue as a function of x.

Past experience shows that the total daily costs (£y) and the number of units produced during the day (x) are related by

$-x + 0.0125y = 5$.

(*b*)   Investigate the company's breakeven point(s).

The solution to (a) is found as follows:
the company can sell daily x units at £P each, and so can obtain a revenue of:

$£Px = (200 - 5x)x$.

Hence

the daily revenue $ = £(200x - 5x^2)$.

Proceeding to (b), the breakeven point(s) occur where the daily revenue equals the daily cost (£y) and so, *at the breakeven point(s),*

$y = 200x - 5x^2$ \hfill (i).

Further, we are told

$-x + 0.0125y = 5$ \hfill (ii).

We must now solve these two simultaneous equations. To do so, we first change equation (ii) into a more familiar form:

$-x + 0.0125y = 5$

$0.0125y = 5 + x$

$$y = \frac{5}{0.0125} + \frac{x}{0.0125}$$

$y = 400 + 80x$ \hfill (iii).

This expression for y can be substituted into equation (i):

$$400 + 80x = 200x - 5x^2$$
$$-200x + 5x^2 + 400 + 80x = 0$$
$$400 - 120x + 5x^2 = 0.$$

This is now a standard quadratic equation which can be solved using an earlier formula. Before doing so, we note that the arithmetic can be made easier by first dividing through by 5:

$$80 - 24x + x^2 = 0.$$

Substituting $a = 80$
$$b = 24$$
$$c = 1$$

into the quadratic formula:

$$x = \frac{24 \pm \sqrt{576 - 320}}{2}$$
$$= \frac{24 \pm 16}{2}$$

and so $x = 20$ or $x = 4$.
The corresponding values of y can now be found from equation (iii):

$$x = 20: \quad y = 400 + 80 \times 20$$
$$= 2000$$
$$x = 4: \quad y = 400 + 80 \times 4$$
$$= 720.$$

Finally, we note that a daily sale of 20 units corresponds to a unit price (£P) of £100, while 4 units corresponds to a price of £180. However, the latter does not lie in the price range for which the price-demand equation is valid, namely £50 to £150. Thus we assert that the company breaks even when its selling price is *£100/unit*, when *20* units are sold per day. At this point, both total costs and revenue are *£2000 per day*.

The above equation had two pairs of solutions (x, y), although one had to be discounted because it lay outside the range of validity of one of the equations. In general a straight line could cross a parabola (a quadratic function has a parabolic graph):

twice, as above;
once, if the line just touches the parabola in one place;
or not at all, if the line completely 'misses' the curve.

Hence simultaneous equations of this type can have zero, one or two pairs of solutions.

Summary

Two equations in two unknowns are known as a pair of *simultaneous equations*. If they are both linear, they can be solved by multiplying one or both equations by suitable values to make the number of x's (or y's) equal, and then subtracting.

The general form of a straight line is

$$rx + sy = t$$

where r, s, t are numbers.

A pair of simultaneous equations, one linear and one quadratic, can be solved by transforming the linear equation into the gradient/intercept form (if it is not already so), and then substituting for y in the quadratic equation.

Exercises on Chapter 4

1   Solve the following pairs of simultaneous equations

(a) $3x + 4y = 25$
      $4x + 3y = 24$

(b) $x + y = 10$
      $3x - 2y = 10$

(c) $y = -20 - x + 2x^2$
      $6x + 2y = 23$

(d) $20x - 4y = 15$
      $y = 15 - 10x + 3x^2.$

2   A company manufactures two products X and Y. Each product has to go through two processes and the amount of time needed on each one is given in the following table:

| | Time per unit needed in | |
	process 1	process 2
product X	2 hours	3 hours
product Y	1 hour	4 hours

In a certain period, there are totals of 600 hours available in process 1 and 1900 hours available in process 2. How many units of X and of Y should the company produce in order to use up all of this available time?
(Hint: suppose x units of X and y units of Y are made, and set up two simultaneous equations).

3   As part of a series of spot-checks on the accuracy of its checkout procedures, the management of a superstore compares the purchases of a number of customers against their receipts. Customer A is found to have bought 3 units of X and 5 units of Y, and was charged £5.99. Customer B bought 4 units of X and 2 units of Y, and was charged £4.21. In the subsequent analysis of the survey, it is found that customer B had been overcharged by 5 pence, while customer A's receipt was accurate. How much do each unit of X and each unit of Y cost?

4   Two equations are given by:

$$4Y = 9X + 1$$
$$Y = X - 1$$

These lines intersect at the following co-ordinates:

A $X = -1, Y = -2$

B $X = \dfrac{3}{5}, \; Y = -\dfrac{2}{5}$

C $X = 1, Y = 2\frac{1}{2}$

D $X = 2, Y = 1$

E   none of these.

ICMA, May 1986

5 (a) The difference between two positive numbers is 5 and the sum of their squares is 193. Find the two numbers.

   (b) A rectangle has a perimeter of 114 metres and an area of 800 square metres. Find the dimensions.

ICMA, November 1978.

6 A company manufactures two products, A and B, by means of two processes, X and Y. The maximum capacity of X is 1900 hours and of Y 5000 hours. One unit of product A requires four hours in process X and two hours in process Y, while one unit of product B requires one hour in process X and five hours in process Y.

   You are required to calculate the number of units to be produced of products A and B to ensure that the maximum capacity available is utilized.

ICMA, November 1979.

Part Two

Data – Their Collection and Representation

5 Obtaining data

Introduction

Many of the problems which face accountants require the acquisition, communication or analysis of information as part of their solution. In this section, we look at each of these aspects in turn. First of all, there is the question of how to obtain information, or *data*, as the individual pieces of information are known.

Data can be classified in two ways: *primary* and *secondary*. Primary data are those collected specifically for the problem in hand, while secondary data are collected for some other purpose. Thus an accountant, working in the budgeting department of a manufacturing company, might get information on raw material costs by contacting the suppliers himself, and so obtain primary data. Alternatively, he could use secondary data in the form of a list of quotations compiled for their own purposes by the company's buying department.

Primary data are the more reliable, since you have obtained them yourself (or have had them collected) and because they relate precisely to the particular problem facing you. Their actual collection, however, does take time, and obtaining them, therefore, tends to be costly, and there may be a considerable delay before the information is ready to use.

On the other hand, secondary data, if available, are relatively inexpensive and quick to obtain: often simply a reference to some relevant publication. The disadvantages here arise from the possibility that there may be no suitable sources for the information and, even if there are, they may not match your requirements too well. In addition, although official or government statistics may be considered reliable, other secondary sources may not.

Primary data: Sampling

We begin by considering how primary data can be obtained. All the information or data relating to a problem is known as the *population*. For reasons of finance and practicality, it is rarely possible to obtain *all* the relevant data, so you normally have to use only part of the population, that is, a *sample*. It is clear that, if the sample data are to be of any use, they must be representative of the population as a whole. If a sample *is* representative of its population, it is said to be *unbiased*; otherwise it is *biased*. Another fundamental point to note is that, because a sample is only a subset, that is, some information has been omitted, any results arising from it cannot be exact representations of the whole population. This deficiency is said to constitute *sampling error*.

By careful choice of sampling method, it is possible to ensure that a sample is representative of its population, thereby avoiding bias. Since the very act of sampling omits some of the data, sampling error is inevitable. In general, if you increase its *size*, the sample will represent a larger proportion, and so will be 'nearer to' the population. Increasing sample size thus tends to reduce sampling error.

An example will illustrate these new concepts and terms.

Example 5.1:
You work as an assistant to the chief accountant of a company which owns a large number of retail stores across the country. The chief accountant asks you to provide him with some up-to-date information on the weekly turnover figures of the stores. Discuss how you would set about this.

Secondary financial data on the stores will no doubt be available, but it may not consist of weekly turnover figures and probably will not be up-to-date. Thus, provided enough time and resources are available, you should consider obtaining primary data. We shall leave discussion of possible methods of actually collecting the information until later in this chapter and concentrate here on the meaning of the various concepts defined above, as applied to this example.

The *population* here consists of all the recent weekly turnover figures for all the stores owned by the company. Clearly it would be practically impossible to collect all these data, and so a *sample* will have to be taken. This will consist of a selection of a certain number of the weekly turnover figures, for example 100 or 1000 of them: the exact number will depend on the time and resources available, and the level of accuracy required by the chief accountant. If the selection of 100 or 1000 (or whatever) weekly turnover figures is representative of all the possible data, then we shall have an *unbiased* sample. However, because a sample consists only of part of the population (possibly just a small proportion), it will give only an approximation to the overall picture: *sampling error* will be present. In general, increasing the sample size from, say, 100 to 1000 will reduce this error.

Probability sampling methods

We now look at various ways of selecting samples, beginning with *probability sampling methods*: those in which there is a known chance of each member of the population appearing in the sample. Such methods eliminate the possibility of bias arising due to (subjective) human selection: it can now only arise by chance. In addition, it is possible to undertake calculations concerning the effects of sampling error when probability sampling methods are used.

Of these methods, the most basic is *(simple) random sampling*, in which each element of the population has an *equal* chance of being selected. As we shall see in later parts of the text, random sampling is the most important method in statistics, since much theory is based on it. Before giving an example of how such a sample can be drawn in practice, we should mention a variation: *stratified random sampling*. In this case, the population is divided into coherent groups, or strata, and the sample is produced by sampling at random within each stratum. This process takes more time than simple random sampling, but can reduce the possibility of bias and can be shown to reduce sampling error.

Example 5.2:
How would a simple random and a stratified random sample be drawn in the situation described in example 5.1?

To begin with, we shall need a list of the population. If, for example, the company owns 100 stores, and the investigation is confined to the last year's (50 trading weeks') trading, then the population will consist of 5000 pieces of data. These might be arranged as follows:

turnover of store 1, week 1	0001
turnover of store 1, week 2	0002
.	
.	
.	
turnover of store 1, week 50	0050
turnover of store 2, week 1	0051
.	
.	
.	
turnover of store 100, week 50	5000.

The members of the population can be numbered 1 to 5000, using 4-digit notation, as shown in the right hand column of the above table. The problem of selecting, say, 200 of these weekly turnover figures, each with an equal chance of being picked, can now be translated into the task of obtaining a similar sample from the digits 0001 to 5000.

There are a number of ways of obtaining the necessary *random numbers*, such as computer generation or by using random number tables. The latter method consists of reading off four-digit numbers from the tables. (Because there are 5000 elements in the population, we ensured

that each one was numbered with a 4-digit number: hence 0001, etc.)
Using the tables in Appendix 1:

0347: week 47 of store 7 is the first member of the sample;
4373: week 23 of store 88 is the second;
8636: this is bigger than 5000, and so is ignored;

.

.

.

We proceed in this way until we have selected the desired sample of size
200. Note that, because each digit in the table has an equal chance of
being 0, 1, 2, ...9, we have ensured that each element of the population
has an equal chance of being sampled, that is, our sample is random.

Following the above procedure, it is possible, by pure chance, that the
200 sampled weeks may come from just a few stores' figures, with many
stores not being represented. If the 100 stores are similar in their
trading patterns, this may not matter, but, if we wish to ensure that
there is a good spread from the stores within the sample, we can *stratify*
before sampling. By way of illustration, this can be done by taking each
store's figures as a stratum and sampling at random within each. Thus
the data on store 1 would form the first stratum:

turnover, week 1	01
turnover, week 2	02
.	
.	
.	
turnover, week 50	50

Note that we need only 2-digit random numbers now. Again, using
Appendix 1 (starting at the bottom and reading backwards, for variety):

33 : the turnover of week 33 is selected;
67 : bigger than 50, so this is ignored;
00 : too small (01 is the lowest in our numbering);
98 : too big;
09 : the turnover of week 9 is selected.

These two figures would form the contribution to the sample from the
first stratum. Repeating this procedure for the 2nd to the 100th stratum
(store's figure) would now produce a randomized sample in which every
store was represented.

Before we leave this example, it should be noted that there are many
other ways of stratifying. For example, it may be that stores number 1
to 10 are far bigger than the others and so should be better represented
in the sample. In such a case, you might work with just two strata
(larger stores' turnover figures and smaller stores' turnover figures) and
then sample (at random) 100 values from each. In practice, situations
like this demand the use of personal judgement when determining how
to stratify and what proportion of the sample to include from each

stratum. In other situations, it is possible to be a little more precise, as the following example illustrates.

Example 5.3:
A market research agency is commissioned to investigate the attitudes of the adult population of a town towards a certain product. Its clients are interested only in a breakdown of the opinions by gender and by age (over or under 35). How might the agency use stratified sampling?

The agency will be able to find fairly reliable secondary data on the characteristics of the town's adult population. Suppose that this shows:

female:	51%	male:	49%
35 and over:	68%	under 35:	32%.

A simple process of multiplication could then be used to produce the following strata:

female, 35 and over	34.68% (0.51 × 0.68, as a percentage)
female, under 35	16.32% (0.51 × 0.32, as a percentage)
male, 35 and over	33.32%
male, under 35	15.68%.

In other words, if a sample size of 1000 were being employed, 347 of the sample would be females aged 35 and over, and so on.

Other sampling methods

If we reconsider the examples in the preceding section, we shall see that there can be great practical problems in using random methods of sampling. First of all, in order to use random number tables (or any other method of ensuring randomness), we need a list of the population. This list is often called a *sampling frame*. As we shall see, there are many instances where a sampling frame is unavailable. Even when one is, *stratified* random sampling may be impossible. For instance, in example 5.3, to stratify the population, it would be necessary to divide the sampling frame (possibly the town's electoral register) into the four categories shown. This would not be possible, since an individual's age could not easily be determined from the register. Note that it would not be sensible to try to find the age of every individual in the town, as one would then be contacting every member of the population – the whole idea of sampling is to avoid such an onerous task!

A second practical problem lies in the cost of random sampling. Imagine taking even a *simple* random sample of 1000 people from a town's electoral register. This would involve counting down the register to find person number 139103 (say), which our random number tables gave us, then contacting her or him to conduct an interview. Multiply this by 1000 and you will appreciate the immense time and expense involved.

A number of alternative sampling methods have been devised to get round the problems posed by the need for a sampling frame and by cost considerations. They are often termed *quasi-random* or *pseudo-random* techniques, because, as we shall see, they are not truly random and can produce biased samples.

Cluster sampling consists of taking one definable subsection of the population as the sample. Thus, you could take the inhabitants of one street as a cluster sample of the population of a town. The way in which this will be biased is clear, and so a variation might be to take the inhabitants of five streets (chosen at random from an alphabetical list) as the sample. The latter example could still be biased, but the great ease of defining the sample is often taken as an overriding consideration.

Systematic sampling involves taking every nth member of the population as the sample. This can be applied with or without a sampling frame, and so may or may not be a probability method. As an example, a sample could be drawn from an electoral register by selecting every 1000th on the list. In a quality control situation, we could take every 100th batch coming off a production line for testing. Note that, in this latter case, we have only part of the sampling frame, those batches produced near the time of sampling. A complete sampling frame, consisting of *all* past and future batches, would be impossible to obtain.

Quota sampling is essentially non-random stratified sampling. The members of the various strata are called *quotas*, which are not chosen at random but are selected by interviewers. The market research agency in example 5.3 could draw its sample by issuing quotas of:

347 females, 35 and over
163 females, under 35
333 males, 35 and over
157 males, under 35.

The actual members of the sample would be selected by the interviewers, as they moved around the town. When the interviewee's age was determined, he or she could be included as part of one of the above quotas. When a quota was complete, no more people from that category would be included. This subjective element is an obvious source of bias which can be reduced in practice by training interviewers to choose a 'spread' within each quota. For example, they would be encouraged not to choose all 40-year-olds in the '35 and over' quotas, but to try to achieve a variety of ages within the range. This method is particularly attractive for those who want *some* degree of control over the composition of the sample but wish to keep the actual sampling process simple.

Multi-stage sampling

We conclude the discussion of sampling techniques by looking at a method commonly used when a survey has to cover a wide geographical area without incurring great expense. *Multi-stage sampling*, as its name implies, involves splitting the process into a number of (typically three) separate steps. An example will illustrate.

Example 5.4:

If you were organizing a nationwide opinion poll, how would you set about organizing the sample, using a multi-stage technique?

The first stage is to divide the country into easily definable regions: in the case of a political survey such as we have here, the 650 parliamentary constituencies are ideal for this. It is now a straightforward matter to select, *at random*, 20 (say) of the constituencies.

In the second stage, the regions are split into smaller, more manageable, districts. There is an ideal subdivision in this example, namely the political wards within each constituency. A random sample of (say) 3 wards might now be selected within each of the 20 constituencies obtained in the first stage. Note that we have now a sample of 60 wards, randomly selected, and that these could be obtained by one person in a matter of minutes, provided that a complete list of constituencies and wards, and a set of random number tables are available.

The time-consuming stage is the third and final one, that of contacting and interviewing a sample of (say) 30 voters in each of the 60 wards. This could be done at random from the electoral registers of the wards, thereby ensuring that the whole process is random. A faster and less expensive alternative, albeit one which risks the introduction of bias, would be a quasi-random method such as quota sampling. The quotas might be by gender and age, or working with a larger budget, might be more sophisticated.

One criticism of multi-stage sampling is that the regions in the first stage and the districts in the second stage will not each contain the same number of people. In the above example, one constituency may have 40,000 electors, while another may have 60,000. As the two are equally likely to be chosen in stage 1, an elector in the former constituency will have 1½ times more chance of appearing in the final sample than does an elector in the latter constituency, (one in 40,000 as opposed to one in 60,000).

A variation which redresses this imbalance is *sampling with probability proportional to size*. Hence you weight the chances of choosing a region (stage 1) and then a district (stage 2) according to the number of people in the region or district, larger regions or districts having proportionately more chance of selection than smaller ones. In the above example, you would ensure that a constituency of 40,000 electors has ⅔ the chance of being selected as does a constituency of 60,000 electors, by allocating ⅔ as many random numbers to the former as compared to the latter. This proportion will then exactly compensate for the imbalance referred to in the preceding paragraph.

Secondary data: Sources

There are numerous potential sources of secondary data which could be used to provide the required information in a given situation. Searching out sources is usually not too problematical: the real difficulty lies in judging whether the data adequately match the requirements or whether primary data should be sought.

Sources of secondary data can be categorized into three types. First of all, there are data collected and compiled internally by the organization, such as its financial reports and accounts, personnel records, and so on. Secondly, there are business data produced by sources external to the organization. Under this heading come the results of surveys by the CBI, the financial press and similar sources. Finally, we have the many government-produced statistics on a whole range of commercial and demographic topics, any one of which might be applicable in solving a business problem. These publications are too numerous to list here, but The Central Statistical Office *Guide to Official Statistics* is published annually and gives a comprehensive catalogue of sources of official statistics.

Summary

Simple random sampling consists of ensuring that every member of the population has an equal chance of being selected. *Stratified random sampling* involves dividing the population into strata before sampling from each.

In *cluster sampling*, the sample is a definable subset of the population. Choosing every nth member of the population constitutes *systematic sampling*. *Quota sampling* is similar to stratified sampling except that the quotas are filled by interviewer selection rather than at random.

Multi-stage sampling consists of selecting regions from a large geographical area (such as the whole country); then selecting districts from these regions; and, finally, sampling people within the districts. The first two stages can usually be at random while the third might use one of the quasi-random methods.

Exercises on Chapter 5

1   In *each* of the following situations, suggest why bias might occur in the sample and suggest ways of reducing or eliminating it:

   (a)   sampling a barrel full of apples by taking a handful from the top;
   (b)   sampling the digits 0 to 9 inclusive by opening a telephone directory and picking telephone numbers;
   (c)   sampling the number of inhabitants per house in a town by house-to-house enquiry in the early afternoon, ignoring those houses at which there is no reply;
   (d)   as (c), but visiting every 20th house between 0900 hours and midday;
   (e)   sampling electors' views on a topic by placing an advertisement in the country's most popular newspaper, inviting readers to write in about the subject;

(f) controlling the quality of a bottling plant by testing the first 100 bottles produced each day.

2 In *each* of the following cases, suggest appropriate method(s) which might be used to obtain the samples and discuss how bias might arise from them:

(a) test marketing a new brand of washing powder in your local town, working within a low budget;

(b) in a nationwide test market of a new brand of washing powder, working for a company owning a chain of department stores and using a relatively high budget;

(c) assessing the number of errors made in trial balances by junior employees of an accountancy concern;

(d) estimating, at the end of each week, the total value of invoices received by a company during the week. (Assume, in this last case, that the company receives many thousands of invoices each week and that the company's information system is geared up only to provide monthly or quarterly figures.)

3 Sampling methods are widely used for the collection of statistical data in industry and business.

Explain *four* of the following, illustrating your answers with practical examples:

(i) simple random sampling;
(ii) stratification;
(iii) quota sampling;
(iv) sampling frame;
(v) cluster sampling;
(vi) systematic sampling.

ICMA, November 1983.

4 The Health Ministry of your Government wishes to know the percentage of people who have a broken leg on, say, 1st June this year. A large random sample is to be chosen from one of the following five populations. Which population is likely to provide the least biased sample?

A Those on a (GP) doctor's list.
B Those shopping in a large department store.
C Those watching a football match.
D Those returning from a skiing holiday.
E The in-patients of a large general hospital.

ICMA, May 1985.

5 Statistical sampling techniques are widely used for the collection of data in industry and business. Explain four of the following, illustrating your answer with examples:

(a) sampling frame;
(b) simple random sampling;
(c) multi-stage sampling;
(d) stratification;
(e) quota sampling;
(f) sampling with probability proportional to size.

ICMA specimen question, published 1986.

6 The presentation of data

Introduction

Data, when first collected, are often not in a form that conveys much information. Such *raw data*, as they are called, may just consist of a list or table of individual datum values: if the list or table is of any appreciable size then it may need some refinement before anyone can draw conclusions from it. In this chapter we look at ways in which raw data can be collated into more meaningful formats, and then go on to see some pictorial representations of data which provide convenient ways of communicating them to others.

Tallying. Frequency distributions

An example will illustrate a simple way of converting raw data into a concise format.

Example 6.1:
In order to monitor the efficiency of his department, the head of the finance section of a large company spot checks the number of invoices left unprocessed at the end of each day. At the end of the first period of this check, (26 working days), he has collected the following data:

1	5	3	3	2
3	0	4	1	4
3	3	2	1	2
1	1	0	3	6
5	0	3	4	2
3				

Collate these raw data into a more meaningful form.

By scanning the table we can see that all the values lie between 0 and

6 inclusive. It might be useful to find out how often each value in this range occurs in the table. This could be achieved simply by counting, but there are no safeguards against human error in doing this. Instead, we use a *tallying* procedure, which is more accurate than counting, especially with large tables of figures. After going along the first row, the tally will look like:

Number of invoices left unprocessed	Tally
0	
1	I
2	I
3	II
4	
5	I
6	

As we go through the table, one 'notch' is put against the appropriate number each time it appears. For ease of counting, when each fifth 'notch' is reached, it is marked: ЖI

Number of invoices left unprocessed	Tally	Total
0	III	3
1	ЖI	5
2	IIII	4
3	ЖI III	8
4	III	3
5	II	2
6	I	1
		26

Note that we have the check that the grand total must equal the sample size: in this case, 26.

The 'totals' in the above table are called *frequencies* and the table is called the *frequency distribution* of the sample. Thus the frequency of 0 invoices is 3, and so on.

The next example will demonstrate that the collation of raw data into a frequency distribution is not always as straightforward as in the case above.

Example 6.2:
In order to assist management negotiations with the trade unions over piece-work rates, the management services department of a factory is asked to obtain information on how long it takes for a certain operation to be completed. Consequently, the members of the department measure the time it takes to complete 30 repetitions of the operation, at random occasions during a month. The times are recorded to the nearest tenth of a minute.

19.8	21.3	24.6	18.7	19.1
15.3	20.6	22.1	19.9	17.2
24.1	23.0	20.1	18.3	19.8
16.5	22.8	18.0	20.0	21.6
19.7	25.9	22.2	17.9	21.1
20.8	19.5	21.6	15.6	23.1

Form the frequency distribution of this sample.

A scan of the table shows that the smallest value is 15.3 minutes and the largest 25.9 minutes. If we tallied as in the previous example

Time (minutes)	Tally
15.3	
15.4	
15.5	
.	
.	
.	
.	
.	
.	
25.9	

we should obtain a format of little more use than the original data, because most of the frequencies would be 0, interspersed by the occasional frequency of 1. A far more sensible approach is to tally the number of values in a certain range or *class*. The choice of classes is somewhat arbitrary, but should be such that they are neither too narrow, which would result in most of the frequencies being zero, as above, nor too wide, which would produce only a small number of classes and thereby tell us little. Following these general guidelines, we tally as follows:

Time (minutes)	Tally	Frequency
15 to under 17	III	3
17 to under 19	ⅢⅡ	5
19 to under 21	ⅢⅡ ⅢⅡ	10
21 to under 23	ⅢⅡ II	7
23 to under 25	IIII	4
25 to under 27	I	1
		30

Even though some precision has been lost, this frequency distribution is considerably more use to the management services department than the raw data, because, for example, one can see at a glance where the bulk of the times lie, how often the time exceeds some target figure such as 23 minutes, say, and so on.

Discrete and continuous variables

There is an essential difference between the two variables considered in examples 6.1 and 6.2. The former is *discrete*, whereas the latter is *continuous*. That is to say, the number of invoices can only consist of certain values

0 or 1 or 2 or ....
never 1.6, 2.3, and so on.

On the other hand, the time taken to undertake a certain operation can theoretically take a value to *any* level of precision

20.2 minutes
20.19 minutes
20.186 minutes
20.1864 minutes, and so on.

In example 6.2, the management services staff *chose* to measure to 1 decimal place: theoretically, they could have chosen to measure to 2, 3, or any number of places. A number of invoices *cannot* be measured any more accurately than 0 or 1 or whatever.

This distinction has a number of consequences in the following chapter. Here, it can affect the way we tally. Continuous variables, such as the times to undertake a certain operation, can rarely be tallied as individual values, since few of them will coincide to give meaningfully large frequencies. Classifying is therefore almost always necessary with continuous variables. As example 6.2 demonstrated, discrete variables can sometimes be tallied with single values. However, with a wider range (0 to 100, for example), the problem of having frequencies being mostly 0, interspersed with a few 1's, could still arise: it is therefore sometimes necessary to use classes for discrete data.

There are numerous ways of classifying, when it is necessary. For instance, in example 6.2, we could have used

	15	to	17	
	17.1	to	19	
	19.1	to	21	and so on
or	15	to	16.95	
	16.95	to	18.95	
	18.95	to	21.95	and so on.

Both of these could be problematical if the measurements were later taken to the nearest twentieth (0.05) of a minute, as we should have difficulty placing 17.05 minutes in the former classification and 18.95 minutes in the latter. For this reason, we recommend that continuous variables are always classified:

15 *to under* 17
17 *to under* 19, and so on.

Cumulative frequency distributions

It is sometimes helpful to develop the idea of frequency further and to look at *cumulative frequencies*. These are the number of data values up to or up to and including a certain point. They can easily be compiled as running totals from the corresponding frequency distribution, as the following will illustrate.

Example 6.3:

Form the cumulative frequency distributions from the data given in examples 6.1 and 6.2. Hence estimate:

(a)   how often there are more than four invoices left unprocessed at the end of a day;

(b)   how often the time taken beats the target of 23 minutes.

The frequency distribution of the number of unprocessed invoices can be used to obtain:

Number of invoices left unprocessed (less than or equal)	Cumulative frequency
0	3 (simply the frequency of '0')
1	8 (that is: 3 + 5)
2	12 (that is: 8 + 4)
3	20
4	23
5	25
6	26

In the same way, for the distribution of times taken to undertake the operation:

Time (minutes) (less than)	Cumulative frequency
15	0 (there are no values below 15 minutes)
17	3 (the frequency of the first class)
19	8 (that is: 3 + 5)
21	18 (8 + 10)
23	25
25	29
27	30

In the latter example, we have to take the *upper* limit of each class, to ensure that *all* the values in the class are definitely *less than* it. We must use 'less than' as opposed to 'less than or equal' here because it corresponds to the way the frequency table has been compiled.

It is now a simple matter to estimate:

(a) $26 - 23 = 3$ occasions out of 26, that is: *11.5* per cent

(b)   25 occasions out of 30, that is: *83.3* per cent.

How reliable these estimates are depends on how typical or representative is the period or month in which the samples are taken.

We shall see further applications of cumulative frequency in the following section.

Histograms and ogives

Many people find it easier to understand numerical information if it is presented in a pictorial form, rather than as a table of figures. In this section, therefore, we look at diagrammatic representations of frequency and cumulative frequency distributions.

A *histogram* is a graph of a frequency distribution. The x–axis is the variable being measured and the y–axis is the corresponding frequency. It differs from the graphs drawn earlier, since in the examples so far, the frequency is represented by the height of a *block*. The base of the block corresponds to the class being represented, so that, in a case of discrete, unclassified distribution, the 'blocks' become vertical lines. The histograms of the two frequency distributions encountered so far are shown in Figure 6.1.

An *ogive* is a graph of a cumulative frequency distribution. The x–axis is the variable being measured and the y–axis is the corresponding cumulative frequency, the x– and y–values being plotted in exactly the same way as we discussed in Chapter 2. The only question is, how to join up the plotted points. In a discrete case, x–values intermediate to those plotted have no meaning in reality (recall 1.6 invoices) and so we do *not* join them up, but simply draw vertical lines. With a continuous variable, the intermediate values *do* have a meaning, and so it makes sense to join the plotted points. This can be done with a series of straight lines, which is tantamount to assuming that the values are evenly spread throughout their classes. The ogives of the two cumulative frequency distributions encountered so far are shown in Figure 6.2.

Before leaving these graphs, we look at one simple example to show how cumulative frequency distributions and ogives can be used in practice.

Example 6.4:

The management of the company discussed in example 6.2 wishes to reduce the target time for the operation to 22 minutes. Assuming the distribution of times remains unaltered, how often will this target be met?

First of all, it is not possible to answer this as a straight reading from the cumulative frequency distribution, as 22 minutes does not correspond to a value in the table. If we look at the ogive, however, we can estimate how many of the 30 occasions took less than 22 minutes, by a reading off the graph, as shown. Thus, we estimate that the target will be met

on 21.5 out of every 30 occasions,
that is: 72 per cent of the time.

We now give two examples to demonstrate problems which can arise when drawing histograms and ogives.

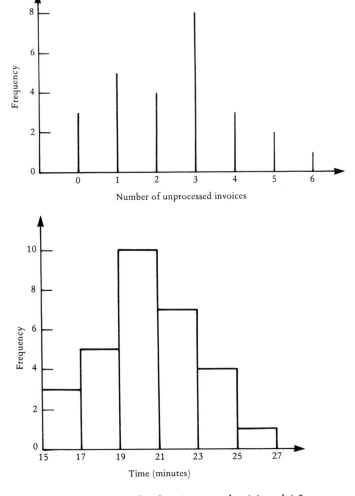

Figure 6.1 *Histograms for data in examples 6.1 and 6.2*

Example 6.5:

The compiler of a careers guide is given the following information on the initial salaries of graduates entering a certain profession during the year prior to the guide's publication.

Annual salary (£)	Number of graduate entrants
4000 – under 6000	108
6000 – under 8000	156
8000 – under 9000	94
9000 – under 9500	80
9500 – under 10000	25

In order to convey the information in a quickly assimilated form, the compiler decides to represent it as a histogram. Draw this histogram.

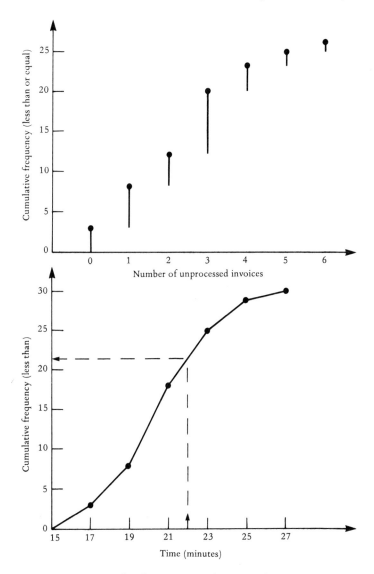

Figure 6.2 *Ogives for data in examples 6.1 and 6.2*

Before referring to the histogram, we point out that, strictly speaking, the data here are discrete. The 'gaps', however, are only of width equal to one penny, which is very small compared to thousands of pounds. We therefore effectively treat this as a continuous case.

If we now draw the histogram as above, we obtain that shown in Figure 6.3(a). Close inspection of this will show that some discrepancies have arisen. For example, the left-hand block is supposed to represent approximately four times more graduates than the right-hand block, and yet the ratio of the size of these two blocks is nearer to sixteen. There are other examples of disproportion in the size of the blocks, the underlying reason being that, by drawing block heights equal to frequencies, we exaggerate those with larger class widths. Thus, in a case like this, where there are *unequal* class widths, one must compensate by adjusting the heights of some of the blocks:

8000 – under 9000 is half the width of the first two,

so height = 94 × 2 = 188

9000 – under 9500 is quarter the width,   height = 80 × 4 = 320

9500 – under 1000   height = 25 × 4 = 100.

(Alternatively, we could leave the frequencies of the last two classes unaltered, and divide the frequency of the first class by four, and so on. This would leave the *shape* of the histogram as in Figure 6.3(b).)

The resulting *correct* version of the histogram is shown in Figure 6.3(b). It will be noted that the areas of the blocks are now in the correct proportion and that the vertical axis of the graph can no longer be labelled 'frequency', but is now 'frequency density'.

Before leaving this example, we point out that the ogive of this distribution would present no extra problems. As this only consists of plotting the upper limit of each class against cumulative frequency, the unequal class intervals do not affect matters. We leave the ogive as an exercise to the reader.

Example 6.6:

The compiler of the careers guide also receives, from a different source, information on the graduate salaries in another profession:

Annual salary (£)	Number of graduate entrants
under 5000	64
5000 – under 7000	131
7000 – under 9000	97
9000 – under 10000	40
10000 and over	11

What problems would the compiler have when drawing the histogram and the ogive of this distribution?

We have seen how to deal with the unequal class intervals, but here we have the extra problem of *open-ended* classes. When drawing the histogram, we can either omit the first and last class or estimate 'closing' values for these two classes. The former would leave the histogram looking rather sparse, and, indeed, as we shall see in ensuing chapters, it is often necessary to close the classes so as to make certain calculations. It might therefore be advisable to estimate values such as

4000 – under   5000

10000 – *under 11000*

to draw the histogram.

In the case of the ogive, only the *upper* limit of each class is needed, and so it would be necessary to close only the last class in order to draw

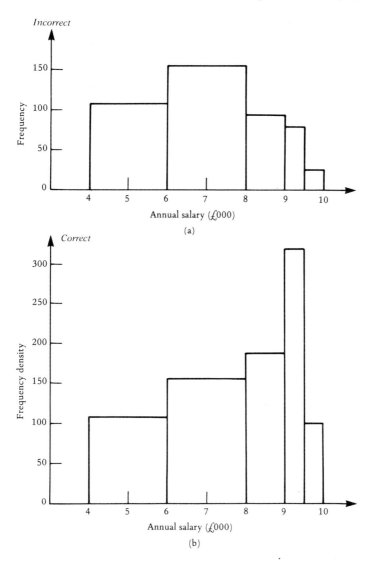

Figure 6.3 *Histograms, example 6.5*

the whole ogive. It would also be possible to draw part of it from just the first four classes, omitting the last.

We leave as exercises for the reader the construction of the histogram and ogive, using the above suggested closing values.

Summary

Tallying is a more reliable method of compiling *frequency distributions* from raw data than is mere counting. Very often we have to tally into *classes* rather than individual values.

Continuous variables can, in theory, be measured to any level of precision, while *discrete* variables can take only certain values.

The *cumulative frequency* of a value is the number of readings up to (or up to and including) that value.

The *histogram* and the *ogive* are graphical representations of a frequency distribution and a cumulative frequency distribution respectively.

Exercises on Chapter 6

1   As part of its annual report, the personnel department of a factory wishes to present the accident statistics. The following weekly numbers of reported accidents are found for the previous year (50 working weeks):

1	3	0	4	2	3	5	2	2	3
5	1	6	1	4	2	3	4	5	6
2	6	3	2	3	5	4	6	3	2
2	4	3	5	5	2	2	7	6	4
3	6	1	4	2	1	6	2	3	2

Tally these data into a frequency distribution and draw its histogram and ogive.

2   A company is conducting an efficiency drive, part of which involves controlling the amount of overtime pay earned by its employees. In order to gauge the current position, a member of the finance department obtains the following data from the company's computerized records:

Total weekly overtime pay (£), last 50 weeks:

8003	5302	7761	8930	9625	6130	7085	8991	7374	9200
9135	7548	10511	6009	8379	7526	9731	8814	5882	7480
8149	8457	7631	9942	7228	5411	8255	6444	7593	6707
7253	6381	10459	8074	6617	8481	7121	10210	7713	8652
9421	8312	8862	9377	7138	8658	9808	8761	6950	7809

(a) To get a better picture of what this information shows, the finance officer decides to compile a frequency distribution. Perform the necessary tallying process, using classes of width around £1,000.

(b) Draw the histogram of this distribution.

(c) Construct the corresponding cumulative frequency distribution and draw its ogive.

(d) The managing director of the company asks if it is feasible to restrict overtime pay to a weekly maximum of £7,500. Use the ogive to estimate what percentage of weeks this target is exceeded. Why might this figure differ from one found from the raw data?

3   The following data show the distribution of prices of houses sold by an estate agent during a year:

House price (£000)	Number of houses sold
under 20	3
20 – under 30	15
30 – under 40	32
40 – under 60	44
60 – under 100	34
100 and over	12

(a) Draw a histogram and an ogive to represent this distribution.
(b) What assumptions have you made in these graphs?
(c) Use the graphs to estimate:
   (i) the most popular range of house prices in the area served by the agent;
   (ii) the proportion of houses selling for over £50,000;
   (iii) the price below which the 20 per cent least expensive houses sell.

(d) To what extent, if any, have the assumptions referred to in (b) affected the answers in (c)?

4 A machine produces the following number of rejects in each successive period of five minutes:

16	21	26	24	11	24	17	25	26	13
27	24	26	3	27	23	24	15	22	22
12	22	29	21	18	22	28	25	7	17
22	28	19	23	23	22	3	19	13	31
23	28	24	9	20	33	30	23	20	8

Construct a frequency distribution from these data, using seven class intervals of equal width. Draw the corresponding histogram.
ICMA, May 1982.

5 The following table gives the annual earnings of the full-time employees of an engineering company:

Earnings (£000)		Number of employees
At least:	Less than:	
	3	36
3	4	100
4	5	46
5	6	140
6	7	608
7	8	200
8	10	50
10	14	15
14 or more		5
		1200

(a) Draw a histogram of the above data.
(b) What percentage of employees earn less than £5,000 per year?
(c) If 75 per cent of those earning less than £5,000 per year are

women, how many employees earning less than £5,000 per year are men?

ICMA, November 1983.

6   The following table shows the income distribution of the middle management of a large industrial company.

Incomes – 1977

Range £	Number of managers
2950 and less than 3150	10
3150 and less than 3350	8
3350 and less than 3550	18
3550 and less than 3750	22
3750 and less than 3950	23
3950 and less than 4150	25
4150 and less than 4350	35
4350 and less than 4550	30
4550 and less than 4750	14
4750 and less than 4950	6
4950 and less than 5150	5
5150 and less than 5350	4

You are required to:

(a)   prepare a cumulative frequency graph of the above situation;
(b)   calculate the salaries above which the highest 25, 50 and 75 per cent salaries lie;
(c)   give a brief note on a business use to which this form of presentation may apply.

ICMA, May 1978.

7 Measures of average

Introduction

In the previous chapter, we saw how a set of raw data can be made more meaningful by forming it into a frequency distribution. Often, it is advantageous to go further and to quote a single value which is representative or descriptive of the whole data set: such a value is termed an *average*. Although most people have an intuitive understanding of the concept of an 'average', we shall see that the word has, in fact, a number of meanings. In this chapter, we shall concentrate on the three most important measures of average for business purposes:

- the arithmetic mean;
- the median;
- the mode.

The arithmetic mean

Most people would understand an 'average' to be the value obtained by dividing the sum of the values in question by the number of values. This measure is the *arithmetic mean*, or, where there is no possibility of confusion, simply *the mean*. Further, if the data being considered are sample data, then we refer to the *sample mean*, to distinguish it from the mean of the population from which the sample is drawn.

In order to introduce some notation, consider the following example.

Example 7.1:
A shopkeeper is about to put his shop up for sale. As part of the details of the business, he wishes to quote the average weekly takings. The takings in each of the last six weeks are:

£1,120; £990; £1,040; £1,030; £1,105; £1,015.

Determine the mean weekly takings which the shopkeeper could quote.

If the weekly takings are denoted by the variable x, then the sample mean value of x is written as $\bar{x}$, pronounced 'x–bar'. Thus

$$\bar{x} = \frac{\text{sum of the values of } x}{\text{number of values of } x}$$

or $\bar{x} = \dfrac{\Sigma x}{n}$

where Σ, a Greek capital letter 'sigma', is the mathematical symbol for 'add up', and n is the number of values of x. In this example

$$\bar{x} = \frac{1120 + 990 + 1040 + 1030 + 1105 + 1015}{6}$$

$$= \frac{6300}{6}$$

$$= £1,050.$$

The shopkeeper could therefore quote a sample mean weekly takings figure of £1,050.

As we can see, this formula is very easy to apply, and, as indicated above, merely reflects the arithmetical procedures most people would recognize as the determination of an average. It will, however, need some modification before it can be used to determine the mean from a frequency distribution, a form in which many data sets appear.

Example 7.2:
A company is implementing an efficiency drive and, as part of a leaflet it is to distribute to its employees, it wishes to point out the average daily absenteeism rate. Duly, the following data are collated from the records of a sample of 200 working days: compute the sample mean number of absentees per day.

Number of absentees per day (x):	Number of days:
0	9
1	28
2	51
3	43
4	29
5	18
6	10
7	7
8	5

It should be noted that the 'number of days' column simply gives the frequency of the corresponding x–values, and so we shall denote this quantity by f. Now, to find the sample mean, the above formula can be applied in a straightforward manner:

$$\bar{x} = \frac{\Sigma x}{n}$$

$$= \frac{\overbrace{0 + 0 + \ldots + 0}^{9 \text{ values}} + \overbrace{1 + \ldots + 1}^{28} + \overbrace{2 + \ldots + 2}^{51 \ldots} + \ldots + \overbrace{8 + \ldots + 8}^{5}}{200}$$

Now, rather than add together nine 0's, then twenty-eight 1's, then fifty-one 2's, and so on, it is clearly simpler to multiply as follows:

$$\bar{x} = \frac{(9 \times 0) + (28 \times 1) + (51 \times 2) + \ldots + (5 \times 8)}{200}$$

$$= \frac{614}{200}$$

$$= 3.07$$

Thus the mean number of absentees in the sample is *3.07* per day.

Note how, in general, each x–value is multiplied by its corresponding frequency, f, and the products are then summed. That is, we evaluate the product fx for each x–value and then add all the values of fx. As we are denoting addition by 'Σ', this sum can be written Σfx. The formula for the sample mean from a frequency distribution is thus:

$$\bar{x} = \frac{\Sigma fx}{\Sigma f}$$

The denominator of this expression, Σf, is simply the sum of the frequencies, which is, of course, the same as n in the earlier expression for $\bar{x}$.

This formula will now prove adequate for all our purposes. In order to illustrate how to deal with a minor problem which can, however, arise and to demonstrate a systematic way of performing and setting out the calculations involved, we give a further example.

Example 7.3:
As part of its preparation for a wage negotiation, the personnel manager of a company has collated the following data from a sample of payslips. She wishes to be able to use the average weekly wage figure in the negotiations: evaluate the mean of the sample.

Weekly wage (£)	Number of employees (f)
180 to under 185	41
185 to under 190	57
190 to under 195	27
195 to under 200	23
200 to under 205	15
205 to under 210	7

The extra difficulty in this problem is clear: as the data have been collated into classes, a certain amount of detail has been lost and hence the values of the variable x to be used in the calculation of $\bar{x}$ are not clearly specified. Short of actually having the raw data, the *actual* wages of the employees in the sample, we can only approximate the value of $\bar{x}$. To do this, we adopt the obvious approach of taking x to be a representative value of each class, the most plausible being the mid-point. Doing this, we have

x	f	fx
182.50	41	7482.5
187.50	57	10687.5
192.50	27	5197.5
197.50	23	4542.5
202.50	15	3037.5
207.50	7	1452.5
	170	32400

It is advisable to set out such statistical calculations in the way shown: very often figures have to be summed, and so they are best arranged in columns. Further, if you are using a calculator with a memory key, each 'fx' figure can be added into the memory as it is calculated, so that the total 'Σfx' is ready for use when the memory total is recalled.

Now we have $\bar{x} = \dfrac{\Sigma fx}{\Sigma f}$

$$= \frac{32400}{170}$$

$$= £190.60 \text{ (approximately).}$$

Hence the manager can use an average weekly wage of *£190.60* in the negotiations.

The median

In example 7.3, we computed a mean weekly wage of £190.60 which the personnel manager could quote in the wage negotiations. An impartial commentator could argue (and the manager might agree) that this is a rather high figure for a supposedly representative average. As 98 out of the sampled 170 (i.e. 58 per cent) actually earn less than £190 per week, it may well be that in excess of 60 per cent of the workforce earn less than the 'average' of £190.60 per week. If we look at this wage distribution, shown in Figure 7.1, it is easy to see the cause of this phenomenon. The two highest frequencies occur at the lowest wage classes and then the frequencies decrease slowly as the wages increase. The relatively small number of large wages has caused the mean value to be so large. Distributions of this type are said to have a long *tail* or to be very *skewed*. It is a criticism of the mean as an average that very skewed distributions can have mean values which appear unrepresentative, in that they are higher or lower than a great deal of the distribution.

   To address this problem, we introduce another measure of average, the *median*. This is defined as the middle of a set of values, when arranged in ascending (or descending) order. This overcomes the above problem, since the median has half the distribution above it, and half below. We leave the wage distribution for now, and look at a simpler example.

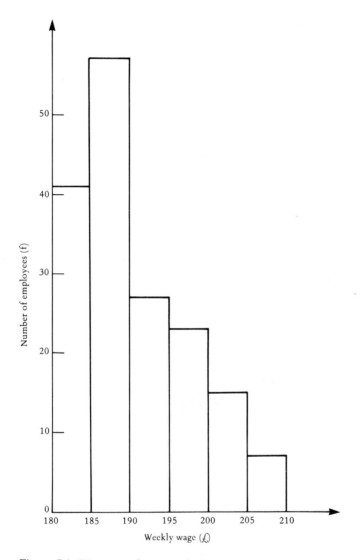

Figure 7.1 *Histogram for example 7.3*

Example 7.4:
A prospective purchaser of the business in example 7.1 notices that the mean value of £1,050 is in fact higher than the takings in four out of the six sampled weeks. He therefore decides to compute a more 'representative' figure as a bargaining ploy. If he chooses the median as his average, what value would be obtained?

First of all, we arrange the takings figures in ascending order:

£990; £1,015; £1,030; £1,040; £1,105; £1,120.

The question now is: what is the middle number of a list of six? With a little thought, you can see that there are two 'middle' values, the third and fourth. The median is thus taken to be the mean of these two values:

$$\text{median} = \frac{1030 + 1040}{2}$$

$$= £1,035.$$

Hence the median weekly takings figure which the prospective purchaser could quote is *£1,035*.

After this example, it is clear that, in the case of an *odd* number of values, the determination of the median is even easier, as there is a clear *single* middle item in an odd number of values. In the case of frequency distributions, the determination of the median is not as straightforward, but can be illustrated by returning to the earlier wage distribution.

Example 7.5:
Using the data of example 7.3, find the more representative median weekly wage figure which the personnel manager could argue in the wage negotiations.

It is clear that the middle wage figure in a set of 170 is halfway between the 85th and the 86th. Unfortunately, we do not have the raw data from which the frequency distribution was compiled, and so cannot tell what these two wage figures are. It is therefore necessary to make an assumption about the wage distribution and to deduce an approximate value from the assumption.

If we consider the wage values to be evenly spread throughout their classes, then we can draw the ogive as in Chapter 6 and then estimate the median from a construction based on this ogive. First of all, we need the cumulative frequency distribution:

Weekly wage (£): (less than)	Cumulative frequency:
185	41
190	98
195	125
200	148
205	163
210	170

Figure 7.2 shows the ogive of this cumulative frequency distribution.

Now, as the median has the property that half of the wage figures lie below it, and half above it, the construction shown on the ogive, drawn at a cumulative frequency of 85 (half of 170), gives the approximate median weekly wage as *£188.80*. This value is arguably more representative of the sample than the earlier mean value, precisely because half the wages lie below and half above it.

Before leaving the median, we remark that it would not be common

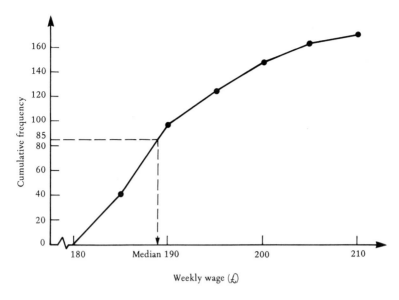

Figure 7.2 *Ogive of wage distribution in example 7.5*

sense to use this construction to estimate the median of every frequency distribution. Take, for example, the absenteeism distribution in example 7.2: you can see from a glance at the frequency distribution that the two middle values of the 200, the 100th and the 101st, are both 3 absentees. The median in this case is thus 3 absentees per day, without further ado. The difference is, of course, that here we have a distribution grouped by single, discrete values, whereas the wage distribution was grouped into classes, thereby losing some detail and necessitating the approximating construction.

The mode

The *mode* or *modal value* of a data set is that value which occurs most often. The determination of this value, when you have raw data to deal with, consists simply of a counting process to find the most frequently occurring value, and so we do not dwell on this case here, but move on to look at frequency distributions.

Example 7.6:
Find the modal daily number of employees absent and the modal weekly wage from the distributions given in examples 7.2 and 7.3 respectively.

The first case is very easy: a glance at the frequency distribution shows that the x–value '2' has the highest frequency and so

modal number of absentees = *2 per day.*

The frequency distribution in the second case shows that the *modal class* (that one with the highest frequency) is £185 to under £190. Now, a number of calculations and constructions exist to find a single approximate value for the mode in such an example. As the values so produced *are* only approximations, and since it is usually unnecessary to have a single estimate of the mode in any case, as the modal class is sufficient, it does not seem appropriate to adopt these methods. Consequently, in this example, we state:

the modal weekly wage class is £185 to under £190.

A comparison of the three measures

As our earlier discussion of the weekly wage distribution indicates, it is often just as important to use a measure of average appropriate to the situation as it is to evaluate the measure accurately. In this section we further discuss the relative merits and demerits of the three averages encountered in this chapter.

It is arguable that the mode is the least useful and important of the three. There are many distributions which have no definite single 'peak' in their histograms, and so it is difficult to attribute any sensible meaning to a modal value in such cases. Further, the mode is often unrepresentative of the whole data set: it may occur at one extremity of a skewed distribution or, at the very least, it takes no account of a high proportion of the data, only representing the most common value. All in all, it is fair to say that, in the vast majority of cases, the mode renders only a general description of one feature of a distribution, and is a relatively unimportant average when compared with the median or the mode.

The mean, on the other hand, has a number of features which usually make it the most appropriate and representative measure. First of all, it has the great advantage of being what most people recognize as 'the average'. It is therefore most easily communicated to non-specialists. Secondly, the mean is the only one of the three which takes account of all the data: like the mode, the median ignores some of a distribution by concentrating only on the middle part. The mean is thus arguably the most representative of *all* of a distribution. Finally, the mean is the measure which is most useful for further statistical analysis, as we shall see as the text develops in later chapters.

Having said that, there are some circumstances in which one might consider the median to be more appropriate than the mean. We have already encountered one important such occasion in the skewed wage distribution of examples 7.3 and 7.5.

In general, the median can often be argued to be the most representative average of a highly skewed distribution, since the mean may then be higher than a large proportion of the data, as in the wage distribution; or lower than a large proportion of the data, if the tail of the distribution extends towards the lower values.

Another instance in which we may doubt the suitability of the mean is when we are dealing with discrete data. In example 7.2 we saw an absenteeism distribution which has

mean   = 3.07 absentees/day
median = 3 absentees/day
mode   = 2 absentees/day.

It is impossible to have 3.07 absentees, whereas the other two values are attainable. This is a common problem when dealing with means of discrete distributions, which sometimes leads to the median being used.

There is no hard and fast rule here, and each such case must be treated on its merits. Rounding the mean off to a 'possible' value of 3 absentees per day only represents a very small (around 2 per cent) change in its value. As this now agrees with the median, this common value can be accepted as the most appropriate measure. The decision would not be so easy with a discrete variate with sample mean of 1.4 and median and mode both 3: rounding the mean to 1 would involve a large (almost 30 per cent) change, and so you would have to accept an unattainable mean value of 1.4 or the common median/modal value of 3 as the 'average'.

A final category in which you might not use the mean is illustrated in the following example.

Example 7.7:
An estate agent wishing to quote the average regional house price in his advertising brochures, collates the following data on the houses he has helped to sell in the last six months.

House price (£000)	Number of houses
Under 20	5
20 – under 25	9
25 – under 30	20
30 – under 40	25
40 – under 50	18
50 – under 70	9
70 and over	6

We have already seen that, in such grouped frequency distributions, all three measures are, of necessity, only approximations. The two open-ended classes in this distribution, however, impose an extra source of inaccuracy in the evaluation of the mean: in order to obtain x–values for use in the formula for $\bar{x}$, we have to assume closing values for these classes. Plausible examples of these values might be:

15 – under 20
70 – under 100.

Of course, the values chosen affect the x–values (the mid-points of the various classes) and thus the value of $\bar{x}$. The estimates of the median and modal values are unaffected by the choice as they both occur towards the centre of this distribution.

Again, there is no rule for resolving this dilemma. Most people would be willing to overlook the extra inaccuracy in the mean value, provided plausible closing values for the open-ended classes are available (as is the case here). If, however, there was some doubt or debate over the closing values, then the median would arguably be the better measure.

Summary

The *mean*, $\bar{x} = \dfrac{\Sigma x}{n}$

or $\bar{x} = \dfrac{\Sigma fx}{\Sigma f}$ for frequency distributions.

The *median* is the middle value when the data are arranged in ascending or descending order. It can be evaluated directly except in grouped frequency distributions, when it can be estimated from an ogive as the *x*–value corresponding to half the total frequency.
The *mode* is the most commonly occurring value.

Exercises on Chapter 7

1   An investor is concerned with determining which companies in a certain sector of the economy he should invest in. First of all, he decides to consider only those companies which are above average in terms of their profitability. Consequently he collates the following distribution of latest gross profit to sales ratios from a sample of 100 of the companies:

Value of Ratio	Number of companies
0 – under 0.1	8
0.1 – under 0.2	14
0.2 – under 0.3	46
0.3 – under 0.4	22
0.4 – under 0.5	7
0.5 – under 0.6	3

(a)   Which measure of average should the investor choose as most representative of this distribution and why?
(b)   Evaluate this average.
(c)   What assumption have you made in calculation (b)?

2   The management of a chain of retail stores has the following data on the turnovers of the stores in the last trading year:

Turnover (£000)	Number of stores
under 150	6
150 – under 180	27
180 – under 210	36
210 – under 240	43
240 – under 270	49
270 – under 300	21
300 and over	4

(a) The management is interested in quoting the average turnover figure for the last trading year: why might the mean not be considered appropriate?

(b) Evaluate the median annual turnover. What assumptions have you made?

3 A member of the finance department of a manufacturing company is attempting to find the cost to the company of industrial accidents amongst its workforce. She is given the following data by the personnel department based on the last two years' (100 working weeks') records:

Number of accidents reported per week	Number of weeks	
0	16	0
1	35	35
2	17	34
3	12	36
4	9	36
5	6	30
6	3	18
7	2	14
	101	203 2.00 *mean*

(a) Evaluate the mean, median and modal number of accidents reported per week during the last two years.

(b) If it is estimated that the average cost per accident to the company (in terms of lost output, compensation, etc.) is £800, which of the above measures should be used to calculate the average weekly cost of accidents? What *is* this average weekly cost?

(c) If, however, the personnel department simply wishes to quote a representative figure for the average weekly number of accidents, which measure would be most appropriate?

4 The data below refer to a survey of large users of computers in the public and private sectors in the United Kingdom. Of these users, 67 reported cases of computer fraud in the previous five-year period.

Fraud incidence and value

Range of financial losses £	Number of cases	Value of losses £	
Nil	17	–	
less than 1,000	18	6,900	124700
1,000 – 4,999	11	26,100	287 100
5,000 – 9,999	6	43,380	260280
10,000 – 14,999	3	33,770	161316
15,000 – 19,999	4	70,000	280000
20,000 – 49,999	4	152,000	608000
50,000 – 99,999	2	143,000	286000
100,000 and over	2	430,000	860000
Total	67	905,150	2806890

Calculate the arithmetic mean and median for these data by the most accurate method:

(*i*)   including all 67 cases;
(*ii*) excluding the first class of 17 cases.

Interpret your results.
ICMA, May 1985.

5   The following distribution is the price charged for exactly the same commodity by a number of retailers in different parts of the country.

Price charged per unit	Number of retailers	
1.00 and less than 1.02	3	3·03
1.02 and less than 1.04	16	16·48
1.04 and less than 1.06	28	29·4
1.06 and less than 1.08	30	32·1
1.08 and less than 1.10	25	27·25
1.10 and less than 1.12	13	14·43
1.12 and less than 1.14	5	5·65
	120	128·9

Calculate (*i*)   the arithmetic mean of the distribution;
          (*ii*) the median of the distribution.

Answer the following questions and for each give a short explanation justifying your answer:

(*iii*) Is the answer to (i) above the same as the following:

$$\frac{\text{Total actual prices charged by the 120 retailers}}{120 \text{ retailers}}$$

(*iv*) Would you agree that 50 per cent of the *units* sold cost less than the answer to (ii);

(*v*)   If the last entry had been '£1.12 and over' instead of '£1.12 and less than £1.14' would this have had any effect on the calculation of the arithmetic mean and of the median?

ICMA, November 1979.

6   An international company, reviewing the orders received by its European sales outlets, has compiled the following information:

Value of orders received July 1977

Monthly value of orders (£000)	Number of sales outlets
180 and less than 220	10
220 and less than 260	30
260 and less than 300	20
300 and less than 340	50
340 and less than 380	40
380 and less than 420	30
420 and less than 460	20

The management wishes to establish an 'average' monthly order value which it can use in budgeting and fixing discounts for the outlets.

   (*i*) State the type of 'average' you would recommend management to use, giving reasons for your choice.

  (*ii*) Calculate the 'average' order value using the measure you have recommended.

ICMA, November 1978.

8 Measures of spread

Introduction

Having obtained an average value to represent a set of data, it is natural to question the extent to which the single value *is* representative of the whole set. Through a simple example we shall see that part of the answer to this lies in how 'spread out' the individual values are around the average. In particular, we shall study four measures of *spread*, or *dispersion*, as it is sometimes called:

- the range;
- the inter-quartile range;
- the mean absolute deviation;
- the standard deviation.

The range

The *range* is the simplest measure of spread and is simply defined as

range = highest value − lowest value.

The following example will illustrate the calculation of the range, and will demonstrate why such a measure may be needed.

Example 8.1:
A recently retired couple are considering investing their pension lump-sums in the purchase of a small shop. Two suitably sited premises, A and B, are discovered. The average weekly takings of the two shops are quoted as £1050 and £1080 for A and B respectively. Upon further investigation, the investors discover that the averages quoted come from the following recent weekly takings figures:

shop A : £1120, £990, £1040, £1030, £1105, £1015.
shop B : £1090, £505, £915, £1005, £2115, £850.

Advise the couple.

The reader can easily check that the 'averages' quoted are, in fact, the means of the two samples. Based on these two figures alone, it might seem sensible for the couple to prefer shop B to shop A, but a glance at the actual data casts doubt on this conclusion. It is clear that the values for shop B are far more spread out than those for shop A, thereby making the mean for shop B arguably less representative. This difference is illustrated well by the ranges of the two sets:

range of A = highest value − lowest value
           = £1120 − £990
           = *£130*

range of B = £2115 − £505
           = *£1610.*

It can be seen that the much larger range in the latter case is almost entirely due to the single value '£2115'. The retired couple would therefore be well-advised to look at larger samples of weekly takings figures to see if this value is some sort of freak and whether shop B does indeed generate higher weekly takings on average. Before leaving this example, we would mention that they should also ensure that the samples are representative: refer back to Chapter 5.

The inter-quartile range

The data on shop B in example 8.1 illustrate a major deficiency in the range as a measure of spread: it can be grossly distorted by just one value. For example, the reader can easily verify that, by removing the possibly freak value £2115 from the sample, the range of weekly takings for shop B is dramatically reduced to £585.

Any value which produces such a distorting effect on the range must be either a very high or a very low figure, relative to the others. One attempt, therefore, to remove this deficiency is to look at the range of the middle part of the data set, when arranged in ascending or descending order. To do this, we begin by defining:

the *third quartile* (denoted Q_3) as the value which has 75 per cent of the data below, it, and
the *first quartile* (Q_1) as the value with 25 per cent of the data below it.

The required measure, the *inter-quartile range*, is then

the range of the middle 50 per cent of the data

or $Q_3 - Q_1$.

It will be noted that, if we referred to the second quartile (Q_2), we should simply be dealing with the median, discussed in Chapter 7.

Example 8.2:

After receiving complaints from trade union representatives concerning the disparity between higher and lower paid workers in his company, the personnel manager of the company asks for information on the current wage structure. He is given the following data:

Basic weekly wage (£)	Number of employees
under 100	16
100 to under 125	153
125 to under 150	101
150 to under 175	92
175 to under 200	68
200 and over	50

The manager decides to calculate a statistical measure of the spread of these data: perform this calculation.

If we had the raw data, it would be a relatively simple counting process to find the wage figures which are 25 per cent and 75 per cent the way along the list, and thus to find the range or the inter-quartile range. As the data are presented, however, the range is unsuitable, as there are 50 employees in the open-ended upper class, any one of which could seriously distort the measure. Also the inter-quartile range cannot be found by a process of mere counting.

In fact, to determine the inter-quartile range, we adopt the same approach as we did for the median in the previous chapter. First of all, we assume that the wage values are evenly spread throughout their classes, and draw the ogive. The necessary cumulative frequency distribution is:

Basic weekly wage (£) (less than)	Cumulative frequency
100	16
125	169
150	270
175	362
200	430

It will be noted that it is unnecessary to close the final class in order to draw the ogive, and so we do not do so. The ogive is shown in Figure 8.1.

We now note that the total frequency is 480, and so, from the constructions shown on the ogive, we have the following approximations:

Q_3 (corresponding to a cumulative frequency of ¾ of 480, or 360)
    = £174
Q_1 (corresponding to a cumulative frequency of ¼ of 480, or 120)
    = £117
and thus the inter-quartile range = £174 − £117
                                  = £57.

Thus the manager could use an approximate measure of the spread of wages of £57.

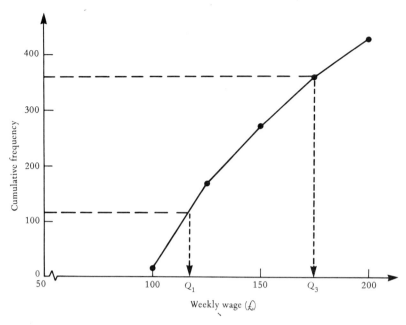

Figure 8.1   *Ogive of wage distribution in example 8.2*

The mean absolute deviation

Many situations arise in which there are no extreme values which could potentially distort a measure of spread. In such cases it seems unreasonable to exclude half the data to hand, as happens if we calculate the inter-quartile range. For this reason we now develop measures of spread which take account of *all* the available data.

Example 8.3:
Measure the spread of shop A's weekly takings (example 8.1), using the whole sample.

A simple way of seeing how far a *single* value is from a (hopefully) representative average figure is to determine the difference between the two. In particular, if we are dealing with the mean, $\bar{x}$, this difference is known as the deviation from the mean or, more simply, *the deviation*. It is clear that, for a widely spread data set, the deviations of the individual values in the set will be relatively large. Similarly, narrowly spread data sets will have relatively small deviation values. We can therefore base our measure on the values of the deviations from the mean. In this case:

deviation $= x - \bar{x}$
values of $x - \bar{x}$:£70, −£60, −£10, −£20, £55, −£35.

The obvious approach might now be to take the mean of these deviations as our measure. Unfortunately, it can be shown that this *always* turns out to be zero, and so the mean deviation will not distinguish one distribution from another. The basic reason for this result is that the negative deviations, when summed, exactly cancel out the positive ones: we must therefore remove this cancellation effect.

One way to remove negative values is simply to ignore the signs, that is, to use the *absolute* values. In this case, the absolute deviations are:

$|x - \bar{x}|$: £70, £60, £10, £20, £55, £35.

The two vertical lines are the mathematical symbol for absolute values. The mean of this list is now a measure of the spread in the data. It is known as *the mean absolute deviation*. Hence

the mean absolute deviation weekly takings for shop A

$$= \frac{70 + 60 + 10 + 20 + 55 + 35}{6}$$

$$= £41.67.$$

Thus our first measure of the spread of shop A's weekly takings is £41.67.

An example will now illustrate how this measure can be calculated in the case of frequency distributions.

Example 8.4:
An analyst is considering two categories of company, X and Y, for possible investment. One of her assistants has compiled the following information on the price-earnings ratios of the shares of companies in the two categories over the past year.

Price-earnings ratios	Number of category X companies	Number of category Y companies
4.95 to under 8.95	3	4
8.95 to under 12.95	5	.8
12.95 to under 16.95	7	8
16.95 to under 20.95	6	3
20.95 to under 24.95	3	3
24.95 to under 28.95	1	4

Compute the mean absolute deviations of these two distributions and comment. (You are given that the means of the two distributions are 15.59 and 15.62 respectively.)

Concentrating first of all on category X, we see that we face the same problem as when we calculated the mean of such a distribution, namely that we have classified data, instead of individual values of x. Adopting a similar approach as before, we take the mid-point of each class and apply the formula for the mean from Chapter 7 to the absolute deviation figures:

Mid-point (x)	$\lvert x - \bar{x}\rvert$	Frequency (f)	$f\lvert x - \bar{x}\rvert$
6.95	8.64	3	25.92
10.95	4.64	5	23.20
14.95	0.64	7	4.48
18.95	3.36	6	20.16
22.95	7.36	3	22.08
26.95	11.36	1	11.36
		25	107.2

Thus the mean of $\lvert x - \bar{x}\rvert$ $= \dfrac{107.2}{25}$.

That is, the mean absolute deviation = *4.29.*

As an exercise, the reader can verify that the mean absolute deviation price-earnings ratio for category Y is *5.16.* These two measures show that the ratios for category Y are considerably more spread about the mean than are those for category X. In view of the virtually identical means (15.59 and 15.62 respectively), this shows that category Y is relatively a more risky investment area than category X, at least in terms of the price-earnings relationship.

Before moving on we note that, in effect, we have used the formula, for a frequency distribution:

$$\text{mean absolute deviation} = \frac{\Sigma f \lvert x - \bar{x}\rvert}{\Sigma f}.$$

The standard deviation

In the preceding section, we solved the problem of negative deviations cancelling out positive ones by using absolute values. There is another way of 'removing' negative signs, namely by *squaring* the figures. If we do that, then we get another, very important, measure of spread, the *standard deviation.*

Example 8.5:

Evaluate the measure of the spread in shop A's weekly takings (example 8.1), using this new approach.

We recall that we have the deviations:

$x - \bar{x}$: £70, −£60, −£10, −£20, £55, −£35;

so, by squaring, we get:

$(x - \bar{x})^2$: 4900, 3600, 100, 400, 3025, 1225.

The mean of these square deviations is now

$$= \frac{13250}{6}$$

$$= 2208.3$$

This is a measure of spread whose units are the square of those of the original data, because we squared the deviations. We thus take the square root, to get back to the original units (£). Our measure of spread is therefore

$$= \sqrt{2208.3}$$
$$= £46.99.$$

This is known as the *standard deviation*, denoted by the letter '*s*'. Its square, the intermediate step before square rooting, is called the *variance*, s^2.

The formula which has been implicitly used here is

$$s = \sqrt{\frac{\Sigma (x - \bar{x})^2}{n}}.$$

Applying the same series of steps to the data in a frequency distribution will give us the corresponding formula in this case:

square the deviations: $(x - \bar{x})^2$

evaluate the mean
(frequency distribution): $\dfrac{\Sigma f (x - \bar{x})^2}{\Sigma f} \quad (= s^2)$

square root: $= \sqrt{\dfrac{\Sigma f (x - x)^2}{\Sigma f}} \quad (= s).$

In practice, this formula can turn out to be very tedious to apply. It can be shown that the following, more easily applicable, formula is the same as the one above:

$$s = \sqrt{\frac{\Sigma f x^2}{\Sigma f} - \left[\frac{\Sigma f x}{\Sigma f} \right]^2}$$

An example will now demonstrate a systematic way of setting out the computations involved with this formula.

Example 8.6:
Evaluate the standard deviation price-earnings ratios for categories X and Y, using the data in example 8.4.

It is advisable to tabulate the calculation columnwise, as it is then easier to do the necessary summations:

x (mid-point)	x^2	f	fx	fx^2
6.95	48.3025	3	20.85	144.9075
10.95	119.9025	5	54.75	599.5125
14.95	223.5025	7	104.65	1564.5175
18.95	359.1025	6	113.70	2154.6150
22.95	526.7025	3	68.85	1580.1075
26.95	726.3025	1	26.95	726.3025
		25	389.75	6769.9625

Thus the standard deviation is

$$s = \sqrt{\frac{\Sigma fx^2}{\Sigma f} - \left[\frac{\Sigma fx}{\Sigma f}\right]^2}$$

$$= \sqrt{\frac{6769.9625}{25} - \left[\frac{389.75}{25}\right]^2}$$

$$= \sqrt{270.7985 - 243.0481}$$

$$= \sqrt{27.7504}$$

i.e. $s = 5.27$.

The standard deviation price-earnings ratio for category X is therefore 5.27. In the same way, the reader can verify that the standard deviation in the case of category Y is 6.29. These statistics again emphasize the wider spread in the category Y data than in the category X data.

The coefficient of variation

In the last example above, it was relatively easy to compare the spread in two sets of data by looking at the standard deviation figures alone, because the means of the two sets were so similar. Another example will show that it is not always so straightforward.

Example 8.7:
Government statistics on the basic weekly wages of workers in two countries show (all figures converted to sterling equivalent):

country V: $\bar{x} = £120$; $s = £55$
country W: $\bar{x} = £90$; $s = £50$.

Can we conclude that country V has a wider spread of basic weekly wages?

By simply looking at the two standard deviation figures, we might be tempted to answer in the affirmative. In doing so, however, we should be ignoring the fact that the two mean values indicate that wages in country V are inherently higher, and so the deviations from the mean and thus the standard deviation will tend to be higher. To make a comparison of like with like, we must use *the coefficient of variation*:

$$\text{coefficient of variation} = \frac{s}{\bar{x}}\%.$$

The coefficient of variation of country V wages $= \frac{55}{120}\%$

$$= 45.8\%$$

and of country W wages $= \frac{50}{90}\%$

$$= 55.6\%.$$

Hence we see that, in fact, it is country W that has the higher variability in basic weekly wages.

A comparison of the measures

In the chapter on averages we saw that there could be considerable room for debate about which measure was most suitable in a given situation. There is less need for such debate here. The standard deviation has a number of properties which have made it a far better basis for the development of statistical theory than the mean absolute deviation. Consequently, the standard deviation has been used almost exclusively in the past, and has become regarded as *the* measure of dispersion.

The only occasions in which the standard deviation might not be considered appropriate are those where a few extremely large (or small) values are present. Unless these extreme values can be shown to be 'freaks', and therefore capable of being ignored, it would be dubious practice to leave them out of the calculation of the standard deviation. In such cases, it would be advisable to use the inter-quartile range, which concentrates on the middle part of the data range, to the exclusion of extreme values.

Summary

The *standard deviation*, $s = \sqrt{\dfrac{\Sigma (x - \bar{x})^2}{n}}$

or $s = \sqrt{\dfrac{\Sigma f x^2}{\Sigma f} - \left[\dfrac{\Sigma f x}{\Sigma f}\right]^2}$ for frequency distributions.

The *coefficient of variation* $= \dfrac{s}{\bar{x}}\%$.

The *mean absolute deviation* $= \dfrac{\Sigma |x - \bar{x}|}{n}$

$or = \dfrac{\Sigma f |x - \bar{x}|}{\Sigma f}$ for frequency distributions.

The *inter-quartile range* $= Q_3 - Q_1$

where Q_3 is the third quartile (which has 75% of the values below it) and Q_1 is the first quartile (which has 25% of the values below it).

The values of the quartiles can be estimated from the ogive, in the case of a frequency distribution.

The *range* = highest value − lowest value.

Exercises on Chapter 8

1 The following data show the weekly number of accidents reported at two different factories over the last two years (100 working weeks):

Number of accidents reported per week	Number of weeks Factory F	Number of weeks Factory G
0	16	25
1	35	27
2	17	20
3	12	5
4	9	7
5	6	7
6	3	4
7	2	5

(a) Evaluate the mean, and hence the mean absolute deviation, number of accidents reported per week in each factory.
(b) Evaluate the standard deviation number of accidents reported per week in each factory.
(c) What do the measures of spread tell us?
(d) In which factory do you think a safety drive would be more effective, and why?

2 The following data show the cash, including banks and building society accounts, possessed by individuals who died in the UK during 1979:

Amount of cash (£)	Number of individuals
less than 1,000	1006
1,000 to under 3,000	2270
3,000 to under 5,000	2045
5,000 to under 10,000	2982
10,000 to under 15,000	2374
15,000 to under 20,000	1674
20,000 to under 50,000	3505
50,000 to under 100,000	644
100,000 to under 200,000	200
200,000 and over	69
	16769

Source: Inland Revenue Statistics, HMSO, 1983.

(a) Why might the standard deviation not be considered an appropriate measure of the spread of this distribution?
(b) Estimate the inter-quartile range of the distribution.
     (*Hint:* when drawing the ogive, ignore the last three classes.)
(c) If you were told that the inter-quartile range of the corresponding distribution in 1985 was £32,000, what reservations would

you have before concluding that the spread of cash possessed by individuals in the UK had widened from 1979 to 1985?

3   A management services study into the delays on production line R in a certain factory shows that the total daily delay times have a mean of 46.2 minutes and a standard deviation of 48.9 minutes. A similar study is undertaken on production line Q in the same factory, and the results, when collated into a frequency distribution show:

Length of delay (minutes)	Number of days
under 5	5
5 to under 10	29
10 to under 20	62
20 to under 30	47
30 to under 60	30
60 to under 120	18
120 to under 240	6
240 to under 480	3

(a) Compute the mean, standard deviation, and hence the coefficient of variation of the length of delay from this sample.
(b) What assumptions have you implicitly made in these calculations?
(c) Why might the standard deviation be considered the 'best' measure of the dispersion of this distribution? Why is it not so appropriate when you compare production line Q with production line R?
(d) Compare the two production lines.

4   A mail-order company is analysing a random sample of its computer records of customers. Among the results are the following distributions:

Size of order £	Number of customers April	September
less than 1	8	4
1 and less than 5	19	18
5 and less than 10	38	39
10 and less than 15	40	69
15 and less than 20	22	41
20 and less than 30	13	20
30 and over	4	5
Total	144	196

You are required to:

(a) calculate the arithmetic mean and standard deviation order size for the *April* sample;
(b) compare the two distributions, given that the arithmetic mean

and standard deviation for the September sample were £13.28 and £7.05 respectively.

ICMA specimen question, published 1986.

5   The following is a distribution of earnings of semi-skilled workers for one week in 1977:

Weekly earnings (£)	Number of workers
20 and under 30	5
30 and under 40	26
40 and under 50	41
50 and under 60	58
60 and under 70	48
70 and under 80	18
80 and under 90	4

You are required to:

(a)   calculate from the distribution given:
   (i)   the median;
   (ii)   the coefficient of variation;

(b)   explain the meaning of the median and the coefficient of variation related to the above example.

ICMA, November 1977.

6   A company has ten sales territories with approximately the same number of sales people working in each territory. Last month the sales orders (£000) achieved were as follows:

Area	A	B	C	D	E	F	G	H	I	J
Sales	150	130	140	150	140	300	110	120	140	120

For these sales data calculate the following:

   (i)   arithmetic mean;
  (ii)   mode;
 (iii)   median;
 (iv)   lower quartile;
  (v)   upper quartile;
 (vi)   quartile deviation (= half the inter-quartile range);
 (vii)   standard deviation;
(viii)   mean absolute deviation.

State clearly the most appropriate average and the most appropriate measure of dispersion for these data.

ICMA, November 1982.

9 Index numbers

Introduction

We conclude this section with a special category of averages, *index numbers*, which measure how a group of related commercial quantities vary, usually over time. As we shall see, index numbers are averages, but they have the extra property that they relate the quantities being measured to a fixed point or *base* period.

Definitions and notation

To illustrate the calculation and use of index numbers, we shall concentrate on those which measure how prices change over time, so-called *price indices*, as these are the most familiar. It is possible, however, to apply the methods to any quantity which varies over space or time.

Average prices which obtain in the base period are represented by the base value 100, and average prices at other times are measured against this nominal value of 100. Thus, if a price index has a value of 105 at a certain point in time, it means that average prices of the goods represented in the index are 5 per cent higher at that time than the average prices were in the base period. The notation used to indicate the base time is

'point in time = 100'.

The best known price index is the *Retail Price Index* (RPI) which is based on average prices in January 1987. Hence we write, for the RPI,

January 1987 = 100.

We now introduce some notation, to be used extensively later. As we have seen above, it is necessary to distinguish between the base time and other times: a subscript 'o' is used to denote the base time, while a subscript 'n' denotes any other time. The latter is often referred to as the *current* time. Thus, if the price of a certain commodity is written as P, we have

P_o = price of the commodity at the base time,
P_n = price of the commodity at the current time.

An example will illustrate these concepts.

Example 9.1:
An index number is to be constructed to represent the 1984 prices of the following commodities, based on their 1983 prices:

	1983 price:	*1984 price:*
commodity A	£1/kilo	£1.10/kilo
commodity B	£2/kilo	£2.10/kilo
commodity C	£1.50/kilo	£1.80/kilo

Express these data in terms of the notation defined above.
As 1983 is to be the base,

$$1983 = 100,$$

and any price in that year will have the subscript 'o'. Hence, for example,

commodity A has P_o = £1.

Since an index is required for 1984, the 'current' year in this example is 1984. Using the subscript 'n':

1984 price of commodity B, P_n = £2.10, and so on.

Calculation of index numbers

A price index can be calculated simply as a mean.

Example 9.2:
Evaluate a price index from the data in example 9.1.
The most simplistic approach would be to add the prices for the two years and express one as the ratio of the other:

1983 total £4.50,
1984 total £5.00,

and the ratio $= \dfrac{5.00}{4.50}$

$$= 1.111$$

Now, with this approach, the 'index' for the base year, 1983, would be

$$\frac{4.50}{4.50} = 1$$

and so, to bring this to the desired notional base value of 100, we multiply by 100. Doing the same for the current year 1984, our index number becomes

$$\frac{5.00}{4.50} \times 100$$

$$= 111.1.$$

This seems a plausible approach, but consider what happens if we had been given the same data, but with the price of commodity C expressed as

1983: 15p per 100 gm. (the same as £1.50/kilo)
1984: 18p per 100 gm.

Then

1983 total = £3.15
1984 total = £3.38

$$\text{and the ratio} = \frac{3.38}{3.15} \times 100$$

$$= 107.3.$$

Thus we have obtained two different values of an 'index' to represent the same set of price changes. This unsatisfactory result arises because our simplistic approach depends on the units of measurement, price per kilo, price per 100 gm, or whatever.

To remove this 'unit dependence', we introduce the ratio of the prices for each commodity

$$\frac{P_n}{P_o}.$$

These are known as *price relatives* and have the property that they do not depend on the units. For example, consider commodity C:

measured in price/kilo, $\quad \dfrac{P_n}{P_o} = \dfrac{£1.80}{£1.50} = 1.20$

measured in price/100 gm, $\quad \dfrac{P_n}{P_o} = \dfrac{18p}{15p} = 1.20.$

Similarly, for the other two commodities:

1984 price relative (based on 1983)
A   1.10
B   1.05

The index is then taken as the mean of these (× 100, as above). This produces the *mean of price relatives* index:

$$\frac{1.10 + 1.05 + 1.20}{3} \times 100$$

$$= 111.7.$$

In other words, our initial index to represent these data is *111.7*. This indicates an *average price increase* for these three commodities of *11.7* per cent from the base, 1983, to 1984. This ease of interpretation is one of the major advantages of index numbers.

Suppose, in the above example, that commodity A was bread and commodity B was pepper. Clearly, bread is an important part of most people's expenditure on food, while pepper is not. Therefore it could be argued that the price index calculated gives too much importance to the 5 per cent increase in B, compared to the 10 per cent increase in A. An improved index takes account of this by *weighting* the more important price relatives more heavily than the less important ones. The resulting *weighted mean of price relatives* has the formula

$$\frac{\Sigma w \frac{P_n}{P_o}}{\Sigma w} \times 100$$

where w stands for the weighting factor.

The effect of these weighting factors is that price changes in important, heavily weighted commodities will cause the index to change far more than relatively unimportant, lightly weighted ones. Thus, in the above example, the price relative of A (bread) would be multiplied by a high value of w, while that of B (pepper) would have only a low multiplying factor.

Example 9.3:
If, in examples 9.1 and 9.2., the relative importance of the commodities is reflected in the factors

    A: 20
    B: 1
    C: 5,

compute the weighted mean of price relatives index.

The price relatives have been calculated earlier, and so can be used to give:

$$\frac{(20 \times 1.10) + (1 \times 1.05) + (5 \times 1.20)}{20 + 1 + 5} \times 100$$

$$= \frac{29.05}{26} \times 100$$

$$= 111.7.$$

The improved index number is thus *111.7*, showing an average price increase of *11.7* per cent.

Although an improvement on the first index, this is still flawed, because the weighting factors used are arbitrary. Even if they are based on an 'expert's' judgement, they will still be subjective. Since the weighting factors are introduced to reflect the relative importance of the commodities, this subjectivity can be eliminated by using the average *expenditures* on each commodity as the weighting factors. If we denote quantity by Q, there are now two choices

$w = P_oQ_o$, the expenditure in the base year;
$w = P_nQ_n$, the expenditure in the current year.

In the former case, the formula for the index number becomes:

$$\frac{\Sigma\, P_oQ_o \cdot \dfrac{P_n}{P_o}}{\Sigma P_oQ_o} \times 100$$

$$= \frac{\Sigma\, P_nQ_o}{\Sigma\, P_oQ_o} \times 100$$

This is the *Laspeyre* or *base weighted* price index.

In the same way, using current year expenditure as weightings, the *Paasche* or *current weighted* price index is

$$\frac{\Sigma\, P_nQ_n}{\Sigma\, P_oQ_n} \times 100$$

Example 9.4:
A company buys in just three raw materials and its management wishes to compute a single value to reflect the average price rise of its raw materials. Calculate the Laspeyre and Paasche price indices for 1985 (1982 = 100) from the following data.

	Average price (£/ton)		Average monthly quantity (tons)	
	1982	1985	1982	1985
Raw material X	2.50	3.00	200	250
Raw material Y	2.20	2.90	200	200
Raw material Z	2.00	2.05	400	650

First of all we determine which symbol in the formula corresponds to which column. Moving from left to right through the table:

1982 average price is base year price; so is P_o;
1985 average price is 'current' year; so is P_n;
1982 tonnage is base year quantity; so is Q_o;
1985 tonnage is 'current' year quantity; so is Q_n.

The Laspeyre index is thus

$$\frac{(3.00 \times 200) + (2.90 \times 200) + (2.05 \times 400)}{(2.50 \times 200) + (2.20 \times 200) + (2.00 \times 400)} \times 100$$

$$= \frac{2000}{1740} \times 100$$

$$= 114.9.$$

The Paasche index is

$$\frac{(3.00 \times 250) + (2.90 \times 200) + (2.05 \times 650)}{(2.50 \times 250) + (2.20 \times 200) + (2.00 \times 650)} \times 100$$

$$= \frac{2662.5}{2365} \times 100$$

$$= 112.6.$$

The company's average price rise has therefore been *14.9* per cent or *12.6* per cent depending on which index is chosen.

Index numbers in practice

Our development of index numbers has now reached the point where the importance of each commodity in the index is reflected by a market-determined, objective weighting. It is rather unsatisfactory, however, that there are two different indices which could be used. There are further index numbers which attempt to reconcile this, but we omit them in this foundation text: the interested reader should consult elsewhere.

The first problem encountered when calculating an index number in practice is, however, which type to choose. Each one has its advantages and disadvantages. The Laspeyre index, for example, has a denominator which does not change from year to year, as it contains only P_o and Q_o, base year data. It is therefore easier to calculate year after year than is a Paasche index, whose denominator must be evaluated anew each year, because of the presence of Q_n. On the other hand, the weighting factors in a Laspeyre index can get out of date as the market changes, whereas a Paasche index uses up-to-date, current, weightings.

The RPI is, in fact, as near to a Paasche index as can be obtained in practice. The *Family Expenditure Survey* (FES) is a massive exercise which collects data on UK families during a mid-year to mid-year time span. The data are then processed during the next six months, ready to be used, inter alia, to provide weightings for the RPI during the following year. The weightings are therefore up to 2½ years out of date by the end of a calendar year, but they are changed each year, and, given the extensive task involved, are as 'current' as is practicable.

The next task in a practical compilation would be the choice of base. There are no hard and fast rules here, but it would clearly be illogical to fix the base of an index at a period during which an abnormal economic event, such as a major industrial dispute, was taking place. Common sense is therefore needed. In addition, the base should not be allowed to go back too far into the past, since we wish to be comparing today's figures with a period of some current relevance. The base should therefore be periodically updated. This leads to the problem of comparing figures across a base change, as happened recently when the base of the RPI was changed from January 1974 to January 1987. The technique involved is known as *splicing*, illustrated below:

Example 9.5:
The price index below changed its base to 1983 after many years with
the base as 1970. How much have prices risen from 1981 to 1985?

Year	Price Index (1970 = 100)
1980	263
1981	271
1982	277
1983	280
	(1983 = 100)
1984	104
1985	107

The clue here is that the 1983 figure has changed from 280 to 100 when
the base was updated. This is a factor of

$$\frac{100}{280}.$$

Applying this to the 1981 figure, the price index for that year with
1983 as base is

$$271 \times \frac{100}{280}$$

or 96.79.

As they are now both to the same base, we can compare directly

1981: 96.79
1985: 107.

This is an increase of 10.21, which is 10.5 per cent of the 1981 figure.
Average prices have therefore increased by *10.5* per cent from 1981 to
1985.

Finally, there is the problem of collecting all the data necessary for
computing the index. This can be an enormous task and involves a
widespread application of the data collection techniques discussed earlier. In the particular case of the RPI, we have already mentioned the
compilation of the weighting factors. As for the prices themselves, these
are collected for a typical 'basket' of goods determined by the RPI
Advisory Committee, a body representative of many interested parties.
There are a number of broad groups in the 'basket' (food, clothing and
footwear, and so on), each divided into subgroups, giving a total of
around 350 items. Officials from the Department of Employment collect
data on the items on a Tuesday in the middle of each month, the
collection being done in such a way as to give a geographical spread
across the nation and to take account of a number of different shops and
varieties for each item. Anything up to 1000 prices could be recorded
for each item in the 'basket'. As these data have to be collected and
processed each month, you may appreciate the complexity of the task.

Applications

Index numbers are in common parlance and widely used. The RPI, for example, is *the* measure of price inflation. Whenever you read that inflation is currently running at 3% (or whatever) this means that, during the previous twelve months, the value of the RPI has increased by 3 per cent. In this section, we look at a number of applications of index numbers, which, though not as often quoted in the media as the above example, are still of great commercial importance.

The first of these is *index linking*. In an attempt to protect people's savings and the incomes of some of the more vulnerable sections of society against the effects of inflation, many saving schemes, pensions and social benefits have, at various times in the past, been *linked* to the RPI in a way illustrated below.

Example 9.6:
At the start of a year, the RPI stood at 340. At that time, a certain person's index-linked pension was £4,200 per annum and she had £360 invested in an index-linked savings bond. At the start of the following year, the RPI had increased to 360: to what level would the pension and the bond investment have risen?

First of all, the RPI has risen by 20 from 340. As a percentage, this is

$$\frac{20}{340} \times 100 = 5.88\%$$

The pension and the investment, being index-linked, would increase by the same percentage. The pension thus increases by

5.88% of £4,200, namely £247 (nearest £)

and the investment by

5.88% of £360, namely £21.17.

Hence, at the start of the year in question, the pension would be £4,447 per annum and the investment would stand at *£381.17.*

Although the RPI is by far the most common index used in linking, there are others. For example, some house insurance policies have premiums and benefits which are linked to the index of house rebuilding costs, a far more suitable index than the RPI, which relates to general retail prices.

At periods of low inflation, the practice of linking pay, pensions, savings, and so on, to the RPI is relatively harmless. When inflation is high, the automatic (and high) rises produced by linking tend to increase costs to industry and commerce, which therefore have to increase their prices. This in turn induces a rise in inflation which triggers off further index-linked rises in pay (and so on). Inflation is therefore seen to be exacerbated by this practice. Indeed, this has been observed in some countries with hyper-inflation and where widespread index-linking has been introduced.

The second common use is in the *deflation of series*, or the removal of inflation from a series of figures, so that they can be compared. An example will illustrate the simple arithmetical process involved.

Example 9.7:
Use the data given below to compare average earnings from 1978 to 1981.

	Average weekly earnings (male manual workers, 21 years +)	RPI (January 1974 = 100)
October 1978	£83.50	201.1
October 1979	£96.94	235.6
October 1980	£113.06	271.9
October 1981	£125.58	303.7

Source: various editions, Monthly Digest of Statistics.

The value of the RPI in October 1978 shows that average prices were 2.011 times higher then than in January 1974. The purchasing power of a pound will therefore have decreased by this factor in the time. An October 1978 wage of £83.50 was therefore 'worth'

$$\frac{83.50}{2.011} = £41.52$$

in January 1974. This is known as the *real* wage, at January 1974 prices. Applying this process to all the figures, we obtain:

	Real *wages, January 1974 prices:*
October 1978	£41.52
October 1979	$\frac{96.94}{2.356} = $ £41.15
October 1980	£41.58
October 1981	£41.35.

The average wages of this section of society can thus be seen not to have changed appreciably *in real terms* over this time period. The apparent rises in wages have been almost exactly cancelled out by similarly sized price rises.

The RPI is not the only index used in deflation, particularly if there is a more suitable index available. For instance, an exporting company interested in its *real* level of profits might well deflate its actual profit figures by an index of *export* prices.

The main criticism of deflation, and indeed another problem of index-linking, is that we are applying an *average* figure (for price rises or whatever) to a *particular* set of people who may or may not be 'average'. To illustrate the effects this could have, consider the cases of,

an old-age pension for a single person being linked to the RPI;
a brewery in the north of England deflating its profit figures by the RPI.

In the first instance, the single pensioner cannot be considered 'average in at least two senses. The RPI measures price rises for the average family, which a single pensioner certainly is not, and the income of a pensioner is generally considerably below average. The effect of this latter factor is that a pensioner will spend a considerably larger portion of his/her income on heating and lighting, and on food than most other people. Thus, at times when prices of these commodities are rising faster than others (a situation which *has* occurred in the recent past), the RPI will underestimate the average price rises in a pensioner's 'basket' of goods and so linking to this index will leave him/her worse off. Indeed, it has been suggested in some quarters that a 'pensioners' price index' be introduced to overcome this problem.

The RPI measures price rises for *all* commodities, not just one type such as beer and related products, which might be rising in price at a different rate from the average. The brewery in the latter example would therefore be advised to deflate by the 'Alcoholic Drinks' section of the RPI. Even then, prices might be rising at a faster or slower rate in the north of England, compared to this average UK figure. The *real* profit figures would then be too high or too low, respectively.

Summary

If we denote

> base period prices by P_o,
> current prices by P_n,
> base period quantities by Q_o,
> current quantities by Q_n,
> general weighting factors by w,

then three possible price indices are:

weighted mean of price relatives

$$\frac{\Sigma \, w \cdot \frac{P_n}{P_o}}{\Sigma w} \times 100;$$

Laspeyre or base weighted

$$\frac{\Sigma P_n Q_o}{\Sigma P_o Q_o} \times 100;$$

Paasche or current weighted

$$\frac{\Sigma P_n Q_n}{\Sigma P_o Q_n} \times 100.$$

In each case the summation is over all commodities in the index.

Exercises on Chapter 9

1   In January 1986 a small manufacturing concern is attempting to calculate the average price rise of its raw materials since it

started business in January 1985. The prices of the four most used materials, together with the owner's estimate of their importance are given in the following table:

	January 1985 price	*January 1986 price*	*'Owner's importance factor'*
Material A	£3.20/kg	£3.80/kg	10
Material B	£105/tonne	£120/tonne	5
Material C	£1500/tonne	£1520/tonne	2
Material D	£45/litre	£48/litre	1

In addition, the books of the company indicate the following typical weekly amounts used;

	January 1985	*January 1986*
Material A	410 kg	405 kg
Material B	1.1 tonnes	1.1 tonnes
Material C	2.6 tonnes	2.7 tonnes
Material D	250 litres	400 litres

Evaluate (*i*)   a weighted mean of price relatives, based on the owner's factors;

(*ii*)   a Laspeyre price index;

and   (*iii*)   a Paasche price index.

Discuss the relative merits of these three as measures of the 'average' price rise of the company's raw materials.

2   In Ruritania, the base period of its retail price index has changed twice recently, in January 1979 and January 1982. The values of the index in the first month of the last few years are:

January of year	*Index*
	(January 1973 = 100)
1977	391.1
1978	401.3
1979	417.2
	(January 1979 = 100)
1980	111.3
1981	126.9
1982	141.7
	(January 1982 = 100)
1983	112.8
1984	129.8
1985	147.1

What have been the percentage rises in average Ruritania prices

(*i*)   from 1981 to 1985;

(*ii*)   from 1978 to 1982;

(*iii*)   from 1977 to 1985?

3(*a*) A company which operates solely in Molvania has the following figures to hand:

	Profits (£ million equivalent)	Average value of Molvanian RPI (January 1973 = 100)
1983	136.6	210.2
1984	150.6	220.3
1985	166.1	230.8

Compute a set of real profit figures for this company and hence comment on its profit performance. Why might this example of deflation of a series be considered invalid?

(*b*) The company has a policy of increasing the price of its major product by an amount index-linked to the RPI over the previous twelve months. During 1985 the product's price has been £12.20 per unit (sterling equivalent). What price will the company policy dictate for the product in 1986? Comment on the policy.

4(*a*) 'A Laspeyre price index is a weighted mean of price relatives.' Explain precisely what this statement means.

(*b*)

Component type	January 1983 price (pence)	May 1983 price (pence)	Weekly quantity of components used, January 1983.
Clips	10	15	3,000
Seals	16	24	6,000
Tubes	12	12	2,000
Widgets	10	11	5,000

Calculate an all-items price index for components for May 1983, using January 1983 = 100.

(*c*) What is involved in the splicing of index numbers?

ICMA, May 1983.

5(*a*) Briefly explain *two* commercial, industrial or business uses of index numbers.

(*b*) A cost accountant has derived the following information about basic weekly wages rate (£*W*) and the number of people employed (*E*) in the factories of a large chemical company.

Technical group of employees	July 1979 W	July 1979 E	July 1980 W	July 1980 E	July 1981 W	July 1981 E
Q	60	5	70	4	80	4
R	60	2	65	3	70	3
S	70	2	85	2	90	1
T	90	1	110	1	120	2

(*i*) Calculate a Laspeyre all-items index number for the July 1980 basic weekly wage rates, with July 1979 = 100.

(*ii*) Calculate a Paasche all-items index number for the July 1981 basic weekly wage rates, with July 1979 = 100.

(*iii*)   Briefly compare your index numbers for the company with the official government figures for the Chemical and Allied Industries, which are given below:

	Yearly annual averages		
	1979	*1980*	*1981*
Weekly wage rates	156.3	187.4	203.4
(July 1976 = 100)			

Source: Employment Gazette, November 1981.

ICMA, November 1982.

6   Your company has a factory, the buildings of which are insured through an index-linked scheme. Under this scheme the sum insured of a policyholder's buildings is automatically changed each month in line with the Cost of Construction Materials Index which is shown below.

Cost of Construction Materials Index (1975 = 100)

	1980	*1981*	*1982*
January	200.3	225.0	244.5
February	205.1	226.8	249.3
March	210.2	229.9	251.4
April	212.9	232.2	253.4
May	217.3	234.3	254.9
June	218.1	235.4	255.6
July	220.2	236.3	
August	221.3	236.6	
September	222.3	237.1	
October	223.1	239.6	
November	223.6	240.4	
December	224.0	241.0	

Source: Monthly Digest of Statistics, July 1982.

(*a*)   Explain briefly why weights would be used in the construction of this index. (No specific technical details of the Construction Materials Index are required.)

(*b*)   What is the importance of the phrase '1975 = 100'?

(*c*)   What was the percentage increase in the cost of construction materials over the two-year period ended in June 1982?

(*d*)   Your company's factory was insured for £1.5 million in January 1981. What was the sum insured for in June 1982? Assuming the percentage increase to be the same in the second half of 1982 as in the first half of 1982, estimate the sum insured on the factory for December 1982.

ICMA, November 1983.

Part Three

Forecasting

10 Correlation

Introduction

In this section we look at one of the major applications of statistics, namely forecasting. Although there are a number of ways of producing forecasts which involve little or no mathematics, we shall concentrate here on two of the most important quantitative approaches, causal and extrapolative. A *causal* approach is based on the assumption that changes in the variable which we wish to forecast are *caused* by changes in one or more other variables. With an *extrapolative* approach, we examine past data on the variable which is to be forecasted, in order to determine any patterns they exhibit. It is then assumed that these patterns will continue into the future: in other words, they are *extrapolated*.

Let us begin with the causal approach, and, to simplify matters, we shall deal with the case in which the variable to be forecasted (the dependent variable, *y*) depends on only *one* other variable (the independent variable, *x*). Before actually looking at how to produce forecasts in such situations, we must consider the question as to how we know that changes in *y* *are* caused by changes in *x* (alternatively: how we know that *y* depends on *x*). The answer to this involves the study of *correlation*.

Correlation

Two variables are said to be *correlated* if they are related to one another, or, more precisely, if changes in the value of one tend to accompany changes in the other. Now, we have already used the (*x*, *y*) notation of the earlier Part One, and this initially suggests a graphical approach: if there are pairs of data available on the variables *x* and *y*, then these can

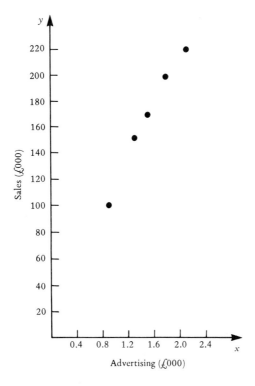

Figure 10.1 *Scatter diagram, example 10.1*

be plotted as points against a set of *x*– and *y*–axes. The result is known as a *scatter diagram* or *scatter graph*.

Example 10.1:
A company is investigating the effects of its advertising on sales. Consequently, data on monthly advertising and sales in the following month are collated to obtain:

Advertising expenditure in month (£000)	Total sales in following month (£000)
1.3	151.6
0.9	100.1
1.8	199.3
2.1	221.2
1.5	170.0

Plot these data on a scatter diagram.

Since the company is interested in how advertising affects sales, it seems that sales should be the dependent variable, *y*, and advertising the independent, *x*. The scatter diagram is shown in Figure 10.1.

The five pairs of data points are marked as crosses on the graph.

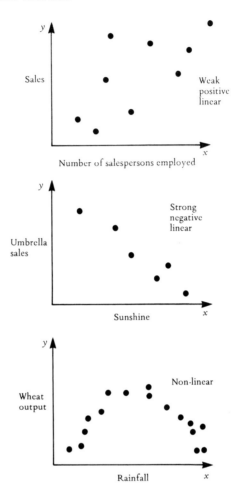

Figure 10.2 *Examples of correlation*

Since, unlike Part One, we have not been told that *y* is a function of *x* here, the points have *not* been joined up. In particular, although the points appear to be *close* to lying on a straight line, they do not lie *exactly* on a line; we do not know that a linear function is involved and so none has been drawn in.

The scatter diagram in the above example seems to show a case where the two variables *are* related to one another. Further, the relationship seems to be of an approximately linear nature: it is an example of *linear* correlation. Since the approximation is so good, and the points are close to a straight line, we talk of *strong* linear correlation. Finally, as the gradient of the 'line' is positive, it is *positive linear* (or direct) correlation. Figure 10.2 shows further examples, of

weak positive linear correlation, in which *y* shows a slight tendency
to increase as *x* does;

strong negative linear (or inverse) correlation, in which *y* shows a
strong tendency to *decrease* as *x* increases;

non-linear correlation, in which *x* and *y* are clearly related, but not in
a linear fashion.

Although such scatter diagrams are useful for getting a feel for the
presence or otherwise of correlation, it is often difficult to judge what is
'weak' and what is 'strong', and, indeed, whether a large number of
points on a diagram constitute any correlation at all. Therefore an
objective *measure* of correlation is needed.

Pearson's correlation coefficient

The statistician Pearson developed a measure of the amount of *linear*
correlation present in a set of pairs of data. This *Pearson's correlation
coefficient*, denoted r, is defined as

$$r = \frac{n\Sigma xy - \Sigma x \cdot \Sigma y}{\sqrt{(n\Sigma x^2 - (\Sigma x)^2)(n\Sigma y^2 - (\Sigma y)^2)}}$$

where *n* is the number of data points.

This measure has the property of always lying in the range -1 to $+1$,
where

$r = +1$ denotes *perfect* positive linear correlation
(the data points lie *exactly* on a straight line);
$r = -1$ denotes perfect negative linear correlation;
$r = 0$ denotes no *linear* correlation.

The strength of a correlation can be judged by its proximity to $+1$ or
-1: the nearer it is (and the farther away from zero), the stronger is the
linear correlation.

Example 10.2:
Evaluate Pearson's correlation coefficient for the data in example 10.1,
and interpret its value.

As with previous calculations involving summations, we facilitate the
calculations by setting them out in columns:

x	y	x^2	y^2	xy
1.3	151.6	1.69	22982.56	197.08
0.9	100.1	0.81	10020.01	90.09
1.8	199.3	3.24	39720.49	358.74
2.1	221.2	4.41	48929.44	464.52
1.5	170.0	2.25	28900.00	255.00
7.6	842.2	12.40	150552.50	1365.43

Thus

$$r = \frac{(5 \times 1365.43) - (7.6 \times 842.2)}{\sqrt{[(5 \times 12.4) - 7.6^2] \, [(5 \times 150552.5) - 842.2^2]}}$$

$$= \frac{426.43}{\sqrt{4.24 \times 43461.66}}$$

$$= 0.993.$$

The value of Pearson's correlation coefficient in this case is *0.993*. The arithmetic in such a calculation can be seen to be potentially very tedious. The reader would therefore be well advised to investigate the availability of any computer packages or special functions on a calculator in order to ease the computation of correlation coefficients.

The value of the coefficient in this case is clearly very close to the value 1, indicating a very strong positive linear correlation, and reflecting the close proximity of the points in Figure 10.1 to a straight line.

In general, it is not always as straightforward to interpret a value of r as in the above case. Although it would be inappropriate for the purpose of this text to go into detailed theory, it must be noted that the sample size (n) has a crucial effect: the smaller the value of n, the 'easier' it is for a large value of r to arise. Thus a value for the correlation coefficient of, say, 0.7 can indicate only a weak correlation for some small samples but a strong one for some large samples. As a very rough guide, the following table shows the sort of value a correlation coefficient should have for the correlation to be considered 'strong':

sample size (n):	minimum r to be considered 'strong':
5	0.88
10	0.63
20	0.44
50	0.27
100	0.19

It should be remembered when referring to this table that negative values of r can indicate 'strong' correlations. Thus, for a sample size of 20, an r–value of −0.6 would show a strong *negative* linear correlation.

We have already mentioned the desirability of using a computer package or the statistical functions on a calculator for determining values of Pearson's correlation coefficient. The next example illustrates a time-saving device which can be used when the calculations are done from the formula.

Example 10.3:
A company has the following data on its sales during the last year in each of its regions and the corresponding number of salespersons employed during this time:

region	sales (units)	number of salespersons
A	236	11
B	234	12
C	298	18

D	250	15
E	246	13
F	202	10

Are the sales in any way connected to the number of salespersons employed?

To answer this question we shall calculate Pearson's correlation co-efficient using the formula. However, before we do so, it would be useful to consider the following. If, on a scatter diagram, we were to move the origin and/or change the scales on the axes, the points would still lie in the same configuration and the correlation would thus remain un-altered. Arithmetically, this means we can add or subtract a *constant* value to *all* the x–values (or y–values) and we can multiply or divide *all* the x–values (or y–values) by a *constant* amount, and leave the value of r unaltered. This fact enables us to simplify the arithmetic considerably.

The way the question is phrased, sales might depend on the number of salespersons, and so we can denote the former y and the latter x. The numbers involved can now be made much smaller if we use

$$\frac{\text{sales figures} - 200}{2}$$

and number of salespersons $- 10$

in the calculations. This gives the modified values of x and y:

y	x
18	1
17	2
49	8
25	5
23	3
1	0

The computation of r can now be performed fairly quickly:

x	y	x^2	y^2	xy
1	18	1	324	18
2	17	4	289	34
8	49	64	2401	392
5	25	25	625	125
3	23	9	529	69
0	1	0	1	0
19	133	103	4169	638

Thus

$$r = \frac{(6 \times 638) - (19 \times 133)}{\sqrt{[(6 \times 103) - 19^2]\,[(6 \times 4169) - 133^2]}}$$

$$= \frac{1301}{\sqrt{257 \times 7325}}$$

$$= 0.948.$$

The earlier table confirms that this value of Pearson's correlation coefficient, *0.948*, shows a strong positive correlation, and so it appears that the number of salespersons *has* had an effect on sales. The fact that the correlation is positive is an encouraging sign for the company: it appears to indicate that, as the number of salespersons increases, so do sales.

There are, however, a number of cautionary notes on this conclusion. It is possible that an apparently high correlation can occur *accidentally* or *spuriously* between two unconnected variables. There is no mathematical way of checking when this is the case, but common sense can help. In the case under discussion, it seems plausible that sales and the number of salespersons *are* connected, and so it would seem reasonable to assume that this is *not* an accidental or spurious correlation.

More importantly here, two variables can be correlated because they are separately correlated to a *hidden third variable*. The size of the region could well be such a variable: larger regions would tend to have larger sales figures and the management of larger regions would tend to employ more salespersons to cover those areas. It is therefore *possible* that this high correlation coefficient may have arisen because

the variable 'sales' is highly correlated with size of region,
the number of salespersons is highly correlated with size of region,
but sales and number of salespersons are not directly connected.

Even if this third variable effect does not obtain, we still cannot conclude that *y depends* on *x*. The strong correlation lends support to the *assumption* that this is so, but does not *prove* it. *Correlation cannot be used to prove causation.*

Rank correlation. Spearman's coefficient

Situations often arise where you could be interested in the degree of correlation between two variables, but where one or both of them do not appear in a suitable quantitative form. In such circumstances, Pearson's coefficient cannot be used. If, however, the variables can be *ranked*, or put into order, then a *rank correlation coefficient*, as developed by Spearman, can be applied. The formula for this coefficient is

$$r' = 1 - \frac{6\Sigma d^2}{n(n^2 - 1)}$$

where *d* denotes the difference in ranks. The interpretation of values of *r'* is similar to that for values of *r*, with similar caveats.

Example 10.4:
Two personnel officers interview seven people for a vacancy. After the interview, they rank the candidates in order of suitability, with 1 = *'best'*:

Candidate	Interviewer A's rank	Interviewer B's rank
Z	1	3
Y	6	4
X	3	1
W	5	6
V	2	5
U	4	2
T	7	7

To what extent have the two interviewers agreed?

To calculate the rank correlation coefficient, we first compute the values of d. Because this number is to be squared, we pay no attention to its sign.

Candidate	d = difference in rank	d^2
Z	2	4
Y	2	4
X	2	4
W	1	1
V	3	9
U	2	4
T	0	0
		26

$$r' = 1 - \frac{6 \times 26}{7\,(7^2 - 1)}$$
$$= 1 - .464$$
$$= 0.536.$$

In view of the sample size (7), this value of Spearman's rank correlation coefficient, *0.536*, is not particularly high, showing a fairly weak positive correlation. The interviewers, therefore, have found some degree of consensus, but not a strong degree.

The next example is one in which the variables must be ranked first.

Example 10.5:
A firm of accountants employs five trainees at the start of a year. At the end of the year, the trainees are given appraisal interviews and awarded ratings from A (excellent) through to E (unsatisfactory). In addition, the firm has a list of average examination marks attained by the trainees on a course at the local college.

Trainee	Appraisal grade	Average examination mark (%)
I	A	60
J	B	61
K	A	50
L	C	72
M	D	70

Compute a correlation coefficient between appraisal grade and examination mark, and comment.

To use Pearson's coefficient, both variables have to be in a numerical form. We could make the grade numerical by allocating numbers to letters, but this would be arbitrary: we do not know, for example, if the 'difference' between A and B is the same as that between B and C. Spearman's coefficient must therefore be used and the data ranked:

Trainee	Rank of grade	Rank of examination mark
I	1.5	4
J	3	3
K	1.5	5
L	4	1
M	5	2

The best in each case has been ranked '1'. We could just as well have ranked the worst as '1', *provided we did so for both variables*. Trainee I and K both have grade A, and so are first equal. They therefore 'share' first and second and so are both allocated the 'average rank' of 1.5. This is known as instance of a *tied rank*.

We can now proceed to calculate the rank correlation coefficient:

d	d^2
2.5	6.25
0	0
3.5	12.25
3	9
3	9
	36.5

$$r' = 1 - \frac{6 \times 36.5}{5(5^2 - 1)}$$
$$= 1 - 1.825$$
$$= -0.825$$

The value of Spearman's rank correlation coefficient, *−0.825*, is quite high, showing a fairly strong *negative* correlation between appraisal grade and examination mark. The firm would be well advised to investigate this further, because trainees with lower appraisal grades are tending to get higher examination marks, while those who are doing better on appraisal are less successful in examinations.

A comparison of Pearson's and Spearman's coefficients

We conclude this chapter by considering the comparative merits of the two correlation coefficients under discussion. If we look back to example 10.5, it can be seen that the process of ranking the examination marks loses some of the detail of the data. For instance, the first three marks are:

1	72
2	70
3	61

and so, by working only with the ranks, we lose the fact that the first mark is only slightly more than the second, while the second is considerably more than the third. This illustrates that, *if it is possible*, Pearson's coefficient should be preferred to Spearman's, since it uses more of the detailed information in the data. In example 10.5, it was *not* possible to use Pearson's coefficient, since one of the variables was not in a numerical form.

When, as is usually the case, we are working with sample data, we might wish to know how well two variables are correlated in their *populations*. In example 10.5, it would be interesting to know to what extent the strong negative correlation would occur in *all* trainees, as opposed to the sample of five who happened to start together at the firm. The theory behind this type of question is too advanced for this text, and so we just point out that it is necessary to make a number of assumptions to be able to infer the population value of Pearson's coefficient, whereas, in the case of Spearman's coefficient, no such assumptions are needed. The practical consequence of this which concerns us here is that care must be taken before assuming that a sample value of r will be reflected in the population as a whole.

Finally, if *Pearson's* coefficient is calculated for a set of *ranked* data which are treated as ordinary numbers, the answer will be the same as Spearman's coefficient, with minor discrepancies introduced if there are tied rankings (as in example 10.5). However, it is clear from earlier worked examples that the rank correlation is by far the easier to compute. Therefore, in a case where one or both variables are ranked, or must be ranked, Spearman's coefficient should be chosen, because of its easier arithmetic.

Summary

Pearson's coefficient of linear correlation, r, is

$$r = \frac{n\Sigma xy - \Sigma x \cdot \Sigma y}{\sqrt{(n\Sigma x^2 - (\Sigma x)^2)(n\Sigma y^2 - (\Sigma y)^2)}}$$

Spearman's rank correlation coefficient, r', is

$$r' = 1 - \frac{6\Sigma d^2}{n(n^2 - 1)}$$

where n is sample size (number of data points) and d is the difference in ranks.

When interpreting correlation coefficients, care should be taken over:
how representative (or otherwise) is the sample;
the sample size;

whether the correlation is spurious or accidental;
whether a hidden third variable is present.

Exercises on Chapter 10

1   In order to determine how soon trainees in her firm can be allowed
to work with minimal supervision, an accountant collates the following data on the accuracy of her current trainees' work:

Trainee	Number of days of employment	Number of errors recorded in the last day
A	3	12
B	10	4
C	9	6
D	8	6
E	11	5
F	5	11

(a)   Plot these data on a scatter diagram.
(b)   Compute Pearson's correlation coefficient between days of employment and number of errors.
(c)   Interpret this value. Would you expect this degree of correlation
to extend as far as trainees who have been employed for 30
days? Why not?

2   The management of a company is comparing the prices it has
charged during the recent past to prices charged by the industry as a
whole. To achieve this, the following table is drawn up, showing the
price of the company's major article and the government's price
index for the sector of the economy in which the firm operates, for
the last seven months.

Price of company's major article (£/unit)	Official price index (January 1976 = 100)
11.20	231.0
11.25	232.1
11.25	232.9
11.35	234.3
11.40	235.0
11.40	236.2
11.50	237.2

(a)   Find Pearson's correlation coefficient between these variables.
(*Hint:* first of all, modify the data as we did in example 10.3.)
(b)   What does this measure tell the company management? What
further information would they need to draw from the data in
order to compare company prices with those of the industry as
a whole?

3   A college is selecting students for a course requiring one 'A'-level
pass. In the post one morning, there are eight application forms for

the course. From these forms, the following data is drawn: the grade of the 'A'-level pass (A, best, to E) and an assessment from the candidate's school of his/her ability (A, excellent, to D, unsatisfactory):

Candidate	'A'-level grade	School assessment
1	D	C
2	A	A
3	C	B
4	D	D
5	B	A
6	E	C
7	C	B
8	B	B

(a) Rank these data and compute Spearman's rank correlation coefficient. (Take care when ranking the *triple* tie of B's under school assessment.)

(b) What does this value mean?

4 A sample of eight employees is taken from the production department of a light engineering factory. The data below relate to the number of weeks' experience in the wiring of components, and the number of components which were rejected as unsatisfactory last week.

Employee	A	B	C	D	E	F	G	H
Weeks of experience (X)	4	5	7	9	10	11	12	14
Number of rejects (Y)	21	22	15	18	14	14	11	13

$\Sigma X = 72$; $\Sigma Y = 128$; $\Sigma XY = 1069$; $\Sigma X^2 = 732$; $\Sigma Y^2 = 2156$.

(a) Draw a scatter diagram of the data.

(b) Calculate a coefficient of correlation for these data and interpret its value.

ICMA, May 1982.

5 Draw scatter diagrams of about ten points to illustrate the following degrees of linear association:

(a) weak, positive correlation;

(b) approximately zero correlation;

(c) $r = -1$;

(d) fairly strong, negative correlation.

ICMA, May 1984.

6 A national consumer protection society investigated seven brands of paint to determine their quality relative to price. The society's conclusions were ranked as follows:

Brand	Price per litre (£)	Quality ranking
T	1.92	2
U	1.58	6
V	1.35	7
W	1.60	4
X	2.05	3
Y	1.39	5
Z	1.77	1

Determine the value of a suitable correlation coefficient and hence whether the customer generally gets value for money.
ICMA, November 1976.

11 Linear regression

Introduction

The topic of correlation was developed in the preceding chapter partly as a way of determining whether one variable, y, depends on another, x. As we emphasized at the time, the presence of a high degree of correlation only lends weight to an *assumption* of dependence or causation. We now proceed to consider *causal forecasting*: how one variable can be forecasted from another, correlated one.

Most of the earlier discussion concentrated on *linear* correlation. For simplicity, we restrict ourselves here also to the linear case. Thus we are interested in situations where the dependence is in the form of a straight line. As we saw in Part One, this involves equations of the type

$$y = a + bx,$$

where a and b are numbers. We are, therefore, initially concerned with determining suitable straight line(s) for the particular problem.

The least squares criterion

The approach is illustrated through an example first seen in Chapter 10.

Example 11.1:
A company has the following data on its sales during the last year in each of its regions and the corresponding number of salespersons employed during this time:

Region	Sales (units)	Number of salespersons
A	236	11
B	234	12
C	298	18
D	250	15
E	246	13
F	202	10

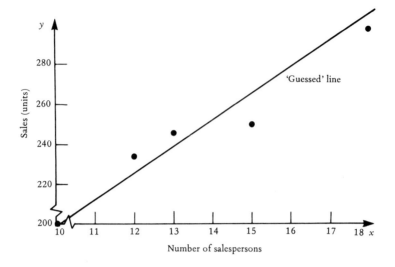

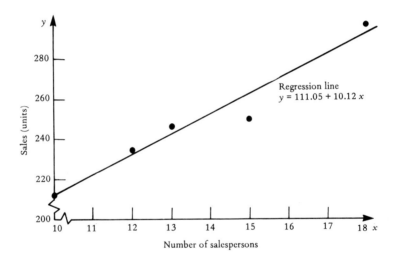

Figure 11.1 *Guessed line and regression line, example 11.1*

Develop a linear model for forecasting sales from the number of sales-persons.

The linear correlation coefficient between these two variables was calculated (in example 10.3) to be 0.948. This high value encourages us to assume that sales, y, might depend on number of salespersons, x, in a linear way.

The scatter diagram for the data is shown in Figure 11.1. For convenience of drawing, the scales on the axes do not start from zero. However, this has the effect of exaggerating the divergences from linearity. A truer impression would be obtained from a graph containing the origin, but this would not be so easy to draw.

In the upper part of the figure, a straight line has been gauged or 'guessed' by using a ruler to draw a line which appears to be 'close' to all five data points. This approximate approach may well be accurate enough in many instances, but is certainly arbitrary. A number of different, equally plausible, lines could be drawn in: the question is how can you judge whether one line is 'better' than another. Indeed, which is the 'best'?

If we look at the 'guessed' line, it is clear that there are discrepancies between actual y–values and y–values obtained from the line. There are y-errors present, and the sizes of these enable us to judge one line against another. Examples of y–errors in this instance are:

$x = 13$: actual $y = 246$
y from line $= 239$ (approximately)
y–error in line $= -7$

$x = 15$: actual $y = 250$
y from line $= 266$
y–error in line $= +16$.

It can be seen that some errors are positive and some negative. Simply adding the errors to judge the 'goodness' of the line, therefore, would not be a sensible idea, as large positive errors would tend to be cancelled out by large negative ones. To eliminate this effect, we *square* the errors, and deem one line 'better' than another if its sum of *squared* errors is lower. The 'best' line is thus the one with the least sum of squared errors: the so-called *least squares regression line*. Without going through the theory, this can be shown to have equation

$$y = a + bx$$

where $b = \dfrac{n\Sigma xy - (\Sigma x)(\Sigma y)}{n\Sigma x^2 - (\Sigma x)^2}$

and $a = \bar{y} - b\bar{x}$ ($\bar{y}, \bar{x}$: means of y and x, respectively).

The calculation of a and b is set out in a familiar tabular form:

x	y	x^2	xy
11	236	121	2596
12	234	144	2808
18	298	324	5364
15	250	225	3750
13	246	169	3198
10	202	100	2020
79	1466	1083	19736

$$b = \frac{(6 \times 19736) - (79 \times 1466)}{(6 \times 1083) - 79^2}$$

$$= \frac{2602}{257}$$

$$= 10.12$$

$$\bar{x} = \frac{79}{6} = 13.17$$

$$\bar{y} = \frac{1466}{6} = 244.33$$

and so

$$a = 244.33 - (10.12 \times 13.17)$$
$$= 111.05.$$

Thus the least squares regression line in this case is

$$y = 111.05 + 10.12x.$$

This line has been plotted on the lower scatter diagram of Figure 11.1. The values of the coefficients in this line are clear: each extra salesperson generates an extra 10.12 sales (on average), while 111.05 units will be sold if no salespersons are used. The latter may well be nonsensical, but we return to this later.

It should be noted that, unlike Pearson's correlation coefficient, these calculations do not use Σy^2, and so no time has been wasted evaluating it. Also, it will be appreciated that calculations such as these can involve potentially large numbers, and so, again, the reader might be advised to use an available computer package or statistical function on a calculator.

Forecasting

Once the equation of the regression line has been computed, it is a relatively straightforward process to obtain forecasts.

Example 11.2:
In the situation of example 11.1, forecast the number of sales which would be expected next year in regions which employed

(a)   14 salespersons;
(b)   25 salespersons.

As we have the 'best' line representing the dependence of sales on the number of salespersons, we will use it for the forecasts. The values could be read off the line drawn on the scattergraph, but it is more accurate to use the equation of the line.

(a)   the regression line is
$$y = 111.05 + 10.12x;$$
so, when $x = 14$
$$y = 111.05 + 10.12 \times 14$$
$$= 252.73.$$

Rounding this to a whole number, we are forecasting that *253 units* will be sold in a region employing 14 salespersons.

(b)   Substituting $x = 25$ into the formula:

$$y = 111.05 + 10.12 \times 25$$
$$= 364.05.$$

Hence the forecast is that *364 units* will be sold in a region employing 25 salespersons.

We give one more example to illustrate the complete process of forecasting from paired samples.

Example 11.3:

A company has the following data on its profits and advertising expenditure over the last six years:

Profits (£m)	Advertising expenditure (£m)
11.3	0.52
12.1	0.61
14.1	0.63
14.6	0.70
15.1	0.70
15.2	0.75

Forecast the profits for next year if an advertising budget of £800,000 is allocated.

First of all, to justify our assumption that there is a relationship between the two variables, the correlation coefficient should be computed. It is left as an exercise to the reader to verify that its value is *0.936*. This high correlation encourages us to proceed with the regression approach.

As we wish to forecast profits, we shall make this the dependent variable, *y*, and advertising expenditure the independent variable, *x*. The next step is to evaluate the parameters *a* and *b*:

x	y	x^2	xy
0.52	11.3	0.2704	5.876
0.61	12.1	0.3721	7.381
0.63	14.1	0.3969	8.883
0.70	14.6	0.49	10.22
0.70	15.1	0.49	10.57
0.75	15.2	0.5625	11.4
3.91	82.4	2.5819	54.33

Thus

$$b = \frac{(6 \times 54.33) - (3.91 \times 82.4)}{(6 \times 2.5819) - 3.91^2}$$

$$= \frac{3.796}{0.2033}$$

$$= 18.67$$

$$\bar{x} = \frac{3.91}{6} = 0.652,$$

$$\bar{y} = \frac{82.4}{6} = 13.73,$$

and so

$$a = 13.73 - (18.67 \times 0.652)$$
$$= 1.56.$$

The least squares regression line relating profits to advertising expenditure therefore has equation

$$y = 1.56 + 18.67x.$$

Hence each extra million pounds' advertising generates an extra £18.67 million profits. Also profits would be £1.56 million without any advertising. The dubious nature of this latter statement will be referred to later.

If advertising expenditure is to be £800,000 ($x = 0.8$), then

$$y = 1.56 + 18.67 \times 0.8$$
$$= 16.496.$$

Rounding this value off to a sensible level of apparent accuracy, we are forecasting profits of *£16.5 million* next year, if advertising expenditure is £800,000.

Judging the validity of forecasts

When we have made forecasts, obvious questions to be asked are

'How accurate are they?'
'What validity do they have?'

Such queries can be addressed in a number of ways.

The importance of using the correlation coefficient as a check on the validity of the assumption of causality has already been stressed. In addition, you should bear in mind the caveats mentioned in Chapter 10. In particular, is there a hidden third variable in the problem? Thus, in examples 11.1 and 11.2, sales might not depend on the number of salespersons at all, but on the size of the region, as we mentioned when first discussing this problem. If this is the case, then simply increasing the number of salespersons within a region would not in itself increase sales. Even if this is not the case, have we got the causation the right way round? In example 11.3, it might be that, as profits increase, the company feels able to spend more on advertising, so that advertising expenditure depends on profits, contrary to the implicit assumption we made when forecasting profits. If this is the case, increasing the advertising would not necessarily increase profits.

Before leaving the correlation coefficient, we mention another, closely related, measure, *the coefficient of determination*, r^2. The value of this measure, when expressed as a percentage, shows the percentage of variations in the variables which can be explained by the regression analysis. The remaining variation is due to factors omitted from the analysis.

Example 11.4:

Evaluate the coefficients of determination for the situations in

   (*a*) examples 11.1 and 11.2
   (*b*) example 11.3,

and interpret their values.

   (*a*) We have seen that $r = 0.948$
   and so $\qquad\qquad r^2 = 0.948^2$
$$= 0.899.$$

Hence *89.9* per cent of the variations in sales and number of sales-persons can be explained by the regression analysis.

   (*b*) From $r = 0.936$
   we get $r^2 = 0.936^2$
$$= 0.876,$$

and so *87.6* per cent of variations in profits and advertising expenditure can be explained by the regression analysis.

Consider now the two forecasts made in example 11.2. The second one is distinctly different from the first, in that we have taken the regression line far beyond the upper data point ($x = 18$ salespersons) to 25 sales-persons. The forecast is an *extrapolation* beyond the range of the data. This is an uncertain step to take, as the sales within a region at a certain time must have a ceiling: there must come a point where extra salespersons will generate no further sales. If this point has been passed with 25 salespersons, then our forecast will be an overestimate. The first case, by contrast, is an *interpolation* within the range of the data, and so can be considered more valid. In the same way, the profit forecast of example 11.3 is a slight extrapolation and so should be treated with some caution.

Extreme cases of extrapolation have already been seen when inter-preting values of the coefficient '*a*' in earlier regression equations. In doing this, we are effectively extrapolating to the *x*–value of zero, and so we should not be surprised if the result seems implausible.

It will be noted that we have always been careful to ensure that the variable to be forecast is the dependent variable, *y*. This is because the regression line only minimizes the sum of squares of *y*–errors: it is the so-called *y on x line*. It would not, in example 11.3 for instance, be valid to use the regression line to forecast advertising expenditure in terms of profits. To do this, you would have to find another, different, regression line. The best way to do this would be to interchange the variables, that is, call

   profits $= x$
   advertising expenditure $= y$

and re-evaluate the formulae accordingly. As we have said, the two regression lines are, in general, different. They only coincide in cases of perfect correlation, that is, when

$r = \pm 1.$

The approach we have adopted is, of course, a considerable simplification of reality. Profits, sales, and so on, depend on a number of factors, not all of them quantifiable, whereas we have assumed here that they depend on just one other quantitative variable. We have studied only *simple* regression.

There is an extension to the topic, known as *multiple* regression, which enables a variable to be forecast in terms of any number of other variables. The interested reader should investigate elsewhere.

All the forecasts made in this chapter have been for 'next year', whereas the data come, of course, from the past. There is, therefore, an implicit assumption that conditions which obtained in the past still obtain now and, more importantly, will continue to obtain during the period of the forecast. There is no mathematical way of checking that this is so, but the forecaster will have qualitative knowledge of the particular company and its market, and so will be able to form a judgement. If, for example, a new company was known to be making a big push in the market of the company in example 11.3, you might doubt the forecast of next year's profit figures.

In conclusion, this section has looked at a number of considerations which should be borne in mind when judging the validity of a regression-based forecast. We will summarize these in the following.

Summary

The *least squares y on x regression line*

is $y = a + bx$

where $b = \dfrac{n\Sigma xy - (\Sigma x)(\Sigma y)}{n\Sigma x^2 - (\Sigma x)^2}$

and $a = \bar{y} - b\bar{x}.$

In using this line to forecast values of y, the following points/questions must be considered:

- is the correlation coefficient, r, (or *the coefficient of determination, r^2*) large enough to support the assumption that y depends on x?
- is there a hidden third variable?
- *does y* depend on x, or is it the case that x depends on y?
- interpolated forecasts are more reliable than extrapolated ones;
- ensure that the y on x line is used only to forecast y;
- are there any other variables which might affect y?
- have there been, or are there likely to be, any changes in background circumstances which might invalidate the forecast?

Exercises on Chapter 11

1   The variable y is assumed to depend on the variable x in a linear way. A sample of eight pairs of values (x, y) is taken:

x	y
1.0	3.0
3.0	6.9
5.0	11.1
6.0	13.0
7.0	14.7
8.0	17.3
10.0	20.5
12.0	24.6

(a)   Plot a scatter diagram of these data.
(b)   Use a ruler to 'guess' a straight line which appears 'close' to the points on the scatter diagram.
(c)   Compute the equation of the least squares y on x regression line for these data. Plot this line on your scatter diagram.
(d)   Evaluate the sum of squares of the y–errors in the two lines plotted. Which is the smaller?

2   A small company employs only part-time salespersons on one-month contracts, and is determining how many to hire for the next month. The company has data on the monthly revenue and numbers of part-time salespersons employed:

Month	Number of salespersons	Revenue (£)
A	11	19,730
B	13	23,590
C	12	21,610
D	17	30,850
E	17	25,110

(a)   Find the equation of a suitable regression line and hence forecast the revenue next month if   (i)   15
   (ii)   20
salespersons are hired.
(b)   If, on average, the total cost (including an apportionment of fixed costs) to the company of hiring one part-time salesperson for a month is £1,100, forecast the profit next month under the two circumstances in (a).
(c)   Comment briefly on the likely reliability of your forecasts.

3 A factory manufactures certain metal items from suitable scrap metal bought in from a supplier. A sample of each batch of scrap is analysed for certain trace elements and the percentage of understrength items made from each batch is recorded. The following data relate to the last six batches of scrap bought in and the items made from them:

Batch number	% of element E in batch sample	% understrength items produced
134	0.09	0.823
135	0.10	0.804
136	0.08	0.829
137	0.07	0.860
138	0.08	0.859
139	0.10	0.790

Batch number 140 is found to have 0.05 per cent of E in its sample. Forecast the percentage of understrength items which will be produced from this batch, and comment on the reliability of this forecast.

4   A cost accountant has derived the following data on the running costs (£ hundreds) and distance travelled (thousands of miles) by twenty of a company's fleet of new cars used by its computer salesmen last year. Ten of the cars are type F and ten are type L.

Car F		Car L	
Distance travelled, X	Running costs, Y	Distance travelled, X	Running costs, Y
4.0	5.3	3.5	6.9
4.6	6.7	4.6	7.6
5.9	7.5	5.3	7.9
6.7	8.8	6.0	8.3
8.0	8.0	7.2	8.8
8.9	9.1	8.4	9.2
8.9	10.5	10.1	9.6
10.1	10.0	11.1	10.3
10.8	11.7	11.5	10.1
12.1	12.4	12.3	11.3
Mean 8.0	9.0	8.0	9.0

(a)   The least squares regression lines were calculated using a standard computer package as follows:

Car F: $Y = 2.650 + 0.794X$
Car L: $Y = 5.585 + 0.427X$

Plot the two scatter diagrams and regression lines on the same graph, distinguishing clearly between the two sets of points.

(b)   Explain the meaning of the four regression coefficients for these data.

(c)   This year the company is expanding into a new region in which travelling distances are expected to be 50 per cent higher, on average, than those in the example above. Given that the car type has to be F or L, which should the company choose for this region and why?

(d)   What will be the expected total running costs for five of these cars in this new region next year, if costs per mile are 10 per cent higher than those in the example above?

ICMA, November 1983.

5 A cost accountant has derived the following data on the weekly output of standard size boxes from a factory.

Week	Output (X)(thousands)	Total cost (Y)(£000)
1	20	60
2	2	25
3	4	26
4	23	66
5	18	49
6	14	48
7	10	35
8	8	18
9	13	40
10	8	33

$\Sigma X = 120$, $\Sigma Y = 400$, $\Sigma X^2 = 1866$, $\Sigma Y^2 = 18{,}200$, $\Sigma XY = 5704$.

(a) Plot a scatter diagram of the data.
(b) Find the least squares regression line of total cost on output, and plot the line on the graph.
(c) What is the fixed cost of the factory?
(d) In a given week it is planned to produce 25,000 standard size boxes. Use your regression equation to estimate the total cost of producing this quantity.

ICMA, November 1982.

6 A book publisher has produced seven comparable books with the following costs:

Quantity produced (000):	Manufacturing costs (£000):
1	5
3	6.2
4	6.5
5	7
7	8
9	9
13	10.8

(Sum of squares = 350)   (Sum of squares = 416.33)
(Sum of cross products, $\Sigma XY = 362$)

Source: Data based on RSS News and Notes, September 1983.

You are required:
(a) to draw an appropriate scatter diagram;
(b) to derive the least squares regression of manufacturing costs on quantity produced and interpret your results;
(c) the company planning a production run of 10,000 copies of an

eighth book, to use the results of your regression to estimate the manufacturing costs for this eighth book;

(*d*)   the publisher receiving £2 per book, to state at what point he will break-even on this eighth book.

ICMA, November 1984.

12 Time series forecasting

Introduction

There are many situations in which there are no plausible or available independent variables from which a dependent variable can be forecast. In such cases alternative approaches have to be adopted. One of these consists of using past values of the variable to be forecast, a so-called *time series*, and looking for patterns in them. These patterns are then assumed to continue into the future, so that an *extrapolative* forecast is produced. The first task is thus to discuss the various patterns which time series data display.

Components and models of times series

There are considered to be four *components of variation* in a time series:

the *trend*, T,
the *seasonal* component, S,
the *cyclical* component, C,
the *irregular* (or random) component, I.

The *trend* in a time series is the general, overall movement of the variable, with any sharp fluctuations largely smoothed out. It is often called the *underlying* trend, and any other components are considered to occur around this trend. There are a number of basic trend patterns which business variables tend to follow, as shown in Figure 12.1. The simplest is a *linear* trend, in which the variable is basically growing (or declining) at a steady rate. A *logistic* trend (Figure 12.1b) is typically followed by the sales figures of a product after its introduction: the level plateau is the market saturation figure which the sales eventually reach. A *compound interest* trend, as the name suggests, is a relatively steeply rising curve followed by variables whose values are compounded on

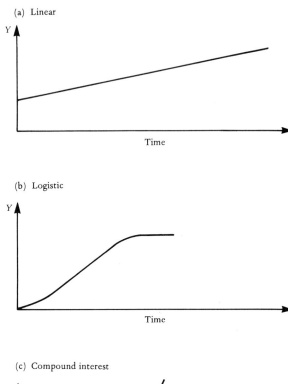

Figure 12.1 *Common forms of trend*

earlier values: for instance, investments subject to compound interest.

The *seasonal* component accounts for the regular variations which certain variables show at various times of the year. Thus, a newly formed ice-cream manufacturing company may have sales figures showing a rising trend. Around that, however, the sales will tend to have peaks in the summer months and troughs in the winter months. These peaks and troughs around the trend are explained by the seasonal component. In general, if a variable is recorded weekly, monthly or quarterly, it will tend to display seasonal variations, while data recorded annually will not.

The *cyclical* component explains much longer-term variations caused by business cycles. For instance, when a country's economy is in a slump, most business variables will be depressed in value, whereas, when a general upturn occurs, variables such as sales and profits will tend to rise. These cyclical variations cover periods of many years and so have little effect in the short term.

The *irregular* component is that part of a variable which cannot be explained by the factors mentioned above. It is caused by random fluctuations and unpredictable or freak events, such as a major fire in a production plant. If the first three components are explaining the variable's behaviour well, then, subject to rare accidents, the irregular component will have little effect.

The four components of variation are assumed to combine to produce the variable in one of two ways: thus we have two mathematical *models* of the variable. In the first case there is the *additive model*, in which the components are assumed to add together to give the variable, Y:

$$Y = T + S + C + I.$$

The second, *multiplicative, model* considers the components as multiplying to give Y:

$$Y = T \times S \times C \times I.$$

Thus, under the additive model, a monthly sales figure of £21,109 might be explained as follows:

the trend might be £20,000;
the seasonal factor: £1,500 (the month in question is a good one for sales, expected to be £1,500 over the trend);
the cyclical factor: −£800 (a general business slump is being experienced, expected to depress sales by £800 per month);
the irregular factor: £409 (due to unpredictable random fluctuations).

The model gives

$$Y = T + S + C + I$$
$$21,109 = 20,000 + 1,500 + (-800) + 409.$$

The multiplicative model might explain the same sales figure in a similar way:

trend: £20,000;
seasonal factor: 1.10 (a good month for sales, expected to be 10 per cent above the trend);
cyclical factor: 0.95 (a business slump, expected to cause a 5 per cent reduction in sales);
irregular factor: 1.01 (random fluctuations of + 1 per cent).

The model gives:

$Y = T \times S \times C \times I$
$21,109 = 20,000 \times 1.10 \times 0.95 \times 1.01$.

It will be noted that, in the additive model, all components are in the same units as the original variable (£ in the above example). In the multiplicative model, the trend is in the same units as the variable, while the other three components are just multiplying factors.

Forecasting linear trends

There are many ways of forecasting time series variables. To give a flavour of extrapolative forecasting we shall concentrate here on just one. The method consists of forecasting each component separately, and then combining them through one of the models to form a forecast of the variable itself. We begin with the trend and, in this first treatment, deal only with the simplest case of *linear* trends. In this case, there is no need for any new theory, since we can find the trend as a linear regression line.

Example 12.1:
The following table gives the quarterly sales figures of a small company over the last three years. Forecast the next four values of the trend in the series.

Time period:	Sales (£000):
1985, quarter 1. (t = 1)	42
quarter 2. (t = 2)	41
quarter 3. (t = 3)	52
quarter 4. (t = 4)	39
1986, quarter 1. (t = 5)	45
quarter 2. (t = 6)	48
quarter 3. (t = 7)	61
quarter 4. (t = 8)	46
1987, quarter 1. (t = 9)	52
quarter 2. (t = 10)	51
quarter 3. (t = 11)	60
quarter 4. (t = 12)	46

The graph of these data, the *time series graph* (or historigram), is shown in Figure 12.2. This shows that the company's sales are following an upward trend, of a more or less linear shape, and that there is a definite seasonal pattern: each third quarter is a peak and each fourth quarter is a trough. The approach and model being used here are therefore appropriate.

It will be noted that the twelve quarters for which we have data have been numbered from one to twelve, for ease of reference and to facilitate the computation of the regression line. It is left as an exercise for the reader to verify that this has equation

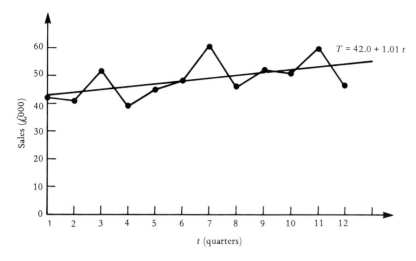

Figure 12.2 *Time series graph and trend line, example 12.1*

$$T = 42.0 + 1.01t,$$

where T is the assumed linear trend in sales (£000) and t is the number of the quarter (1985, quarter 1: $t = 1$, and so on). This line has been superimposed on the graph in Figure 12.2.

It is now a simple matter to forecast the trend in sales during 1988:

1988 quarter 1: $t = 13$, giving
$$\hat{T} = 42.0 + 1.01 \times 13$$
$$= 55.1 \ (£000)$$

1988 quarter 2: $t = 14$, so $\hat{T} = 56.1$ (£000)

1988 quarter 3: $t = 15$: $\hat{T} = 57.2$ (£000)

1988 quarter 4: $t = 16$: $\hat{T} = 58.2$ (£000).

The notation $\hat{T}$ is used to denote a *forecast* value of the trend, as distinct from a historical or actual value, T. The next four trend values are therefore forecast to be £55,000, £56,000, £57,000 and £58,000 (nearest £000), respectively.

Forecasting seasonal components. Seasonal adjustments

Up to now, we have not had to concern ourselves with the choice of model. Since the nature of the seasonal component is so different in the two models, we now have to make a choice. The multiplicative model is usually considered the better, because it ensures that seasonal variations are assumed to be a constant *proportion* of the sales. The additive model, in contrast, assumes that the seasonal variations are a constant *amount*, and thus would constitute a diminishing part of, say, an increasing sales trend. Because there is generally no reason to believe that seasonality does become a less important factor, the multiplicative model is adopted more frequently, as demonstrated here.

The arithmetic involved in computing seasonal components is somewhat tedious but essentially simple. Considering the two components discussed so far,

the actual value, $Y = T \times S$
and so $\quad\quad S = Y/T$.

The seasonal component, S, is therefore found as the ratio of the actual values to the trend, averaged over all available data (so as to use as much information as possible). For forecasting purposes, the same degree of seasonality is assumed to continue into the future, and so the historical seasonal components are simply projected unaltered into the future.

Example 12.2:
Forecast the seasonal components for 1988 from the sales data and trend of example 12.1.

The first, tedious step is to calculate the ratio of sales trend for each of the twelve quarters given. We show the first and last here, leaving the intermediate ten calculations as exercises:

$t = 1$: $T = 42.0 + (1.01 \times 1)$
$\quad\quad = 43.01$

and so $S = Y/T$

$\quad\quad = \dfrac{42}{43.01}$

$\quad\quad = 0.9765$

$t = 12$: $T = 42.0 + (1.01 \times 12)$
$\quad\quad = 54.12$

and so $S = Y/T$

$\quad\quad = \dfrac{46}{54.12}$

$\quad\quad = 0.8500.$

The complete set of ratios, arranged by quarter is:

	Quarter 1	Quarter 2	Quarter 3	Quarter 4
1985	0.9765	0.9314	1.1548	0.8471
1986	0.9564	0.9988	1.2431	0.9185
1987	1.0178	0.9789	1.1297	0.8500
Total	2.9507	2.9091	3.5276	2.6156
Mean	0.9836	0.9697	1.1759	0.8719

When arranged like this, the averaging process for each quarter is facilitated. The resulting values constitute the mean seasonal component for each quarter from the given data: they show that, on average in the past, quarter 1 sales have been 98 per cent (approximately) of the trend, quarter 2 sales 97 per cent of the trend, and so on. These values are now adopted as the required *forecast* seasonal components (denoted $\hat{S}$). In this case the forecasts for the four quarters of 1988 are thus:

0.9836, 0.9697, 1.1759 and 0.8719, respectively.

Before proceeding we digress slightly to look at a closely related topic, *seasonal adjustment*. This is important, because we are often presented with a single figure for weekly revenue, monthly profit, or whatever, and it is difficult to make judgements without some idea of whether the quantity given represents a seasonal peak or trough (or neither). One approach is to *deseasonalize* or remove the seasonal effects from the figure. In the multiplicative model, in which the factor S *multiplies* with all the other components, seasonal adjustment consists of *dividing* by S.

Example 12.4:
The company of examples 12.1 and 12.2 reports sales of £50,000 during the fourth quarter of a certain year. Seasonally adjust this figure.

We saw earlier that the seasonal component for the fourth quarter in this series is 0.8719. Dividing by this

$$\frac{50,000}{0.8719} = 57346.0.$$

We see that the *seasonally adjusted sales* for the quarter in question are *£57,350* (approximately).

Producing the final forecast

We must now consider the final two components of variation. Isolating the cyclical component of time series has proved to be a controversial area in economics and statistics. There is no consensus on an approach to the problem. Also, as we have already mentioned, cyclical variations have little effect in the short term. For these reasons, we shall omit the factor C from this first treatment.

The irregular component is by nature unpredictable. The best that we can do is to hope that any random fluctuations are small and that no freak events occur, so that the factor I has no overall effect.

For a component to be omitted or to have no effect, it must have the value 1 in the multiplicative model, since multiplying anything by 1 leaves it unchanged. We have thus simplified our model, for the purposes of forecasting, to

$$\hat{Y} = \hat{T} \times \hat{S}.$$

Example 12.5:
In the example under discussion here, forecast the sales during 1988.

We have already found values for $\hat{T}$ and $\hat{S}$, and so it is now a matter of pulling these values together to find $\hat{Y}$:

1988 quarter 1: $\hat{Y} = \hat{T} \times \hat{S}$
$$= 55.1 \times 0.9836$$
$$= 54.20$$

1988 quarter 2: $\hat{Y} = 56.1 \times 0.9697$
$$= 54.40$$

1988 quarter 3: $\hat{Y} = 57.2 \times 1.1759$
$$= 67.26$$

1988 quarter 4: $\hat{Y} = 58.2 \times 0.8719$
$$= 50.74.$$

The forecast sales for the four quarters of 1988 are thus £54,000, £54,000, £67,000 and £51,000 respectively.

Judging the validity of forecasts

As in the preceding chapter, we now have to consider how valid are these and other extrapolative forecasts. First of all, as the name implies, they are extrapolations, and so there is the possibility of error, as discussed earlier. In particular, you should monitor background circumstances to detect any changes which might invalidate the assumption that these are constant. Further, the adoption of a linear trend carries the danger of extrapolating too far: if the trend is, in fact, logistic (see Figure 12.1(b)), as many are, then extending the near linear middle portion too far, beyond the 'market saturation' plateau, will lead to overestimates of future values. For this reason, each successive step into the future becomes increasingly less reliable.

Refinements on this basic method can remove the necessity to assume that the trend is linear and the seasonality constant. If the assumptions *are* to be made, however, they can be checked to some extent by draw-ing the time series graph. For example, this might show that the peaks and troughs do *not* occur at the same time each year, invalidating the assumption of constant seasonal components; or the graph might start to plateau out, showing that the trend was indeed following a logistic form, as referred to above.

The method of this chapter, and any amendments to it, depend on the assumptions that a time series has a certain number of components of variation, and that these combine in a certain way ('the model'). One way of checking on these assumptions is to assess the values of the irregular component from past data. To do this, we re-introduce I into our model:

$$Y = T \times S \times I$$

so that

$$I = \frac{Y}{T \times S}.$$

Thus, in 1985 quarter 1 of the time series under discussion here,

$Y = 42$
$T = 43.01$ (evaluated in example 12.2)
$S = 0.9836$

so that

$$I = \frac{42}{43.01 \times 0.9836}$$
$$= 0.99.$$

Proceeding in this way, all twelve past values of the irregular component can be found. Now, ideally, this component should be having little effect, and so should be close to 1: examining whether this is so is a check on how well the model has matched the actual data. In particular, if the values gradually moved away from 1, the model would be getting progressively less reliable, so casting doubt on any forecasts from it. Another assumption which might be invalidated by this process is that of constant seasonality: the presence of a seasonal variation in the supposedly random component, I, would again cast doubt on the validity of the model and its forecasts.

Finally, the reader will have noticed the great amount of arithmetic needed to produce the forecasts of this chapter. It is therefore highly advantageous to use one of the many available computer packages which deal with such extrapolative models.

Summary

We are modelling the values, Y, in a time series by

$$Y = T \times S \times C \times I$$

where T is the trend component of variation,

S is the seasonal component
C is the cyclical component
I is the irregular component.

If we ignore the cyclical component and omit the unpredictable, irregular component, the model becomes, for forecasting purposes,

$$\hat{Y} = \hat{T} \times \hat{S}.$$

Assuming a linear trend and constant seasonality, $\hat{T}$ can be found from a linear regression analysis and $\hat{S}$ can be found as the average past ratio of actual value to trend (that is: Y/T).

A numerical check on the validity of the model can be obtained by inspecting the past values of the irregular component, found from

$$I = Y/T \times S.$$

Exercises on Chapter 12

1 As part of the preparation of next year's budgets, an accountant working for a large manufacturing company feeds data on the last four years' monthly sales of one of the company's products into a computer package. The package is designed to fit a linear trend to past data, and then to evaluate monthly (seasonal) components of variation around the trend, assuming a multiplicative model. The package produces the following results:

$$T = 193.1 + 0.62t$$

where T is trend sales (£000)

and $t = 1$ indicates the first month of the four-year period,
    $t = 48$ indicates the last month of the four-year period,
    $t = 49$ indicates next month, and so on.

Month number		Seasonal variation
1	(corresponding to $t = 1, 13$, and so on)	0.841
2		0.900
3		0.933
4		0.988
5		1.020
6		1.227
7		1.259
8		1.102
9		0.991
10		0.954
11		0.887
12	(corresponding to $t = 12, 24$, 36, 48, and so on)	0.819

(a) Forecast the sales for the year being budgeted, namely time periods 55 to 66 inclusive.
(b) Discuss how the accountant might check on the likely reliability of these forecasts.

2 In the example discussed in the chapter, forecast the company's sales for the four quarters of 1989, and state how reliable you think these forecasts will be, compared to those found on page 130. Further, complete the process started on page 131 by evaluating the remaining eleven past values of the irregular component. Inspect these in the ways suggested in the chapter, and hence comment on how well the model has matched the past data.

3 A business consultant has been asked to investigate the need for extra machinery and manpower in an expanding company. As one of the first stages of the investigation, she decides to forecast the future sales of the company's major product. Consequently, she obtains data from the last three years' available figures:

	Sales (000 units):
1984 quarter 1	9.8
quarter 2	7.3
quarter 3	9.5
quarter 4	9.6
1985 quarter 1	12.1
quarter 2	9.9
quarter 3	11.5
quarter 4	13.0
1986 quarter 1	14.1
quarter 2	12.9
quarter 3	14.3
quarter 4	15.3

(a) Assuming a linear trend, find the equation of the trend line in terms of time ($t = 1$ indicates 1984 quarter 1, and so on).

(b) Evaluate the seasonal component for each quarter as the average of past values of Y/T.

(c) Hence forecast sales for the years 1989 and 1990.

(d) How valid do you think these forecasts are?

4 A company has found that the trend in the quarterly sales of its furniture is well described by the regression equation

$$Y = 150 + 10X$$

where Y equals quarterly sales (£000)

$X = 1$ represents the first quarter of 1980,
$X = 2$ represents the second quarter of 1980,

.
.
.

$X = 5$ represents the first quarter of 1981, etc.

It has also been found that, based on the multiplicative model

Sales = Trend × Seasonal × Irregular,

the mean seasonal quarterly index for its furniture sales is as follows:

Quarter	1	2	3	4
Seasonal index	80	110	140	70

You are required:

(a) to explain the meaning of *this* equation and *this* set of seasonal index numbers;

(b) using the regression equation, to estimate the trend values in the company's furniture sales for each quarter in 1985;

(c) using the seasonal index, to prepare sales forecasts for the company's quarterly furniture sales in 1985;

(*d*)   to state what factors might cause your sales forecasts to be in error.

ICMA, May 1985.

5   Index numbers of retail sales in Great Britain (1978 = 100)

	1980	1981	1982	1983
Q1	–	131	141	153
Q2	124	134	145	–
Q3	129	139	151	–
Q4	155	168	184	–

Source: Monthly Digest of Statistics, August 1983.

(*a*)   Evaluate the trend in these data as a linear regression equation. (*Hint:* subtract a constant figure, 120 say from each index, so as to ease the arithmetic.)

(*b*)   Adopting a multiplicative model, find the mean seasonal sales to trend ratio for each quarter, and hence predict the index of retail sales for the *fourth* quarter of 1983.

ICMA, November 1984.

6   A company is carrying out a time series analysis on one of its products. It finds that the *trend* in ex-factory sales is satisfactorily described by the equation

$$S = 409 + 11t,$$

where S represents sales, and $t = 1$ to 11 represents the quarters from the start of 1983 to the third quarter of 1985.

Quarterly sales

t:	1	2	3	4	5	6	7	8	9	10	11
S:	400	430	490	440	420	535	490	460	480	550	530

You are required:

(*a*)   Using the equation above to find the estimated trend value for each quarter and hence to find the seasonal component for each quarter, assuming a multiplicative model;

(*b*)   to prepare a sales forecast for each quarter of 1986;

(*c*)   to de-seasonalize the data given above and plot both this and the original series on one graph.

ICMA, November 1985.

Part Four
Probability

13 Probability I

Introduction

Probability concerns the study of uncertainty or chance. The need for accountants and business people to understand this area can be seen from the following typical statements:

'On past evidence, there seems to be a fifty-fifty chance of this project succeeding'.

'I reckon that, if we stay on this course, we will have only a one in ten chance of making a profit next year'.

'The consultants' report says that our project launch has a 60 per cent chance of success'.

Each of the above sentences contains a term attempting to quantify the degree of uncertainty in a business situation. In this chapter we begin the formal study of such quantification, initially looking at several different approaches to the subject.

Definitions of probability

One way of viewing a probability is as a *proportion*, as the following simple example will illustrate.

Example 13.1:
An ordinary six-sided dice is rolled. What is the probability that it will show a number less than three?

Here it is possible to list all the possible equally likely outcomes of rolling a dice, namely the whole numbers from one to six inclusive:

1 2 3 4 5 6

The outcomes which constitute the 'event' under consideration, that is, 'a number less than three' are:

1 2

Hence the proportion of outcomes which constitute the event is

$$\frac{2}{6}$$

or ⅓, which is therefore the desired probability.

Note that this answer agrees with the intuitive statements you might make about this situation, such as 'the chances are one in three'.

In situations like this, where it is possible to compile a *complete* list of all the *equally likely* outcomes, we can define the probability of an event, denoted *p*(event), in a way which agrees with the above intuitive approach:

$$p(\text{event}) = \frac{\text{total number of outcomes which constitute the event}}{\text{total number of outcomes}}$$

This is known as *exact* probability because it involves having a complete list of all possible outcomes and counting the exact number which constitute the event. This definition, however, is not always practical for business purposes, as you can rarely state all the possible outcomes. To illustrate this, and to demonstrate a way of overcoming the problem, we consider the following.

Example 13.2:
A quality controller wishes to specify the probability of a component failing within one year of installation. How might she proceed?

To find this probability from an exact approach would necessitate obtaining a list of the lifetimes of *all* the components, and counting those of less than one year. It is clearly impossible to keep such a detailed record of *every* component, after sale.

An alternative, feasible, approach is to take a *sample* of components, rather than the whole population, and test them under working conditions, to see what proportion fail within one year. Probabilities produced in this way are known as *empirical* and are essentially *approximations* to the true, but unobtainable, exact probabilities.

In this case, the quality controller may choose to sample 1000 components. If she then finds that 16 fail within one year,

$$p(\text{component failing within one year}) = \frac{16}{1000} \text{ or } 0.016.$$

For this approximation to be valid, it is essential that the sample is representative. Further, for a more accurate approximation, a larger sample could be taken, provided the time and money are available.

We make two comments before moving on. First of all, since we are defining probabilities as proportions, probabilities will lie in the range 0–1, with 0 denoting an impossibility and 1 denoting a certainty. Secondly, there are many practical instances in which a suitable sample is unavailable; so an empirical probability cannot be found. In such cases, a *subjective* probability could be estimated, based on judgement and experience. Although such estimates are not entirely reliable, they can occasionally be useful, as we shall see later. The second quotation in section 13.1 is an example of the use of judgement to estimate a subjective probability.

Rules of probability

In principle, it is possible to find any probability by a method discussed above. In practice, however, there are many complex cases which can be simplified by using the so-called *rules of probability*. We shall develop these via examples.

Example 13.3:
According to personnel records, the 111 employees of an accountancy practice can be classified by their workbase (A, B or C) and by their professional qualifications thus:

	Office A	Office B	Office C	Total
Qualified	26	29	24	79
Not qualified	11	9	12	32
Total	37	38	36	111

What is the probability that an employee, chosen at random, will be employed at office A *or* be professionally qualified?
    Examining the table, we can apply our earlier rule:

37 are employed at office A
79 are qualified,

making a total of 116. It is clear, however, that we have 'double counted' the 26 employees who both work at office A and are qualified. Subtracting this doubly counted amount, we see that

$$116 - 26 = 90$$

employees have the desired property. Hence

$$p(\text{employed at office A } or \text{ professionally qualified}) = \frac{90}{111}.$$

We can generalize from the above argument. We have:

$$p(\text{employed at office A } or \text{ professionally qualified}) = \frac{90}{111}$$

$$= \frac{37 + 79 - 26}{111}$$

$$= \frac{37}{111} + \frac{79}{111} - \frac{26}{111}$$

$$= p(\text{employed at office A}) + p(\text{professionally qualified}) - p(\text{office A } and \text{ qualified}).$$

This is an example of the *additive law of probability*:

$p(X \text{ or } Y) = p(X) + p(Y) - p(X \text{ and } Y)$.

The last term in this law compensates, as we have seen, for double counting. *If*, however, there is no possibility of double counting: that is, if X and Y cannot occur together, or

$p(X \text{ and } Y) = 0$,

then this term can be omitted and the law simplified to

$p(X \text{ or } Y) = p(X) + p(Y)$.

In this last case, X and Y are said to be *mutually exclusive*.

Example 13.4:
In the situation described in example 13.3, what is the probability that a randomly selected employee will come from office B *and* not be qualified?

A reading from the table shows that 9 of the 111 employees come under the required category. Hence

$p(\text{employed at office B } and \text{ not qualified}) = \dfrac{9}{111}$.

Developing this, as above, to derive a general rule:

$$= \dfrac{38}{111} \times \dfrac{9}{38}$$

$= p(\text{office B}) \times p(\text{not qualified}, if \text{ from B})$.

This is an example of the general *multiplicative law of probability*:

$p(X \text{ and } Y) = p(X) \cdot p(Y, \text{ if } X)$
or: $p(X \text{ and } Y) = p(X) \cdot p(Y|X)$.

In the latter form of this law we see the symbolism

$p(Y|X)$

which is read as 'the probability of Y *if* (or *given*)X'. Such a probability is called a *conditional probability*. It is used because the fact that X occurs affects the probability that Y will occur. In the above, for example,

$p(\text{not professionally qualified}) = \dfrac{32}{111}$.

Yet the value we must use in the calculation is

$p(\text{not professionally qualified}, if \text{ from office B}) = \dfrac{9}{38}$

On occasion, X and Y are statistically *independent*. That is, the fact that X occurs has no effect on the probability of Y occurring (and vice-versa), or

$p(Y|X) = p(Y).$

In this case, the rule can be simplified to

$p(X \text{ and } Y) = p(X) \cdot p(Y).$

Probability trees

Armed with the two laws of probability and using a device called a *probability tree*, we can now look at some more complex and practical situations. A major application of probability theory is in the calculation of insurance and similar premiums. A real example would be too complicated for this text, but the following will give a flavour of the actuarial calculations involved.

Example 13.5:
Past data show that the probability of a married woman of age 32 being alive in 30 years' time is 0.69. Similarly, the probability of a married man of age 35 being alive in 30 years' time is 0.51. Calculate, for a married couple (woman aged 32, man aged 35), the probabilities that in 30 years' time

(*i*)   they are both alive,
(*ii*)   only (exactly) one is alive,
(*iii*)   neither are alive,

If we consider the woman first, there are two possibilities: she will be alive (probability 0.69) or she will not (probability 0.31). Independently of these, there are two possibilities concerning the man: alive (probability 0.51) or not (0.49). There are thus four possible combinations, as shown in the *probability tree* of Figure 13.1. Note how, as we move along each 'branch' of the tree, the *multiplicative* law of probability is applied. For example, point A is reached via

woman alive *and* man alive,

hence, for this branch,

$p = .69 \times .51 = .3519.$

(*i*)   This is the case A discussed above; so the probability is *0.3519.*
(*ii*)   There are two ways this situation can arise:

woman alive *and* man not (B on the tree)
or woman not alive *and* man alive (C on the tree).

Thus, as B and C are mutually exclusive, we simply add ('*or*') the two values from the tree to get

$p(B) + p(C) = .3381 + .1581$
$= .4962.$

Thus the probability that only (exactly) one of the couple is alive is *0.4962.*

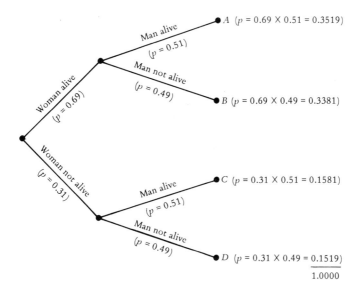

Note: how the total probabilities at the end of each branch should add up to 1. This simply reflects that one of the end points *must* happen, i.e. is certain.

Figure 13.1 *Probability tree for example 13.5*

(*iii*) This case is simply branch D; so the probability that neither is alive is *0.1519*.

Before leaving this example, we point out one simplification (and therefore one assumption) we have made. The probabilities quoted in the question (0.69 and 0.51) are empirical, arising from the histories of many people in the past. To apply these values to the couple in the question requires the assumption that the people are 'typical' of the sample from which the basic probabilities came. If, for example, either spouse had a dangerous occupation, this assumption would be invalid: in practice, actuaries would have data, and therefore empirical probabilities to deal with such 'untypical' people.

Our second, more complex, example shows another practical application of empirical probabilities.

Example 13.6:
A manufacturing company's accountant wishes to estimate the costs arising from faults in a new product, which is soon to be launched. Tests show:

2 per cent of the product are faulty; and, independently of this,
6 per cent of the packaging is faulty.

Further, it is known from past experience of similar items that cus-

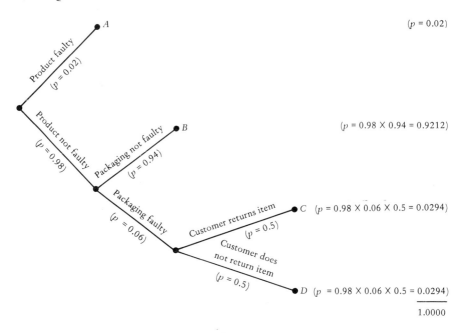

Figure 13.2 *Probability tree for example 13.6*

tomers *always* return faulty products. However, they return items with faulty packaging (product not faulty) only *half* the time.

Since costs associated with defective products differ from those relating to packaging, the accountant wishes to estimate the percentage of products which will be returned due to

(*i*)   faulty product;
(*ii*) faulty packaging, but no problems with the product itself;
(*iii*) any fault.

Before proceeding, we point out that this is essentially a problem on probabilities. For example 2 per cent of the product being faulty is the same as

p(product is faulty) $= 0.02$.

To begin the tree, we consider the product: it is either faulty or not, and so we have two branches. In the former case, we are anticipating that customers will always return the item, and so there is no need to develop this branch. In the latter case, we consider the packaging, which is either faulty or not. Of the two branches that this implies, the one corresponding to 'faulty' will have to be continued, since half of these customers will return the item, while the other half will not. See Figure 13.2.

As before, moving along each route in the tree implies the use of the multiplicative law of probability ('*and*').

(i)   This is simply point A on the tree: so $p = 0.02$. That is, 2 per cent of product will be returned under this category.
(ii) Reading along the tree, we see that this is point C, so $p = 0.0294$. Thus *2.94* per cent of product will be returned due only to faulty packaging.
(iii) Points A *or* C on the tree correspond to situations in which the product is returned due to *any* fault. Applying the additive rule of probability to this mutually exclusive case

$$p(A \text{ or } C) = p(A) + p(C)$$
$$= 0.02 + 0.0294$$
$$= 0.0494.$$

Hence a total of *4.94* per cent of product will be returned due to some fault or other.

It should be emphasized that these estimates are valid only if the test results are representative of the actual product performance and if this product *does* resemble the previous 'similar items' regarding return rates of faulty product (100 per cent) and faulty packaging (50 per cent).

Bayes' Theorem

The multiplicative law of probability states

$$p(X \text{ and } Y) = p(X) \cdot p(Y|X).$$

Similarly, reversing the order of X, Y

$$p(Y \text{ and } X) = p(Y) \cdot p(X|Y).$$

Now '*X and Y*' and '*Y and X*' are precisely the same thing, and so the two right-hand sides of the above equations must be equal; that is

$$p(X) \cdot p(Y|X) = p(Y) \cdot p(X|Y)$$

and so

$$p(Y|X) = \frac{p(Y) \cdot p(X|Y)}{p(X)}.$$

This is known as *Bayes' Theorem*, named after Thomas Bayes who first proposed it. Used together with a probability tree, it enables us to tackle some more complicated problems involving probabilities.

Example 13.7:
An oil drilling company knows from past experience that the probability of a test drill giving a correct indication of the presence of economic quantities of oil is 0.7. The success rate of indicating the *lack* of economic quantities is, however, 0.8.

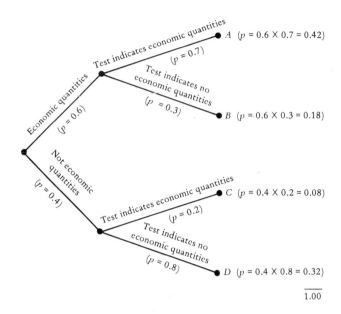

Figure 13.3 *Probability tree for example 13.7*

That is:

> p(test indicates economic quantities of oil|
>   economic quantities are present) = 0.7
> p(test indicates *no* economic quantities of oil|
>   economic quantities *not* present) = 0.8.

The company is considering drilling in a certain field. The project engineer estimates a 60 per cent chance of economic quantities of oil being present; so a test drill is undertaken, which subsequently indicates that economic quantities *are* present: use Bayes' Theorem to revise the project engineer's original estimate.

We begin by drawing the probability tree. First, in any given field, there will either be economic quantities of oil or not. Further, in both cases, a test drill could show the presence or otherwise of economic quantities. There are thus four end points on the tree, as shown in Figure 13.3. Note that we use the engineer's original estimate of 60 per cent for the field in question, as that is all we have to go on, and that we use the given conditional probabilities in the multiplicative law of probability.

Bayes' Theorem can now be applied. If we denote

'oil is present in economic quantities' by Y
'the test indicates economic quantities' by X,

the theorem gives

p(oil is present in economic quantitiesǀ
  test indicates economic quantities)

$$= \frac{p(\text{oil present in economic quantities}) \cdot p(\text{test indicates economic quantities} | \text{oil present in economic quantities})}{p(\text{test indicates economic quantities})}$$

$$= \frac{p(A)}{p(A \text{ or } C)} \qquad \text{(compare the probability tree)}.$$

$$= \frac{p(A)}{p(A) + p(C)}$$

$$= \frac{.42}{.42 + .08}$$

$$= 0.84.$$

Thus the revised probability of the presence of economic quantities of oil is *0.84 or 84 per cent.*

This example gives a typical appliction of Bayes' Theorem. There is an initial estimate of the required probability (the engineer's subjective estimate of 60 per cent) and some further information (that the test drill has positive results) with which the first value can be revised. Even though the 'further information' is imperfect (the probability of the test drill giving a correct positive indication being 0.7), Bayes' Theorem still enables it to be used in our calculations.

Summary

Probability can be defined from a complete list of equally likely outcomes as

$$p(\text{event}) = \frac{\text{total number of outcomes constituting the event}}{\text{total number of outcomes}}.$$

This can be used in an *exact* sense when applied to the population of outcomes, or in an *empirical*, approximate sense when applied to a sample.

The *additive* law of probability states

$$p(X \text{ or } Y) = p(X) + p(Y) - p(X \text{ and } Y).$$

The *multiplicative* law of probability states

$$p(X \text{ and } Y) = p(X) \cdot p(Y|X)$$

where $p(Y|X)$ denotes the conditional probability of Y, *if* (or *given*) X.

Bayes' Theorem states

$$p(Y|X) = \frac{p(Y) \cdot p(X|Y)}{p(X)}.$$

A *probability tree* is a diagrammatic representation of the probabilities in a problem. It is particularly useful in more complex examples and in those involving Bayes' Theorem.

Exercises on Chapter 13

1   Three trainees, X, Y and Z, are given a number of trial balances to perform as part of their training. The balances are then checked and the number of major and minor errors that each trainee commits are counted and collated into the following table:

		Trainees			
		X	Y	Z	
Errors	Minor	17	28	25	70
	Major	3	11	4	18
		20	39	29	88

From this table, evaluate the probability that a randomly selected error

(a)   was minor;
(b)   was committed by Y;
(c)   was major *and* committed by X;
(d)   was minor *or* committed by Z.

(e)   Using the same table, find the conditional probabilities
        (i)   p(error was major|was committed by Y)
and (ii)   p(error was committed by Y|was major).

2   The organizers of an outdoor event are considering insuring against there being measurable rainfall on the day. Meteorological records indicate that there is an 80 per cent chance of the day being dry. Further the organizers' experiences of similar past occasions show that, if it is dry, the probability of the event being profitable is 0.9, whereas this falls to 0.3 if it is wet.

(a)   Draw a tree to represent the probabilities in this situation.
(b)   Use the tree to evaluate the probability of the event being profitable.
(c)   If an insurance policy is taken out to cover for any losses on a wet day, under what set of circumstances could the event *still* not make a profit? What is the probability of this happening?

3   The managing director of a company feels that a new product (K) about to be launched has a 90 per cent chance of success. A team of market research consultants feels that the launch will *not* succeed. The consultants are not infallible; indeed their past performance suggests that their forecasts are right 80 per cent of the time for successful launches, and 70 per cent of the time for unsuccessful launches. That is:

p(consultants forecast product successful|product does succeed)
    = 0.8

p(consultants forecast product not successful|product does not succeed) = 0.7.

(a) Draw a probability tree to represent this situation.
(b) Use Bayes' Theorem to revise the managing director's estimate of a successful launch of K.

4 A proposal, to put more emphasis on improved superannuation rather than wage increases, was put by the union executive to the members. The following results were received:

		In favour	*Opinion* *Opposed*	*Undecided*	
Members	Skilled	800	200	300	1300
	Unskilled	100	600	200	900
		900	800	500	2200

Calculate the probability that a member selected at random will be:

(i)   skilled and in favour of the proposal;
(ii) undecided;
(iii) either unskilled or opposed to the proposal.

ICMA, November 1980.

5 The independent probabilities that the three sections of a costing department will encounter a computer error are respectively 0.1, 0.2 and 0.3 each week. Calculate the probability that there will be:

(i)   at least one computer error;
(ii) one (and only one) computer error;

encountered by the costing department next week.
ICMA, May 1982.

6 (a) A glass bottle manufacturer has three inspection points – one for size, one for colour, and another for flaws such as cracks and bubbles in the glass. The probability that each inspection point will incorrectly accept or reject a bottle is 0.02. What is the probability that:

(i)   a perfect bottle will pass through all inspection points;
(ii) a bottle faulty in colour and with a crack will be passed;
(iii) a bottle faulty in size will be passed?

(b) Two machines produce the same type of product. The older machine produces 35 per cent of the total output but 8 in every 100 are usually defective. The newer machine produces 65 per cent of the total output and 2 in every 100 are defective. Determine the probability that a defective product picked at random was produced by the older machine. (*Hint*: Bayes' Theorem should be used here.)

ICMA, May 1981.

14 Probability II

Introduction

In this chapter we develop further the theory of probability to introduce the concepts of a *probability distribution* and an *expected value*. These two topics will concern us greatly during the four chapters following: here we apply them, with the idea of a *decision tree*, to the area of financial decision-making.

Discrete probability distributions. Expectations

We use the word discrete here in the same sense as in Part Two, namely to describe a variable which can assume only certain values, regardless of the level of precision to which it is measured. For example, the number of errors made on an invoice is a discrete variable as it can be only

0 or 1 or 2 or ...

and never 2.3.

A *discrete probability distribution* is similar to a discrete frequency distribution (see Part Two) in that it consists of a list of all the values the variable can have (in the case of exact probabilities) or has had (in the case of empirical probabilities), together with the appropriate corresponding probabilities. A simple example will illustrate.

Example 14.1:
The records of a shop show that, during the previous 50 weeks' trading, the number of sales of a certain item are:

148

Number of sales/week	Number of weeks
0	4
1	16
2	22
3	6
4 or more	2

Construct the corresponding probability distribution.

The variable here is clearly *discrete* (number of sales) and the probabilities are to be based on the *empirical* data given. Hence we shall have a discrete distribution of empirical probabilities. Now, using the definition of the preceding chapter,

$$p(0 \text{ sales in a week}) = \frac{4}{50}$$
$$= 0.08.$$

Proceeding in this way, we can build up the distribution:

Number of sales/week	p(number of sales/week)
0	0.08
1	0.32
2	0.44
3	0.12
4 or more	0.04
	1.00

The *expected value* of a discrete probability distribution, $E(x)$, is defined as

$$E(x) = \Sigma x \cdot p(x),$$

where the summation is over all values of the variable, x, and $p(x)$ denotes the *exact* probability of the variable attaining the value x. At first sight, this appears to be an abstract concept, but an example will show that it has both a practical and an intuitively clear meaning.

Example 14.2:
What is the expected number of weekly sales of the item in example 14.1? What meaning does this value have?

We note that we have only *empirical* probabilities here, and so our answer will be an approximation. Using a familiar tabular format for the calculations:

x	p(x)	x·p(x)
0	0.08	0
1	0.32	0.32
2	0.44	0.88
3	0.12	0.36
4	0.04	0.16
		1.72

(For convenience, we have taken '4 or more' as 4 in the calculation.) Thus the expected number of sales per week is approximately *1.72*.

Consider now what the probabilities in the distribution mean. In the past, the item has had weekly sales of:

0 in 8% of the weeks,
1 in 32% of the weeks,
2 in 44% of the weeks, and so on.

An intuitive approach to 'expectation' would therefore be to take

8% of 0,
32% of 1, and so on,

and add the resulting values. Looking at the computation above, we see that this is precisely what the formula has done.

Having shown that our definition corresponds exactly with our intuition, we can now see another meaning of an expected value. Since the empirical probabilities have been calculated simply by dividing the individual frequencies by the total frequency, that is

$$\frac{f}{\Sigma f}$$

we have in fact calculated the value of

$$\Sigma x \cdot p(x)$$
$$= \Sigma x \cdot \frac{f}{\Sigma f}$$
$$= \frac{\Sigma xf}{\Sigma f}$$
$$= \bar{x},\text{ the sample mean, as encountered in Chapter 7.}$$

Hence the expected value of a probability distribution is similar to the mean of the corresponding frequency distribution. In fact, if we have *exact* probabilities to work with, the two are *precisely* the same.

Before looking at an important application, there is a special case of expected values worth mention. In the example above, on how many weeks would you expect there to be no sales during a trading period (4 weeks) and during a trading year (50 weeks)?

The intuitive answers to these questions are that, since the probability of no sales in any one week is 0.08, we should 'expect'

in 4 weeks, no sales to occur in 4 × 0.08 = 0.32 weeks, and
in 50 weeks, no sales to occur in 50 × 0.08 = 4 weeks.

In fact, to fit in with these intuitive ideas, we extend the definition of expectation. If there are n *independent* repeats of a circumstance, and the *constant* probability of a certain outcome is *p*, then the *expected number* of times the outcome will arise in the n repeats is *np*.

In the above, when we have n = 4 weeks, our (assumedly independent) repeated circumstances, and the constant probability *p* = 0.08 (outcome of no sales in a week), then the expected value is

$np = 4 \times 0.08$
$\quad = 0.32$, as our intuition told us.

Probability and financial decision-making. Decision trees

Many business situations require a choice between numerous courses of action whose results are uncertain. Clearly, the decision-maker's experience and judgement are important in making 'good' choices in such instances. The question does arise, however, as to whether there are objective aids to decision-making, which, if not entirely replacing personal judgement, can at least assist it. In this section, we look at one such possible aid in the area of *financial* decision-making.

In order to introduce a degree of objectivity, we begin by seeking *criteria* for classing one option as 'better' than another. One criterion is to assume that the worst will happen in all circumstances and to choose the option which gives the optimal results under this assumption. This is often called the *maximin* criterion in that you are *maxi*mizing under the assumption that the *mini*mum will occur. The opposite of this most pessimistic decision criterion is that of *maximax*: you assume that the best will happen in all circumstances and maximize accordingly.

Before giving an illustrative example, we note that, in addition to the obvious criticism of being over-pessimistic or over-optimistic, these criteria have a further drawback. We have already stated that the results of our actions are *uncertain*, and so some outcomes may be more likely than others: maximin and maximax effectively ignore this, implicitly assuming that all outcomes are equally likely. If it is possible to assign probabilities to all the possible outcomes, then we have a third, arguably better, decision criterion: choose the option which gives the maximum *expected* outcome ('expected' in the sense of the preceding section). This is usually called the *expected monetary value* or the *EMV* criterion. An example will now demonstrate all three criteria.

Example 14.3:
A decision has to be made between three options, A, B and C. The possible profits and losses are:

option A: + £2000 (probability 0.5), − £500 (probability 0.5);
option B: + £800 (probability 0.3), + £500 (probability 0.7);
option C: + £1000 (probability 0.8), + £500 (probability 0.1),
$\qquad\qquad\qquad\qquad$ − £400 (probability 0.1).

Which option should be chosen under (*i*) the maximin
$\qquad\qquad\qquad\qquad\qquad\qquad$ (*ii*)   the maximax
$\qquad\qquad\qquad\qquad\qquad\qquad$ (*iii*) the EMV criterion?

(*i*) The worst (the 'min') that can happen in each case is

$\quad$ A: − £500
$\quad$ B: + £500
$\quad$ C: − £400.

Choosing the option providing the maximum of these gives us
option B.
(*ii*)   The best (the 'max') that can happen in each case is

A: + £2000
B: + £800
C: + £1000.

Choosing the option providing the maximum of these gives us
option A.
(*iii*)   The expected profit (EMV) obtained from each option is, using
the formula of the preceding section:

EMV(A) = (.5 × 2000) + (.5 − 500) = £750
EMV(B) = (.3 ×   800) + (.7 × 500) = £590
EMV(C) = (.8 × 1000) + (.1 × 500) + (.1 × −400) = £810.

Thus we should choose *option C* in order to maximize expected profit.
We are asserting that this is a 'better' decision because it uses more
information than the previous two, namely the probabilities. However,
it is arguable that a person or organization which cannot afford a
loss would opt for the 'safe' option B (the choice under the maximin
criterion).

Real-life decisions are more complex than this example, often involving a *sequence* of decisions (logical or chronological). In such cases, a
decision tree can be used to depict the decisions and their associated
outcomes. The notation used is:

 a square *decision node* depicts a point in the tree where a
decision is made, with each line-off representing one of the
options open to the decision-maker;

 a circular *outcome node* depicts a position in the tree
following a decision, with each line-off representing a possible outcome.

A decision tree, with the above criteria, can assist financial decision-
making, as illustrated below.

Example 14.4:
A storeholder has to decide how many of the perishable commodity X to
buy each day. Past demand has followed the distribution:

Demand (units):	p(this demand):
1	0.2
2	0.4
3	0.4

Each unit is bought for £10 and sold for £20; and, at the end of each
day, any unsold units must be disposed of with no financial return.
Using the EMV criterion, how many units should be bought daily?

If we assume that the past demand pattern will obtain in the future,
we see that, logically, the storeholder has only three initial choices: buy

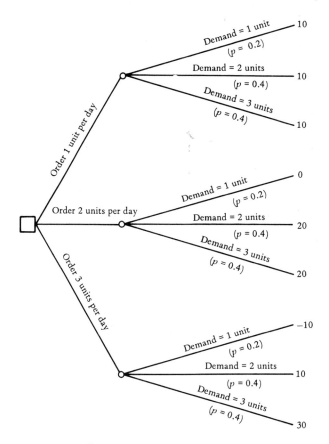

Figure 14.1 *Decision tree for example 14.4*

one, two or three units per day. The decision tree therefore begins with
a decision node to represent this choice, with three branches off, one for
each option. Once this decision has been made, demand factors beyond
the direct control of the storeholder take over. There is thus an outcome
node at the end of each of the three initial (decision) branches, with
three (outcome) branches emanating from each node, one representing
each of the possible demands (one, two or three units). This decision
tree is shown in Figure 14.1.

We have marked some further information on the tree. The probabilities following the outcome nodes come from the given table. It is vitally
important that there are no probabilities following a *decision* node: this
is a *decision*, and so what follows is not an uncontrollable, probabilistic
event, but is under the direct control of the decision-maker. The monetary values at the end of each branch show the daily profit from each
combination of decision and outcome. We give three examples here and
leave the others to the reader:

order 1, demand 1: cost = £10, revenue = £20; so profit = £10;

order 2, demand 1: cost = £20, revenue £20; so profit = £0
(in this case, one valueless unit would be left at the end of the day);

order 2, demand 3: cost = £20, revenue = £40; so profit = £20
(in this case, the demand for the third unit would be unsatisfied).

We can now calculate the expected daily profit for each option:

EMV (order 1) = £10 (no need for calculations here, as the profit is
£10, regardless of the outcome)

EMV (order 2) = (0.2 × 0) + (0.4 × 20) + (0.4 × 20)
= £16

EMV (order 3) = (0.2 × −10) + (0.4 × 10) + (0.4 × 30)
= £14.

Thus, in order to maximize daily profit, the storeholder should order
2 units per day.

Example 14.5:
A company has to decide whether to launch a new product. If the
launch goes ahead, the managing director estimates a 50:50 chance of
success or failure. In the latter circumstance, he has already stated that
the product must be withdrawn from the market and abandoned. In the
former, the level of marketing support (high or low) must be determined. Profits are estimated by the financial director to depend on the
market size as follows:

	High marketing support	*Low marketing support*
Large market	£2,000,000	£300,000
Small market	£ 200,000	£200,000.

(*Note:* these are from sales *only*, and so do *not* include launch costs.)
The marketing director feels there is a 40 per cent chance of the
market being large.
If the initial launch would cost £400,000, should it be undertaken?
The decision tree is more complex in this instance, since two decisions are involved. Logically (and chronologically), the first choice is
between launching the product and not doing so, and so the tree begins
with a node to depict this decision. Following the branch denoting the
option to launch there is an outcome node, since two things could
happen: success or failure. According to the managing director's edict,
the tree ends in the latter case. In the former, the decision arises as to
the level of marketing support, hence there is a second decision node at
this point. Finally, after the two branches following this node (one for
high level of support and one for low), we have the uncertainty over
market size and so outcome nodes occur.
The decision tree is shown in Figure 14.2(a). The decision nodes have
been numbered for ease of reference. The monetary figures at each end
point of the tree come from tracing through the tree to that point. We
give one example:

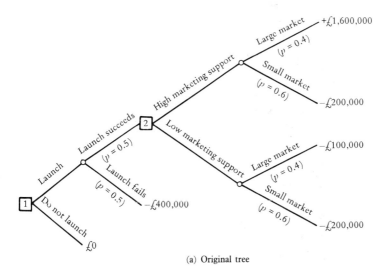

(a) Original tree

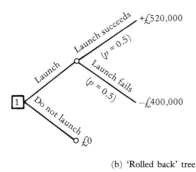

(b) 'Rolled back' tree

Figure 14.2 *Decision trees for example 14.5*

the figure − £100,000, comes from
the product is launched (cost £400,000), then
the launch succeeds, then
a low level of marketing support is allocated and the market turns out
   to be large (gain £300,000).

The analysis of this tree is complicated by the sequential nature of the
decisions. We approach the problem by asking the question

'*if* we reached decision node 2, what should we do?'

This is answered via the EMV criterion:

EMV (high marketing support) = (0.4 × 1,600,000) +
                               (0.6 × −200,000)
                             = +£520,000

$$\text{EMV (low marketing support)} = (0.4 \times -100{,}000) + $$
$$(0.6 \times -200{,}000)$$
$$= -£160{,}000$$

Therefore a *high* level of marketing support would be chosen, with an expected profit of £520,000.

We can thus replace the decision represented by node 2 by its expected profit, and 'roll back' the tree into that shown in Figure 14.2(b). It is now a simple matter to analyse decision 1:

$$\text{EMV (launch)} = (0.5 \times 520{,}000) + (0.5 \times -400{,}000)$$
$$= +£60{,}000$$

EMV (not launch) = 0.

Hence, in order to maximize expected profit, *the product should be launched*. Note that the earlier part of our analysis also shows that, if the launch turns out to be successful, a high level of marketing support should be used.

This method of analysing the decisions in reverse order (right to left through the table) and 'rolling back' each decision into its expected value, is known as the *rollback technique*.

Limitations of this approach

We are not advocating that the above approach is ideal: merely an *aid* to decision-making. Indeed, many texts which develop so-called 'decision theory' further address at some length the limitations we shall discuss here. Suffice it to say, at this point, that attempts to overcome these problems meet with varying degrees of success, and so it is inconceivable that an 'objective' approach can ever replace the human decision-maker.

Looking at examples 14.4 and 14.5, there is a clear difference in the nature of the probabilities being used. In the former case, they are empirical, arising from past experience, and so are presumably reliable, unless the demand pattern changes dramatically. In the latter, they all arise from subjective estimates of various directors and their reliability cannot be judged. There is therefore a question mark over this approach when *subjective* probabilities are used.

There is another difference between the two examples. The storeholder's problem is a decision repeated daily, and so the expected values have a commercial meaning: they are long-term *average* profits. Thus if he buys 2 units per day, he will average £16 per day profit. As this is higher than the average profit attainable from any other choice, this is a valid and sensible decision. In the other example, however, the company is facing a *one-off* decision. The analysis shows which option would give the best average profits over a long run of many *repeats* of the decision, a situation which does not obtain here. Thus one must question the use of the EMV criterion in one-off decisions.

Looking at example 14.5 more closely, we must question whether the company *would* launch the product in practice. The decision tree shows that the *only* way the project can be profitable is if the project is launched and is successful (probability 0.5) *and* if high marketing support is given in a large market (probability 0.4). The overall chance of being profitable is therefore

$$0.5 \times 0.4 = 0.2.$$

Many companies would not undertake a project launch with only a 20 per cent chance of making a profit, even if the potential profits were very high. The factor we are discussing here is *risk*: would the company risk such a venture? Our EMV-based analysis completely ignores this.

Finally, we briefly mention two other criticisms. Both examples are clearly simplifications of reality. In practical applications, decision trees can be much more complex, but you can never be certain that they are complete: how can you tell that a complete set of *all* possible options has been included? Also, business decisions are obviously concerned to a large extent with finance, but not exclusively so. It is a limitation of the method discussed here that other factors, such as time, labour relations, customer goodwill, which come into real-life decisions, cannot be included in the analysis.

Summary

In this chapter, we saw the concept of a *discrete probability distribution* with its associated *expected value*

$$E(x) = \Sigma x \cdot p(x).$$

If, further, the probability of a certain outcome in a certain circumstance is p, then, in n independent repeats of the circumstance, the expected number of times the circumstance will occur is np.

The three criteria for financial decision-making we encountered are:

maximin, in which we assume the worst will happen, and then choose the option that gives the best of these worst outcomes;
maximax, in which we assume the best will happen, and then choose the option that gives the best of these best outcomes;
the EMV criterion, in which we choose the option which gives the maximum expected return.

A decision tree is a graphical way of showing the logical/chronological decision-outcome-decision-outcome-... sequence in a given situation. The rollback technique consists of applying the EMV criterion to the last decision(s) in a tree first, replacing each decision by the expected value of the option with the highest expected value, and proceeding in this way, right to left through the tree until the first decision can be analysed.

Exercises on Chapter 14

1   As part of a costing exercise, the finance department of a manufacturing company receives from the quality control department the following data on rejects of product Y, which is despatched in batches of 50:

Number of rejects per batch	Number of batches (in quality control sample)
0	77
1	19
2	3
3	1

It is estimated that each reject costs the company £3.

   (a)   Form the empirical probability distribution of the number of rejects per batch.
   (b)   Evaluate the expected number of rejects per batch. What is the meaning of this value? (Note that, as you are using empirical probabilities, your answer will be an approximation to the expected value.)
   (c)   If the company despatches an average of 2500 batches of Y per week, what are the expected weekly costs to the company of defective Y's?
   (d)   What assumptions have been made in the above calculations?

2   A decision-maker is faced with a choice between three courses of action, A, B or C. Option A would yield a certain payoff of £2,000. Option B has two equally likely possible payoffs, £1,000 and £3,500. Option C has three equally likely possible outcomes, £500, £1,500 and £3,700.

   (a)   Construct a decision tree to represent these options.
   (b)   Which choice is best under the   (i)   maximin
                                         (ii)   maximax
                                         (iii)   EMV criterion?

   (c)   The decision based on expected values is arguably better as it uses more information, namely the probabilities of the various outcomes. Why might the decision-maker *not* choose the option indicated by this criterion?

3   A component supplier is deciding what price to quote to a car manufacturer for the supply of a number of components. The supplier is considering three possible prices and, based on her experience of the car manufacturer, the salesperson directly involved with the tender estimates the probabilities of their acceptance as:

Quoted price per component	Probability of acceptance
3.20	0.25
2.60	0.65
2.40	0.90

After the quotation has been made and *if* it is accepted, the supplier must decide how to make the components to fulfil the order. There are two options: use existing machinery, in which case the components cost £2.40 each to produce, or hire new machinery. If new machinery is hired, the production engineer reckons there is a 70 per cent chance it will perform adequately and reduce the production cost to £1.90 per component. However, there is a 30 per cent chance the new machinery will not prove adequate, in which case the original existing machinery will still have to be used and the unit production cost will rise to £2.90 each.

(a) Draw a decision tree to depict the situation facing the supplier.
(b) Using the EMV criterion and the rollback technique on the three secondary decisions, determine the price the supplier should quote.
(c) What are the limitations of this analysis?

4 One of the products your company manufactures and sells has a stable selling price of £30 per unit but the monthly sales volume is uncertain. The fixed costs are stable at £6,000 per month, but the variable cost per unit is also subject to uncertainty.

Based on past experience, management has developed the following probability distributions of sales and variable cost per unit:

Sales per month (units)	Probability
400	0.3
500	0.4
600	0.3
Variable cost per unit (£)	
10	0.2
15	0.5
20	0.3

Evaluate the expected total monthly profit for the product.
ICMA, November 1978.

5 For the past 200 days the sales of bread from a bakery have been as follows:

Daily sales (loaves)	Number of days
0	10
100	60
200	60
300	50
400	20

(a) What are the expected daily sales of bread? (*Hint:* first construct the appropriate probability distribution.)
(b) The bakery's production costs are £0.20 per loaf, selling price is £0.40 per loaf, and any bread unsold at the end of a day is contracted to a local farmer who pays £0.10 per loaf. Draw up a

table showing the profit for each combination of daily sales and production (in the range 0 to 400, in steps of 100).

(c) Compute the expected daily profit arising from each level of production and hence advise the bakery on its optimum production level.

ICMA, May 1984.

6 A manager in a department store has to decide how many luxury gift packs of cosmetics to buy for the forthcoming Christmas season. These gift packs have to be bought from a manufacturer in cases of 50 packs and the profit per pack sold is £20. The manager decides to use probability theory to aid her decision. On the basis of trading conditions last Christmas, the current economic climate, and competitive market factors, the manager's estimate of sales of this gift pack this Christmas is:

Sales (cases of 50 packs)	Probability
5	0.2
10	0.2
15	0.3
20	0.2
25	0.1

Any unsatisfied demand is assumed not to affect the probability of future sales. Any unsold gift packs will be sold in the New Year Sale at a loss of £10 per pack.

Assuming between 5 and 25 cases are bought (in steps of 5), draw a decision tree to represent this situation and hence advise the manager on the number of cases to buy.

ICMA, May 1983.

15 The binomial distribution

Introduction

With this chapter we begin the study of three major probability distributions. First of all, however, we must complete the set of definitions concerning probability distributions in general, and then we can go on to look at the *binomial distribution*, which has a particularly important application to quality control situations.

Variance and standard deviation of probability distributions

We restrict our attention for the time being to *discrete* probability distributions. In Chapter 14, we saw the mean or expected value of such a distribution, and we used the notation E(x). Here, however, we shall be considering *exact* probabilities, or those arising from a *population*, and so different symbolism is introduced: μ (pronounced 'mu', the Greek letter 'm'). Thus

mean, $\mu = \Sigma x \cdot p(x)$.

(Note the distinction between this and $\bar{x}$, which is used to denote *sample* means of *empirical* probability distributions.)

We now complete the parallel between this area of study and that of Part Two by defining a measure of dispersion of an exact discrete probability distribution

variance, $\sigma^2 = \Sigma x^2 \cdot p(x) - \mu^2$.

The symbol σ is 'sigma' (Greek letter 's'). Again, this σ^2 is distinct from s^2, the variance from a sample or from empirical probabilities. The square root of this variance, namely σ, is the *standard deviation*.

Example 15.1:
Evaluate the mean and standard deviation of the following probability distribution. What do these values mean?

x	$p(x)$
0	0.64
1	0.32
2	0.04

We set out the calculations in a systematic tabular form similar to that already used on a number of occasions:

x	x^2	$p(x)$	$x \cdot p(x)$	$x^2 \cdot p(x)$
0	0	0.64	0	0
1	1	0.32	0.32	0.32
2	4	0.04	0.08	0.16
			0.40	0.48

Thus the mean, $\mu = \Sigma x \cdot p(x) = 0.40$,

and
$$\sigma^2 = \Sigma x^2 \cdot p(x) - \mu^2$$
$$= 0.48 - (0.4)^2$$
$$= 0.32,$$

giving $\sigma = 0.566$.

Hence this distribution has a *mean of 0.4* and a *standard deviation of 0.566*.

These measures have similar meanings to those encountered earlier: the mean is the 'common or garden' average, while the standard deviation indicates the extent to which the distribution is spread around the mean.

The binomial distribution: how it arises

We develop this distribution with an example.

Example 15.2:
A component is known to have a defective rate of 20 per cent. If two of these components are bought, what is the probability that

neither,
exactly one,
both will be defective?

We tackle this problem by using a probability tree, as in Chapter 13. The first of the components can be either defective or not, and so the tree starts with two branches. After both of these, the second component can also be defective or not, and so we get four end points to the tree, which is drawn in Figure 15.1.

Now, p(neither are defective) $= p(D) = 0.64$

p(exactly one is defective) $= p(B \text{ or } C)$
$$= p(B) + p(C)$$
$$= 0.32$$

p(both are defective) $= p(A) = 0.04$.

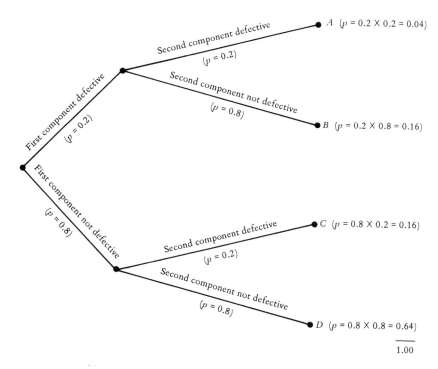

First component defective
$(p = 0.2)$

First component not defective
$(p = 0.8)$

Second component defective
$(p = 0.2)$

Second component not defective
$(p = 0.8)$

Second component defective
$(p = 0.2)$

Second component not defective
$(p = 0.8)$

A $(p = 0.2 \times 0.2 = 0.04)$

B $(p = 0.2 \times 0.8 = 0.16)$

C $(p = 0.8 \times 0.2 = 0.16)$

D $(p = 0.8 \times 0.8 = 0.64)$

1.00

Figure 15.1 *Probability tree for example 15.2*

Hence we have the distribution of the number (x) of defective components:

x	$p(x)$
0	0.64
1	0.32
2	0.04.

The above distribution is an example of a *binomial distribution*. The distinguishing features of this distribution are:

a circumstance is repeated n times, each repeat being *independent* of all others; the probability of each repeat of the circumstance having a certain outcome is a *constant p*.

In these circumstances, the binomial distribution is the exact probability distribution of x, the number of times the outcome occurs in the n repeats.

In example 15.2, the 'repeat circumstance' is each individual component being purchased. It is repeated

$n = 2$

times and each component is assumed to be independent of all others. The 'outcome' is a component being defective, and so the constant probability is

$p = 0.2$.

The probability distribution we have formed is thus known as the *binomial distribution for* $n = 2$, $p = 0.2$.

Evaluation of binomial probabilities

In theory, you could evaluate all probabilities arising from a binomial distribution in the same way as in example 15.2, by drawing a probability tree. If, however, we were considering buying ten of the components ($n = 10$ in the binomial distribution), there would be

$2^{10} = 1024$

end points to the tree! It is therefore necessary to use easier devices for calculating such probabilities.

Two such easier methods are the use of computer programs or statistical tables. As there are many different computer packages available for dealing with binomial distributions, we cannot look at them here. The reader might, however, be advised to use the packages on any accessible computer facilities. Similarly, it is not possible to study the many different ways of tabulating the probabilities, but the reader may wish to investigate further.

There is a formula for calculating binomial probabilities:

$p(x) = {}^nC_x \, p^x \, q^{n-x}$,

where ${}^nC_x = \dfrac{n!}{(n - x)! \, x!}$

and $q = (1 - p)$.

This appears daunting at first sight, but a few words of explanation will provide clarification. The '!' is the *factorial notation*:

$0! = 1$
$1! = 1$
$2! = 2 \times 1 = 2$
$3! = 3 \times 2 \times 1 = 6$
.
.
.
$6! = 6 \times 5 \times 4 \times 3 \times 2 \times 1 = 720$, and so on.

The 'C' notation is *combinatorial notation* and is, in fact, the number of ways x items can be chosen from n items, provided the order does not count. Before using the formula, we give an example to demonstrate these two new notations.

Example 15.3:
A chess team captain has nine players from which to choose a team of six: how many ways can this be done, assuming the order does not count? How many ways can it be done if one of the nine cries off through illness?

In the first case, we require $^9C_6$, which equals

$$\frac{9!}{(9-6)!6!} = \frac{9!}{3!\,6!}$$

Now, factorials can be very big numbers, for example

$$9! = 362880,$$

and so, even with a calculator, it is advisable to simplify the calculations.

$$\frac{9!}{3!\,6!} = \frac{9 \times 8 \times 7 \times 6 \times 5 \times 4 \times 3 \times 2 \times 1}{3 \times 2 \times 1 \times 6 \times 5 \times 4 \times 3 \times 2 \times 1}$$

$$= \frac{9 \times 8 \times 7}{3 \times 2 \times 1}$$

$$= 84.$$

Simplification is often possible through the use of such cancellations.

In the second case, the captain will have to choose six from eight: this can be done in $^8C_6$ ways:

$$^8C_6 = \frac{8!}{2!\,6!}$$

$$= \frac{8 \times 7 \times 6 \times 5 \times 4 \times 3 \times 2 \times 1}{2 \times 1 \times 6 \times 5 \times 4 \times 3 \times 2 \times 1}$$

$$= \frac{8 \times 7}{2 \times 1}$$

$$= 28$$

Thus the captain has *84 choices* of team in the first case and *28 choices* in the second.

Before moving on to an example of the binomial distribution, we note that, provided n is no more than twenty and x no more than 10, Appendix 1 can be used to find the values of combinations.

Example 15.4:
In the situation of example 15.2, five of the components are bought. What is the probability of having 0
1
2
3
4
5 defectives?

We are effectively being asked to find the complete binomial distribution for $n = 5$, $p = 0.2$. For convenience, the table in Appendix 1 will be used to evaluate the combinations, although, for practice, the reader may wish to calculate them from the formula involving factorials:

$$p(x = 0) = {}^5C_0 \cdot 0.2^0 \cdot 0.8^5$$
$$= 1 \times 1 \times 0.32768.$$
$$= 0.32768.$$

$$p(x = 1) = {}^5C_1 \cdot 0.2^1 \cdot 0.8^4$$
$$= 5 \times 0.2 \times 0.4096$$
$$= 0.4096$$

$$p(x = 2) = {}^5C_2 \cdot 0.2^2 \cdot 0.8^3$$
$$= 10 \times 0.04 \times 0.512$$
$$= 0.2048$$

$$p(x = 3) = {}^5C_3 \cdot 0.2^3 \cdot 0.8^2$$
$$= 10 \times 0.008 \times 0.64$$
$$= 0.0512$$

$$p(x = 4) = {}^5C_4 \cdot 0.2^4 \cdot 0.8^1$$
$$= 5 \times 0.0016 \times 0.8$$
$$= 0.0064$$

$$p(x = 5) = {}^5C_5 \cdot 0.2^5 \cdot 0.8^0$$
$$= 1 \times 0.00032 \times 1$$
$$= 0.00032$$

Thus the (binomial) distribution of the probabilities of the number of defectives is

number of defectives, x	probability, p(x)
0	0.32768
1	0.4096
2	0.2048
3	0.0512
4	0.0064
5	0.00032

Example 15.5:

(a) A mass producer of glassware knows from experience that 10 per cent of product A will be classifiable as 'seconds'. Product A is sold in boxes of 20. What proportion of boxes will be free of all seconds?

(b) Further, the producer is considering a money-back offer if any box contains two or more seconds: to what proportion of boxes would this offer apply?

Since proportions and probabilities are essentially the same thing, we are dealing here with the binomial distribution with $n = 20$, $p = 0.1$, provided we make the reasonable assumption that each item of A is independent of the others (a requirement for the binomial distribution to obtain). Also we are required to find only part of the distribution, rather than all of it.

(*a*) We require $p(x = 0)$

$$= {}^{20}C_0 \cdot 0.1^0 \cdot 0.9^{20}$$
$$= 1 \times 1 \times 0.1216$$
$$= 0.1216.$$

Thus 0.1216 or *12.16* per cent of all boxes will be free of seconds.
(*b*) Now, '2 or more' (out of 20) means

2 *or* 3 *or* 4 *or* ... *or* 20,

and so it appears that we have to calculate

$$p(x = 2), p(x = 3), p(x = 4), \ldots, p(x = 20)$$

and then *add* these mutually exclusive probabilities. This would be an exceedingly long process; so we seek an alternative.

As we have seen, the sum of all the probabilities in a distribution is 1. Thus, in this case,

$$p(x = 0) + p(x = 1) + p(x = 2) + \ldots + p(x = 20) = 1,$$

and so

$$p(x = 2) + \ldots + p(x = 20) = 1 - p(x = 0) - p(x = 1).$$

This, then, is our simplification: to obtain the desired left-hand side of this expression, we calculate the far easier right-hand side.

The value of $p(x = 0)$ has been found in (a).

$$p(x = 1) = {}^{20}C_1 \cdot 0.1^1 \cdot 0.9^{19}$$
$$= 20 \times 0.1 \times 0.1351$$
$$= 0.2702.$$

Hence $p(2 \text{ or more}) = 1 - 0.1216 - 0.2702$
$$= 0.6082.$$

That is, 0.6082 or *60.82* per cent of boxes would qualify for the money-back guarantee.

Mean, variance of a binomial distribution

Like any other probability distribution, a binomial distribution has a mean and a variance. Indeed, looking back to the first two examples of this chapter, it can be seen that we have, in fact, already found these parameters of the binomial distribution with $n = 2, p = 0.2$. If, however, the value of n was larger, then the use of the general formulae would be rather tedious. To avoid lengthy calculations, we have, for the binomial distribution:

$$\mu = np$$
$$\sigma^2 = npq.$$

It will be noted that this formula for the mean has already been encountered: see the section on expected values in Chapter 13.

Example 15.6:
In the situation of example 15.5, what are the mean and standard deviation number of seconds per box?
As $n = 20$ and $p = 0.1$, we have

$$\mu = 20 \times 0.1$$
$$= 2$$
$$\sigma^2 = 20 \times 0.1 \times 0.9$$
$$= 1.8$$
and so $\sigma = 1.34$.

Hence boxes of A contain a *mean of 2 seconds* with a *standard deviation of 1.34 seconds*.

Summary

The *mean* of an exact, discrete probability distribution is

$$\mu = \Sigma x \cdot p(x)$$

and the *variance* is

$$\sigma^2 = \Sigma x^2 \cdot p(x) - \mu^2.$$

For a binomial distribution with n independent repeats and a constant probability p of the outcome,

$$p(\text{outcome occurring } x \text{ times in the } n \text{ repeats}) = {}^nC_x \cdot p^x \cdot q^{n-x}$$

where ${}^nC_x = \dfrac{n!}{(n-x)!\, x!}$

and $q = (1 - p)$.

The mean of such a binomial distribution is

$$\mu = np$$

and the variance is

$$\sigma^2 = npq.$$

Exercises on Chapter 15

1 An insurance agent knows that, of all personal interviews he conducts, 70 per cent result in a policy being bought. On a certain day, the agent conducts three personal interviews.

(a) Draw the probability tree to represent this situation. (Hint: it should have *eight* end points.)

(b) Use the tree to evaluate the probability that, on the given day,
  (i)   0
  (ii) 1
  (iii) 2
  (iv) 3 contracts will be bought.

(c) Use the *general* formulae (pages 161–2) to find the mean and standard deviation of the above distribution.

(d) The distribution involved here is the binomial distribution with $n = 3, p = 0.7$. Use the formulae for the binomial distribution to verify your answers in (b) and (c).

(e) All of the above assumes that each repeated occurrence (that is, each interview) is independent of all others. Can you think of any circumstances in which this assumption, and therefore the calculations, are invalid?

2   A manufacturer wishes to cost the effects of defective items of a new product, which is sold in boxes of 100. Extensive quality control tests have shown that 1 per cent of items of the product do not function adequately.

(a) Evaluate the probability that, in any box of 100 of these items, there will be
  (i)   0
  (ii) 1
  (iii) 2 which do not function adequately.

(b) It is proposed that, in the event of there being more than two items in a box which do not function adequately, the purchaser will be offered a 'money-back plus' compensation scheme. Use the answers in (a) to find the probability that any one box will qualify for this scheme.

(c) The cost per box to the company of any box which falls under the proposed compensation scheme is estimated to be £15. If a total of 50,000 boxes are expected to be sold per annum, estimate the annual cost to the company of the scheme.

3   A large company uses an aptitude test as the initial part of its graduate recruitment programme. The organization which developed the test states that an average of 40 per cent of graduates pass the test. One September, after the results of finals are known, 20 graduates turn up for the initial aptitude test.

(a) What is the mean and variance of the number of these who will pass the test?

(b) The company wishes to recruit four graduates in the year concerned: what is the probability that less than this number will pass the initial test?

(c)   Why might these calculations be invalid if 2 of the 20 graduates were twins?

4   (a)   A fair dice with six sides is thrown three times. Find by means of a probability tree the probabilities of getting 0, 1, 2 or 3 sixes.

(b)   A department produces a standard product. It is known that 60 per cent of defective products can be satisfactorily reworked. What is the probability that, in a batch of five such defective products, at least four can be satisfactorily reworked?

ICMA, November 1976.

5   An airline deliberately overbooks its local mini flights because it knows from experience that not all passengers who book for a given flight actually arrive for that flight. It is assumed that the probability of any booked passenger arriving for a given flight is 0.8; this is independent of the probability of any other passenger arriving.

   The airline takes ten bookings for an 8-seater aircraft. Use the binomial distribution to find the probability:

(a)   that the aircraft takes off full;
(b)   that the aircraft takes off with at least two empty seats.

ICMA, November 1983.

6   A company mass produces electronic calculators. From past experience it knows that 90 per cent of the calculators will be in working order and 10 per cent will be faulty if the production process is working satisfactorily. An inspector randomly selects five calculators from the production line every hour and carries out a rigorous check.

(a)   What is the probability that a random sample of five will contain at least three defective calculators?
(b)   A sample of five calculators is found to contain three defectives; do you consider the production process to be working satisfactorily?

ICMA, November 1982.

16 The Poisson distribution

Introduction

The next discrete probability distribution we consider is the *Poisson distribution*, so named after the mathematician who first published details of it in 1837. This distribution has similarities to the binomial, but also has special properties which make it particularly suitable for modelling *rare* events.

The Poisson distribution: definition and calculations

The Poisson distribution arises from situations similar to the binomial, in that we must have a repeated circumstance with each repeat being *independent* of all others and each one having a *constant* probability of a certain outcome. Further, if

the number of repeats is *very large* and the probability of the outcome *very small*, and
there is *no* chance of two or more of the outcomes occurring simultaneously,

then we are said to have a *Poisson process*. The *Poisson distribution* consists of the discrete probabilities arising from such a process.

Poisson probabilities can be calculated in a number of ways, and arguably the best of these is the use of a suitable computer package. As in the case of the binomial distribution, the reader is encouraged to investigate any such packages which may be available. Another relatively easy device is the use of statistical tables such as those in Appendix 1. These cannot always be applied, and in such a case a formula must be used. This states

$$p \,(x \text{ occurrences}) = \frac{e^{-m} \cdot m^x}{x!}$$

where m is the mean of the distribution (alternatively denoted μ),

$x!$ is the factorial notation (first seen in Chapter 15),
and e^{-m} concerns the *exponential function, e^x.*

Before looking at examples of the Poisson distribution, we say a few words about the exponential function, which may be unfamiliar. This function is based on the number e, called 'the exponential e', which has the value

$$e = 2.71828\ldots$$

(Like π, the decimal expansion of this number never ends, and so only the first five significant figures after the decimal point have been given.)
Thus

$$e^x = 2.71828\ldots^x$$

and so, for example,

$$e^2 = 2.71828\ldots^2 = 7.3890\ldots$$

Although we only encounter this number and its associated function here, its wide importance in mathematics has led it to be included as an 'e^x-button' on virtually every modern calculator. It is this facility that the reader is urged to use.

We are now in a position to tackle some examples.

Example 16.1:
The mean daily number of accidents reported to the police on a certain stretch of road is 0.35. Use the Poisson distribution to evaluate the probabilities of any given day having (*a*)   zero;
(*b*)   less than three, accidents reported

to the police on that stretch of road.
(*a*)   The mean, m (or μ), is given to be 0.35, and so, noting that the tables in Appendix 1 do not apply, the formula gives

$$p(x = 0) = \frac{e^{-0.35} \cdot 0.35^0}{0!}$$

Using the exponential function facility on a calculator, and recalling that

$$x^0 = 1 \text{ (any } x\text{)}$$
$$\text{and } 0! = 1 \text{ (see Chapter 15),}$$

this gives

$$p(x = 0) = \frac{0.705 \times 1}{1}$$
$$= 0.705.$$

Thus *70.5 per cent of days* will be accident-free.
(*b*)   Now, 'less than three' means

0 *or* 1 *or* 2;

so

p (less than three accidents) = p (0 *or* 1 *or* 2)
                              = p(0) + p(1) + p(2).

The formula gives

$$p(x = 1) = \frac{e^{-0.35} \cdot 0.35^1}{1!}$$

$$= \frac{0.705 \times 0.35}{1}$$

$$= 0.247$$

and

$$p(x = 2) = \frac{e^{-0.35} \cdot 0.35^2}{2!}$$

$$= \frac{0.705 \times 0.1225}{2}$$

$$= 0.043$$

Hence

p(less than three accidents) = 0.705 + 0.247 + 0.043
                             = 0.995.

Thus *99.5 per cent of days* will have less than three accidents.

Before leaving this example, we make a few observations. We have assumed that accidents on this particular stretch of road constitute a Poisson process – what does this involve? The number of repeat circumstances (vehicles on the road) is indeed very large and the probability of the outcome (a vehicle having an accident in any one day) is certainly very small. It seems plausible to assume that each car is independent of all others and that the probability of a car having an accident is constant – even if one believes in 'accident-proneness', there will not be sufficient people of this type to distort this assumption. The only property of a Poisson process which may not apply is therefore the necessity that there should be *no* chance of two or more simultaneous 'outcomes' – what of multiple accidents? *If* a multiple accident is counted as just one accident, rather than many individual ones, then this requirement is satisfied. Otherwise, our calculations will be invalid.

Further, notice that we could not use the binomial distribution here. We do not know n, the daily number of vehicles on the stretch of road, or p, the probability of any one vehicle having an accident during the day. We *do*, however, know the mean, m or μ, which equals np, which is all that is needed for the Poisson distribution.

Example 16.2:
A battery farm processes 10,000 chickens a week in the immediate pre-Christmas period. It is known that only 0.03 per cent of chickens

suffer from a certain condition which makes them unfit for consumption. Use the Poisson distribution to find the probability that, in a week immediately prior to Christmas, the farm will process

(*a*)   no chickens,
(*b*)   one chicken,
(*c*)   more than three chickens,

with the condition.

This is, in fact, a binomial situation, with $n = 10{,}000$ and $p = 0.0003$ (0.03 per cent). Often, with such a large n and small p, the Poisson is considered an equally valid distribution but, first, we need its mean. The formula for the binomial distribution gives

$$\mu = np$$
$$= 10{,}000 \times 0.0003$$
$$= 3,$$

and so we use $m = 3$.

(*a*)   This value for m occurs in the Poisson tables of Appendix 1, and so we shall use them. The reader may wish to repeat the calculations using the formula, for practice.

$$p(x = 0) = 0.0498.$$

Hence, on *4.98 per cent of occasions*, a week will be free of the condition.

(*b*)   Again using the tables,

$$p(x = 1) = 0.1494,$$

so, on *14.94 per cent of occasions*, precisely one chicken will have the condition.

(*c*)   'More than three' means

4 *or* 5 *or* 6 *or* ...

This now illustrates a difference between the Poisson and binomial distributions. In the former case there is theoretically no upper limit to the number of times the outcome can occur, while in the latter there is, namely n. Thus, while it was advisable to use an alternative approach for an example such as this in the binomial case, it is *essential* to do so in the Poisson case (compare example 15.5(b)):

$$p(x = 4 \text{ or } 5 \text{ or } 6 \text{ or } \ldots)$$
$$= 1 - p(x = 0) - p(x = 1) - p(x = 2) - p(x = 3).$$

From the tables,

$$p(x = 2) = 0.2240,$$
$$\text{and } p(x = 3) = 0.2240,$$

so

$$p(\text{'more than three'}) = 1 - 0.0498 - 0.1494 - 0.2240 - 0.2240$$
$$= 0.3528.$$

Hence, on *35.28 per cent of occasions*, more than three chickens will have the condition during a week.

The variance of a Poisson distribution. The additive property

To complete our discussion of the Poisson distribution, we mention two further properties. First, we have seen the concept of the variance of a probability distribution, and so the question arises as to what is the variance of a Poisson distribution. It is perhaps a remarkable property that

the variance = the mean,

or

$$\sigma^2 = \mu \text{ (or } m).$$

A major property of Poisson distributions is their *additive property*. This property provides that, if the variables x and y are Poisson distributed, then so is $(x + y)$. This usually manifests itself in the useful result that if x is Poisson distributed, then so is

$x + x = 2x$, and
$2x + x = 3x$, and so on.

Hence any *multiple* of x follows a Poisson distribution.

Example 16.3:
The manager of a canteen is attempting to model the arrivals of customers, in order to optimize, within his budget, the facilities on offer. A works study exercise shows that, at peak times, customers arrive at a mean rate of 2.04 every 10 seconds.

The information is not entirely in the correct form for the manager who wishes to consider *30*-second intervals. Assuming a Poisson process is occurring, find (for peak times):

    (a) the mean and standard deviation number of customers arriving per 30 seconds;
    (b) the probability of less than two customers arriving during a 30-second time period.

(a) The number of customers arriving per 10 seconds is Poisson distributed, and so the number arriving per

    3×10 seconds

is *also* Poisson distributed (by the additive property above). The mean of this latter distribution is clearly

    3×2.04
    $= 6.12$ *customers.*

As, for a Poisson distribution,

    $\sigma^2 = \mu,$

we have

$$\sigma^2 = 6.12$$
$$\sigma = 2.47.$$

Hence the standard deviation number of customers arriving per 30 seconds is *2.47*.

(*b*)   We want

$$p(\text{less than } 2) = p(0 \text{ or } 1)$$
$$= p(0) + p(1)$$

Now, the tables do not apply for a mean of 6.12; so, from the formula:

$$p(x = 0) = \frac{e^{-6.12} \cdot 6.12^0}{0!}$$
$$= \frac{.0022 \times 1}{1}$$
$$= 0.0022$$
$$p(x = 1) = \frac{e^{-6.12} \cdot 6.12^1}{1!}$$
$$= \frac{.0022 \times 6.12}{1}$$
$$= .0135.$$

Thus $p(\text{less than } 2) = .0157$.

So, on *1.57* per cent of occasions, there will be fewer than two customers arriving in a 30-second period.

Histograms of probability distributions

We have already seen a number of parallels between discrete probability distributions and frequency distributions. There is a further similarity, in that it is possible to draw *histograms* of discrete probability distributions.

Example 16.4:
Draw the histograms of

(*a*)   the binomial distribution with $n = 4$, $p = 0.3$;
(*b*)   the Poisson distribution with m (μ) = 0.75.

(*a*)   We omit the calculations of the probabilities here, leaving them as exercises for the reader:

x	$p(x)$
0	.2401
1	.4116
2	.2646
3	.0756
4	.0081.

The histogram is shown in Figure 16.1(a). Note that this is very similar to a histogram of a discrete frequency distribution which has not been grouped into classes (see Chapter 6). The only essential difference is that the vertical axis now measures probability.

(b)   Again, the calculations are left to the reader:

x	p(x)
0	.4724
1	.3543
2	.1329
3	.0332
4	.0062
5 or more	.0010

As we have already mentioned, the Poisson distribution theoretically has no upper limit for x, and so we have to decide at which point the probabilities have become so small that we can stop calculating them. In the above example, the value

p(x is 5 or more)

has been found by adding the preceding values and subtracting from 1, since the sum of the probabilities must equal 1.

The histogram is shown in Figure 16.1(b). It can be seen from this that we could have ended the distribution at the point '4 or more'.

Summary

A *Poisson distribution* arises from a situation similar to a binomial distribution, but occurs where n is very large and p is very small and there is no chance of two or more simultaneous outcomes. If the mean of such a distribution is m, then

$$p(x \text{ outcomes or occurrences}) = \frac{e^{-m} \cdot m^x}{x!}.$$

The variance is

$$\sigma^2 = m.$$

If the variables x and y are Poisson distributed, then so are

$(x + y)$

and any whole number multiple of x.

A histogram of a discrete probability distribution is exactly the same as in the corresponding frequency case, but for the vertical lines indicating probability values.

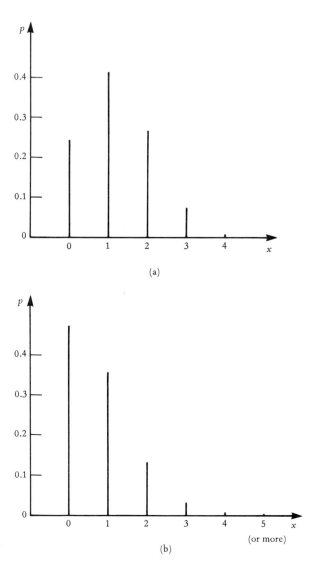

Figure 16.1(a) *Histogram for example 16.4(a).* (b) *Histogram for example 16.4(b)*

Exercises on Chapter 16

1   The manager of a port is trying to determine the optimal level of facilities needed at the port. She estimates from past data that the mean arrival rate is 1.2 ships per day.

   (*a*)   Assuming that ship arrivals at the port constitute a Poisson process, evaluate the probabilities of 0, 1, 2, 3, 4, and 5 or more ships arriving at the port on any given day.

(b) What is the mean and standard deviation number of daily arrivals?

(c) What precisely does the assumption that we are dealing with a Poisson process mean?

2 Accidents are reported to the management of a factory at a rate of 2.5 per week (5 working days). Use the Poisson distribution to evaluate the probability that

(a) a working *day* is accident-free;

(b) a working *week* is accident-free;

(c) a working *month* is accident-free. (A working month is four working weeks.)

In an effort to improve the factory's safety record, the management offers to make a payment into the trade union welfare fund for each week there are two or fewer accidents reported. If the accident rate does *not* change, on what percentage of weeks will the payment be made? On what percentage of weeks will it be made if the accident rate reduces to 2.2 per week?

3 A small town has a population of 1000. A certain rare disease has an incidence rate of 0.001 cases per head of population per year. Use the binomial and the Poisson distributions to find the probability that

(a) the town will have no incidences of the disease next year;

(b) there will be no more than two incidences of the disease in the town next year.

If the disease is highly contagious, common sense might suggest that, if one person in the town contracts it, then many will, and so the above calculations would be in error. What assumption about the binomial and Poisson distributions is invalidated in the case of a highly contagious disease, thereby making their application inappropriate?

4 In a certain large factory the mean number of stoppages per week is 1.5. What is the probability that:

(a) in a given week there will be no stoppages;

(b) in a given week there will be three or more stoppages;

(c) in a given 2-week period there will be at most one stoppage?

What assumptions have you implicitly made in using the Poisson distribution here?
ICMA, May 1983.

5 One per cent of calculators produced by a company is known to be defective. If a random sample of 50 calculators is selected for inspection, calculate the probability of getting no defectives by using:

(a) the binomial distribution;

(b) the Poisson distribution.

Comment on the relative merits of these two distributions in this situation.
ICMA, May 1984.

6. Experience has shown that, on average, 2 per cent of an airline's flights suffer a minor equipment failure in an aircraft. Use the Poisson distribution to estimate the probability that the number of minor equipment failures in the next 50 flights will be:

(*a*)   zero;
(*b*)   at least two.

ICMA, May 1982.

17 The normal distribution

Introduction. Continuous probability distributions

So far we have studied only discrete probability distributions. A *continuous* probability distribution is a distribution of a variable which can take *any* value, subject only to the precision of measurement. As there is now a theoretically infinite number of values the variable could take, it is no longer possible to have a complete list as in the previous discrete distributions. Instead, probabilities in a continuous case are given by graphical representations which have similarities to the histograms seen in the preceding chapter. We give an illustrative example.

Example 17.1:
A clock stops at a random time and the number of minutes after the hour it indicates is read. What does the histogram of the probability distribution of this variable look like?

This is clearly a continuous variable, and so we approach the problem as in the corresponding frequency case, by looking at *classes*. Suppose the variable is measured in classes of width 10 minutes. The distribution would be:

x (minutes)	p(x)
0 to under 10	1/6
10 to under 20	1/6
20 to under 30	1/6
30 to under 40	1/6
40 to under 50	1/6
50 to under 60	1/6

The histogram of this distribution is shown in Figure 17.1(a).

If we now measure in classes of width five minutes, the distribution would consist of 12 classes, each with a probability of 1/12. The corresponding histogram, given in Figure 17.1(b), shows the same rectangular shape, but with more constituent 'blocks' and a different scale on the vertical axis.

Thus, as we increase the precision of measurement, through classes of width

1 minute

$\dfrac{1}{10}$ minute

$\dfrac{1}{100}$ minute

and so on, we can see that the basic shape of the histogram will remain unaltered, only there will be more and more constituent blocks. Ultimately, we shall reach the position shown in Figure 17.1(c) in which the many blocks have become so thin that they cannot be distinguished.

The question remains: what is the height of this block in this ultimate 'histogram'? As we have already seen, the heights of blocks in frequency histograms are somewhat arbitrary, provided they are in the correct proportions to one another. We therefore have a certain element of choice here. So, as we are going to *equate probabilities with areas*, we choose the height to be $\dfrac{1}{60}$, so that

total area = total probability = 1.

The resulting 'histogram' shown is called the graph of the *probability density function*.

Using this concept of a graphical representation of a continuous variable, with areas equalling probabilities, we can now study the normal distribution.

The normal distribution: its importance and characteristics

The normal distribution has been described as the single most important topic in the whole of statistics. This is because it arises in many practical situations and it has numerous theoretical applications, one of which we shall see later. Naturally occurring variables, such as the dimensions and weights of mass-produced items, often turn out to be normally distributed and so a study of this topic is essential in areas such as quality control.

A normal distribution is completely defined by its mean (μ) and its standard deviation (σ). It is bell-shaped and symmetric about its mean, and, as Figure 17.2 indicates, although the probability of a normal variable taking a value far away from the mean is small, it is never quite zero. The graphs in the figure also demonstrate the role of the mean and standard deviation. As before, the mean determines the general position or *location* of the variable, while the standard deviation determines how *spread* the variable is around its mean.

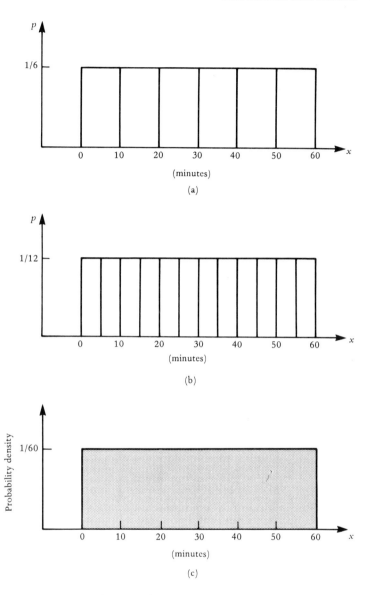

Figure 17.1 *Histograms for example 17.1*

Use of tables of the normal distribution

The above information describes the normal distribution but is insufficient to enable us to calculate probabilities based upon it, even though we know, from the introduction, that the total area under a normal curve must be 1. To evaluate normal probabilities, we must use either a

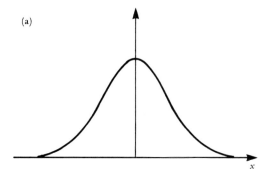

(a)

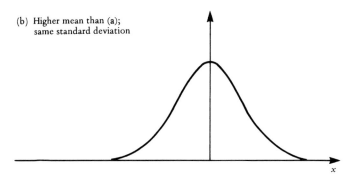

(b) Higher mean than (a);
    same standard deviation

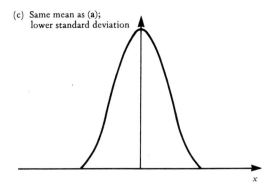

(c) Same mean as (a);
    lower standard deviation

Figure 17.2 *Examples of the normal distribution*

suitable computer package or statistical tables. We look at the latter method here.

The tables in Appendix 1 are for the *standard* normal distribution, that is, that with

mean of 0,
standard deviation of 1.

This special distribution is always denoted by the variable z. Any other normal distribution, denoted x, with mean, μ, and standard deviation, σ, can be converted to the standard one (or '*standardized*') by

$$z = \frac{x - \mu}{\sigma}.$$

Example 17.2:
A machine produces components with diameter of mean 5 cm and standard deviation 0.1 cm. Knowing that the dimensions of many such products follow a normal distribution, the production manager of the manufacturing company decides to use a normal model for the machine's production.

What proportion of the production will have diameters

(a) between 5 cm and 5.2 cm;
(b) between 4.9 cm and 5 cm;
(c) over 5.15 cm;
(d) between 4.8 cm and 5.1 cm;
(e) between 5.1 cm and 5.2 cm?

Although this question concerns proportions, we have seen before that such a problem is essentially a question on probabilities. We are dealing with a normal distribution with

$\mu = 5$
$\sigma = 0.1$.

(a) Denoting the components' diameters by x, we need

$p\,(5 \leq x \leq 5.2)$

which reads as 'the probability of 5 being less than or equal to x, and x being less than or equal to 5.2'.
Standardizing the x–values in this expression:

$x = 5:\quad z = \dfrac{5 - 5}{0.1} = 0$

$x = 5.2:\; z = \dfrac{5.2 - 5}{0.1} = 2,$

we get the equivalent probability involving z:

$p(0 \leq z \leq 2)$.

This probability (area) is depicted as the shaded area in Figure 17.3(a). Comparing this diagram with the one in Appendix 1 we see this is a direct reading from the tables giving 0.4772.

Hence *0.4772* (47.72 per cent) of components produced will have diameters between 5 cm and 5.2 cm.

(b) The probability involved here is

$$p(4.9 \leq x \leq 5).$$

Standardizing,

$$x = 4.9: z = \frac{4.9 - 5}{0.1} = -1$$

$$x = 5: \quad z = 0 \ (\text{above}),$$

we get

$$p(-1 \leq z \leq 0).$$

This is the area shown in Figure 17.3(b), which does not correspond to Appendix 1. However, we recall that the normal curve is *symmetric* about its mean; hence the shaded area is the same as the corresponding area to the *right* of the central dividing line, between the z–values 0 and 1. The tables give this area to be 0.3413.

Thus *0.3413* (34.13 per cent) of components produced will have diameters between 4.9 cm and 5 cm.

(c) We want

$$p(x \geq 5.15)$$

which standardizes, as before, to

$$p(z \geq 1.5).$$

This area, shown in Figure 17.3(c), cannot be read directly from the table of probabilities. However, the area immediately to its left (between the z–values 0 and 1.5) *can*: it is 0.4332. Now, as the *total* area under the curve is 1 and the central dividing line splits the area into two symmetrical halves, the area to the right of the dividing line is 0.5. Hence the area required is

$$0.5 - 0.4332$$
$$= 0.0668,$$

and so *0.0668* (6.68 per cent) of components produced will have diameters over 5.15 cm.

(d) In this case, the probability is

$$p(4.8 \leq x \leq 5.1)$$

which standardizes to

$$p(-2 \leq z \leq 1),$$

the shaded area in Figure 17.3(d). The central dividing line splits this area into two parts convenient for direct readings from the table:

z from -2 to 0: 0.4772 (the symmetry property has been used here, as in (b)).

z from 0 to 1: 0.3413
        total = 0.8185.

That is, *0.8185* (81.85 per cent) of components produced will have diameters between 4.8 cm and 5.1 cm.

(e) This final case is

$p(5.1 \leq x \leq 5.2)$

or

$p(1 \leq z \leq 2)$.

The tables show that the area between

z–values 0 and 1 is 0.3413,
z–values 0 and 2 is 0.4772.

Now, the shaded area in Figure 17.3(e) can be seen to be the *difference* between these, that is

0.4772 − 0.3413
= 0.1359,

so *0.1359* (13.59 per cent) of components produced will have diameters between 5.1 cm and 5.2 cm.

The crucial role of the diagrams in Figure 17.3 should be noted. Such graphs need not be drawn very accurately, but their use is strongly advised in order to make correct use of the probabilities taken from the table. Our next example involves the use of the tables in a slightly different way.

Example 17.3:
The finance department of a pharmaceutical company is concerned that the ageing machinery on their production line is causing losses by putting too much, on average, of a certain product into each container. A check on the line shows that the mean amount being put into a container is 499.5 ml, with a standard deviation of 0.8 ml.

(a) Adopting a normal distribution, what percentage of containers will contain more than the notional contents of 500 ml?
(b) There are two courses of remedial action available: one would reduce the mean amount inserted (leaving the standard deviation unaltered), while the other would reduce the standard deviation (mean unaltered). If the production manager wishes to reduce the percentage of containers containing over 500 ml to 10 per cent, how could this be achieved by reducing
        (i)   the mean
and (ii)   the standard deviation amount inserted?
(a) Initially, we are working with a normal distribution having

$\mu = 499.5$
$\sigma = 0.8$,

and we want

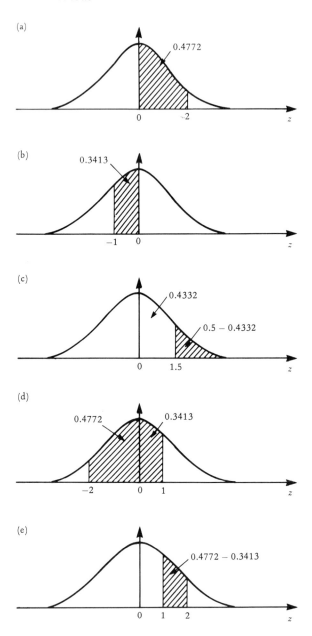

Figure 17.3 *Graphs for example 17.2*

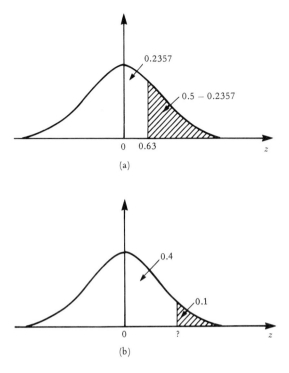

Figure 17.4 *Graphs for example 17.3*

$p(x > 500)$.

Standardizing, we get

$p(z > 0.63)$,

which is the shaded area in Figure 17.4(a). This is similar to part
(c) above, and so equals

$0.5 - 0.2357$
$= 0.2643$.

Thus *26.43* per cent of containers have contents of over 500 ml.

(b) This problem is different from the earlier ones: we now *know* the
probability (10 per cent or 0.1) and we need to 'work backwards' to
find a new value for (i) μ
  (ii) σ.

Figure 17.4(b) shows the standard normal distribution, with the
upper 10 per cent of area shaded. To find the unknown z–value
marked, we must look through the body of the table to find the
z–value corresponding to an area of 0.4. The nearest to this is

$z = 1.28$.

Before moving on, we point out that all we have done is use the table 'backwards' to see that

$p(z \geq 1.28) = 0.4$ (or $0.5 - 0.1$).

(*i*)   Now we have

$$z = \frac{x - \mu}{\sigma}.$$

So, using the value of z we have found:

$$1.28 = \frac{500 - \mu}{0.8};$$

therefore $1.28 \times 0.8 = 500 - \mu$,
giving $\mu = 499.0$ (to 1 decimal place).

Hence reducing the mean input to *499.0 ml* would reduce the percentage of containers with over 500 ml to 10 per cent.

(*ii*)   Similarly, if we regard μ as fixed and change σ:

$$1.28 = \frac{500 - 499.5}{\sigma};$$

so $1.28\,\sigma = 0.5$,
giving $\sigma = 0.39$ (to 2 decimal places).

Thus the standard deviation input must be reduced to *0.39 ml* to achieve the reduction to 10 per cent of containers with contents over 500 ml.

Part (*b*) of the above example shows how, for a given probability, the normal tables can be used to work 'backwards' through the usual steps to find a revised value of the mean or standard deviation. In other words,

use the value of the probability (or area) to find z from the tables; then use the standardization formula to calculate μ or σ.

Summary

A continuous probability distribution is represented by its probability density function. Areas under the graph of this function represent probabilities, so that the total area must equal 1.

A *normal distribution* is a bell-shaped continuous distribution, symmetric about its mean. It is completely defined by its mean, μ, and standard deviation, σ, and can be transformed to the *standard* normal distribution (mean 0 and standard deviation 1) by

$$z = \frac{x - \mu}{\sigma}.$$

Exercises on Chapter 17

1   Past records indicate that the daily output of a certain group of workers is approximately normally distributed with a mean of 250 units and a standard deviation of 20 units. The trade union representing the workers proposes that a bonus should be paid on any day in which the output exceeds 275 units.

   (a) If circumstances do not change, what is the probability that the bonus will have to be paid on any given day?
   (b) If the bonus would cost £250 per day, estimate the annual cost of the bonus. (Assume 300 working days per year.)
   (c) Repeat these calculations on the assumption that the mean daily output increases to 270 units. (Standard deviation unchanged.)
   (d) Why cannot the daily outputs be *exactly* normally distributed?

2   A machine has been used to manufacture ball-bearings for many years. Although the diameters of the bearings produced seem to be *on average* within tolerance, it is suspected the age of the machine is manifesting itself in too wide a variation around the mean. With the diameter set at 2 cm, a test shows that the machine is producing bearings with a mean of 2 cm and a standard deviation of 0.002 cm. At this setting, the desired tolerance for diameters is 1.995 cm to 2.005 cm.

   (a) Assuming that the dimensions of the bearings, like those of many mass-produced articles, are normally distributed, evaluate the percentage of production which lies within the tolerance limits.
   (b) To what value must the standard deviation of the diameters be reduced in order that 99.4 per cent of production would lie within tolerance? (That is, only 0.3 per cent below 1.995 cm and 0.3 per cent above 2.005 cm.) Assume that the adjustments necessary to attain this do not change the mean diameter.

3   An automatic filling machine is designed to put 1 kg of sugar into a bag. In practice, due to small random fluctuations, the weight of sugar put into bags is found to be normally distributed with a mean of 1 kg and a standard deviation of 0.003 kg.

   (a) Any bag containing less than 0.995 kg of sugar is classed as underweight. What proportion of bags will be underweight?
   (b) This proportion is considered to be too high, and so it is desired to reduce it to 0.02 (2 per cent). The machine is running to its maximum efficiency and so the standard deviation cannot be improved. The only way, therefore, to achieve this is to adjust the setting of the machine so as to increase the mean weight of sugar put into the bags. To what value must the mean be increased so that only 2 per cent of bags are underweight?

(c)   If the machine fills 1000 bags per hour, how much extra sugar will be used per hour, if the above change is implemented?

4   Your company requires a special type of inelastic rope which is available from only two suppliers. Supplier A's ropes have a mean breaking strength of 1,000 kg with a standard deviation of 100 kg. Supplier B's ropes have a mean breaking strength of 900 kg with a standard deviation of 50 kg. The distribution of the breaking strength of each type of rope is normal.

   Your company requires that the breaking strength of a rope be not less than 750 kg. All other things being equal, which rope should you buy, and why?
   ICMA, May 1984.

5   A company produces batteries whose lifetimes are normally distributed with a mean of 100 hours. It is known that 90 per cent of the batteries last at least 40 hours.

   (a)   Estimate the standard deviation lifetime.
   (b)   What percentage of batteries will not last 70 hours?

   ICMA, November 1982.

6   A company has invested £50,000 in a plant which should meet all foreseeable demand for a patented product. The annual demand is known to be approximately normally distributed with a mean of 20,000 units and a standard deviation of 4000 units. If the contribution on each unit sold is £2, what is the probability that the company will recover its investment within one year?
   ICMA, November 1985.

18 Confidence intervals

Introduction

We mentioned in the preceding chapter that there are many useful applications of the normal distribution. In this introductory text, we look at just one of these: the idea of a *confidence interval*.

Suppose, in a certain situation, we are interested in finding the mean value of some variable. Ideally, we should like the *population* value, μ, as this represents the totality of all possible information on the variable. For a variety of practical reasons already discussed, however, we have to *sample* and use the mean of this, $\bar{x}$. These two values will not generally be the same, as the sample mean arises only from a subset of the information from which the population value is calculated. We *can* say, however, that

$\bar{x}$ is an *estimate* of the (unknown) μ.

Since μ is what we are really after, the question now arises as to *how good* an estimate $\bar{x}$ is. It is this question that we address here. Its answer initially involves some theory.

The sampling distribution of the mean

Suppose we have a population of a variable and we take many random samples all of the same size, n, from it. The means of these samples can then be evaluated, and so, theoretically, we could build up a list of *all* the possible values of $\bar{x}$ for samples of size n. This 'list' is called *the sampling distribution of the mean*. We give an illustrative example.

Example 18.1:
Consider the population consisting of the three numbers (1, 2, 3). Draw up a list of all the possible samples (with replacement) of size 2, and calculate their sample means.

If we systematically list the samples and evaluate their means, we get:

Sample:	$\bar{x}$:
1,1	1
1,2	1.5
1,3	2
2,1	1.5
2,2	2
2,3	2.5
3,1	2
3,2	2.5
3,3	3

The list of $\bar{x}$–values above constitutes *the sampling distribution of the mean* (for samples of size 2 from the population given). It could be arranged into a neater form:

value of $\bar{x}$:	frequency
1	1
1.5	2
2	3
2.5	2
3	1

The above example is untypical in that we 'know' the population, a situation which rarely arises in practice. It is, however, very illustrative. It is possible, for instance, to evaluate the population mean (again an untypical situation), which can easily be seen to be

$\mu = 2$.

Now, how does the distribution of $\bar{x}$'s compare to this value? Clearly, $\bar{x}$ does not equal μ in all cases, but the distribution does seem to be clustered around the population value. In fact, it is easy to check that the mean of all the $\bar{x}$–values is in fact 2, the population mean value.

Statistical theory states that this *always* happens. That is,

on average, $\bar{x} = \mu$.

The sample mean is said to be an *unbiased* estimate of the population mean. In this sense, we have partially answered the question: $\bar{x}$ is the '*best*' estimate available for μ, in that it gives the correct value, on average.

Although it is the 'best' estimate, the sample mean is not perfect, since the distribution is *spread* around the population mean, as the example illustrated. Further theory, therefore, exists to investigate the *amount* of this spread and the *shape* of the sampling distribution. We do not attempt to justify this theory here, but simply state the results needed later.

It can be shown that the standard deviation of the sampling distribution of the mean equals

$\sigma/\sqrt{n}$,

where σ is the standard deviation of the *population*. This value is termed the *standard error* of the mean, in that, in a sense, it measures the error made when estimating μ by $\bar{x}$. These values can easily be calculated in example 18.1 as:

$\sigma = 0.8165$

and the standard error

$\sigma/\sqrt{n} = 0.5774$

The latter value is also the standard deviation of the 9 $\bar{x}$–values.

Further, provided n is 'large' (usually over 30), the sampling distribution of the mean is approximately *normal*. This fact is quite remarkable, as it assumes *nothing* about the population: the normal distribution can therefore arise out of *any* population, once you consider how the sample mean is distributed. This is one of the reasons why the normal distribution is considered so important.

We now have sufficient theory to look at confidence intervals for the mean.

Confidence intervals for the mean

The sample mean is the 'best' available estimate of the population mean, but it is not perfect. One of the reasons for the imperfection is the spread in $\bar{x}$–values around the population value, as indicated in example 18.1. We take account of this spread, or error, by trying to find a *range* or interval of values within which the true population mean will lie.

Looking at Figure 18.1(a), and using the techniques of the preceding chapter, it can be seen that the central 95 per cent of the area under the standard normal curve lies within the range -1.96 to $+1.96$. Now, if the sample size, n, is large, we have seen that $\bar{x}$ has a distribution which

is approximately normal
has mean $= \mu$ (population mean)
has standard deviation $= \sigma/\sqrt{n}$ (standard error).

Thus, using the standardizing transformation on *this* normal distribution, we get from

$p(-1.96 \le z \le +1.96) = 0.95$

the fact that

$p(\mu - 1.96\sigma/\sqrt{n} \le \bar{x} \le \mu + 1.96\sigma/\sqrt{n}) = 0.95$

(*Note:* $\bar{x}$ is the normally distributed variable here.)

Now, by a simple piece of algebraic manipulation, this can be changed into the statement:

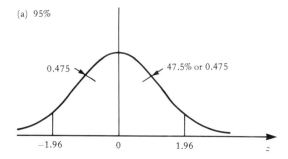

(a) 95%

0.475

47.5% or 0.475

−1.96   0   1.96

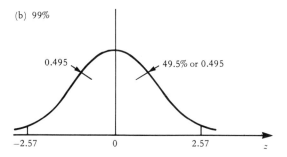

(b) 99%

0.495

49.5% or 0.495

−2.57   0   2.57

Figure 18.1 *Determination of z–values for confidence intervals*

there is a 95 per cent probability that

$$\bar{x} - 1.96\sigma/\sqrt{n} \leq \mu \leq \bar{x} + 1.96\sigma/\sqrt{n}.$$

This range of vaues is known as the *95 per cent confidence interval for* μ. It means that we are 95 per cent confident or certain that the true population mean will lie in the given range.

Now, there is nothing special about '95 per cent': it was simply chosen to illustrate the process. In general, any level of confidence can be adopted, and the normal distribution tables used to find the corresponding z–value. The resulting general formula for *a confidence interval for* μ is:

$$\bar{x} - z\sigma/\sqrt{n} \leq \mu \leq \bar{x} + z\sigma/\sqrt{n}.$$

Example 18.2:
The accounts department of a mail order company wishes to have some idea of the average size order the company receives. Consequently, a random sample of 100 past invoices is taken, and the mean and standard deviation order values of these is found to be

$\bar{x}$ = £11.05
s = £3.20.

(a)   What is the best value the company can assume for the mean value of *all* past orders?

(b)   Find (i)   95 per cent
         (ii)   99 per cent confidence intervals for the mean value of all past orders.

(c)   What do these two intervals indicate?

(a)   The phrase 'the mean value of *all* past orders' is referring to the mean of the *population* of orders, namely μ. Thus, by our earlier theory, the best estimate we can make of μ is the sample mean, *£11.05*.

(b)   At the outset, we notice a problem: the formula we are going to use contains σ, the *population* standard deviation, which we do not know. This therefore has to be estimated, and the only value available, *s*, the sample standard deviation, will be used. There exists, in fact, statistical theory which shows that such an estimation is valid for large samples such as this.

   (i)   Substituting the given values into the formula:

$$11.05 - 1.96 \times 3.20/\sqrt{100} \le \mu \le 11.05 + 1.96 \times 3.20/\sqrt{100}.$$

   This gives *$10.42 \le \mu \le 11.68$*.

   (ii)   Before using the general formula, we need to find the *z*–value corresponding to 99 per cent confidence. Figure 18.1(b) shows this to be

$$z = \pm 2.57 \text{ (or 2.58)}.$$

   The formula therefore gives

$$11.05 - 2.57 \times 3.20/\sqrt{100} \le \mu \le 11.05 + 2.57 \times 3.20/\sqrt{100}$$

   and thus *$10.23 \le \mu \le 11.87$*.

(c)   The confidence intervals can be interpreted by saying that there is a 95 per cent chance the true population mean order lies between £10.42 and £11.68, and there is a 99 per cent chance it lies between £10.23 and £11.87. It may be noted that, as common sense might dictate, the more confident or certain we are about where μ lies, the wider is the range of the interval.

Sample sizes to attain a desired level of accuracy

A question commonly asked of statisticians is, 'How big a sample should I take?' This is so vague that a sensible response is, 'It depends'. One thing that it might depend upon is the level of accuracy that is required. In the case of a mean, the formulae for confidence intervals can be used to relate the level of accuracy to sample size.

   Suppose that, working to a certain level of confidence, we wish to determine the value of a population mean, μ, accurate to $\pm d$. Figure 18.2 shows how we can make this desired interval of accuracy coincide with a confidence interval, and thus have

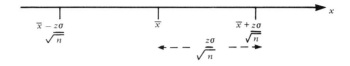

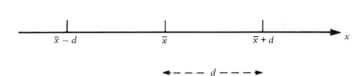

Figure 18.2 *Superimposition of confidence and accuracy intervals*

$d = z\sigma/\sqrt{n};$

so $\sqrt{n} = z\sigma/d,$

giving $n = [z\sigma/d]^2$

as the required minimum sample size. It is a *minimum* because, if we go over this, the confidence interval will be narrowed and we will have *increased* accuracy.

Example 18.3:
The accounts department discussed in example 18.2 feels that the estimates of the mean value of all past orders were not accurate enough. An accuracy of ±£0.40 would be preferred. How large a sample would be needed for this if we work to (a) 95 per cent
(b) 99 per cent confidence?

The formula for n contains the standard deviation, and so, provided we have no reason to doubt the validity of the earlier sample, we can use that value of s here. The sample of size 100 was *random*, and so its use does seem valid.

(a) We have $z = 1.96$
$\sigma = 3.20$ (estimated)
$d = 0.40;$

so

$$n = \left[\frac{1.96 \times 3.20}{0.40}\right]^2$$

$$n = 245.9.$$

Hence a minimum sample size of *246* invoices would be needed.

(*b*)   The only change here is the level of confidence, and so, using the z–value found earlier for 99 per cent confidence intervals (z = 2.57):

$$n = \left[\frac{2.57 \times 3.20}{0.40} \right]^2$$

$$n = 422.7;$$

so a minimum sample size of *423* invoices would be needed at this level of confidence.

Confidence intervals for a proportion

Confidence intervals can be placed on many statistical measures: we look at one further example here, that of proportions. As this is an introductory text, we shall not go through the theory here, but leave that for further investigation by the interested reader.

The notation used is:

p = *sample* proportion
π = *population* proportion (not to be confused with the *number* π).

The statistical theory shows that

p is an *unbiased* estimate of π (or: *on average, p = π*);
the confidence interval on π is, for *large sample size, n*:

$$p - z \sqrt{\frac{p(1-p)}{n}} \leq \pi \leq p + z \sqrt{\frac{p(1-p)}{n}},$$

where z is found from the normal distribution, as before;
to attain a level of accuracy, d, the minimum sample size is

$$n = p(1-p) \left[\frac{z}{d} \right]^2.$$

In the last expression, p can be estimated from a reliable previous sample or, if such is not available should be set equal to 0.5.

Example 18.4:
A cigarette company wishes to measure the popularity of one of its brands, C, before starting a promotion campaign. A market research survey of 1000 smokers shows that 215 choose brand C as their favourite.

(*a*)   What is the best estimate of the proportion of *all* smokers who prefer brand C?

(*b*)   Place a 96 per cent confidence interval on this population proportion.

(*c*)   What does this interval mean? What reservations might you have about its validity?

(d) If the above results are insufficiently accurate and it is desired to find the proportion of all smokers favouring brand C accurate to 0.01, what sample size would be needed if
  (i) the market research survey is considered reliable;
  (ii) the reservations referred to in (c) are such that the market research survey is *not* considered reliable?
(Work to 96 per cent confidence.)

(a) The phrase 'proportion of *all* smokers' refers to the population proportion, π. As p, the sample proportion, is an unbiased estimate, our 'best' value here is p. Now,

$$p = \frac{215}{1000} = 0.215.$$

So our best estimate is

$$\pi = 0.215.$$

(b) It is left to the reader to verify that the z–value corresponding to 96 per cent confidence is 2.05. Thus the interval is

$$0.215 - 2.05 \sqrt{\frac{0.215 \times 0.785}{1000}} \le \pi \le 0.215 + 2.05 \sqrt{\frac{0.215 \times 0.785}{1000}};$$

that is $0.188 \le \pi \le 0.242$.

(c) The confidence interval indicates that we are 96 per cent confident or certain that the proportion of all smokers favouring brand C lies *between 0.188 and 0.242*. The major reservation about this concerns the nature of the sample: is it representative of the population of smokers? Strictly speaking, it should be random, something which might be difficult to achieve in a survey such as this.

(d) (i) As the survey *is* considered reliable in this case, we use the value

$$p = 0.215$$

as an estimate in the expression for n, to get

$$n = 0.215 \times 0.785 \times \left[\frac{2.05}{0.01}\right]^2$$

$$n = 7092.8;$$

that is, a *minimum sample size of 7,093* is needed to measure accurate to 0.01.

(ii) In this instance, we have no reliable estimate for p, and so we have to fall back to the value 0.5:

$$n = 0.5 \times 0.5 \times \left[\frac{2.05}{0.01}\right]^2$$

$$n = 10506.3,$$

and so a *minimum sample size of 10,507* would be needed now.

Note how, in the latter case, we rounded *up* to ensure the sample size was *bigger* than the computed value of *n*. It can also be seen from this example how large these samples need to be in order to achieve great accuracy when measuring a proportion.

Summary

If μ denotes the *population* mean and $\bar{x}$ the *sample* mean, then

$\bar{x}$ is an *unbiased* estimate of μ.

Further, a confidence interval on μ is

$$x - \frac{z\sigma}{\sqrt{n}} \le \mu \le x + \frac{z\sigma}{\sqrt{n}}$$

where z is the value of the standard normal variable corresponding to the required level of confidence.

If we wish to measure μ accurate to $\pm d$, then the minimum sample size required is

$$n = \left[\frac{z\sigma}{d}\right]^2.$$

If π denotes the *population* proportion and p the *sample* proportion, then

p is an *unbiased* estimate of π.

Further, a confidence interval on π is

$$p - z\sqrt{\frac{p(1-p)}{n}} \le \pi \le p + z\sqrt{\frac{p(1-p)}{n}}.$$

If we wish to measure π accurate to $\pm d$, then the minimum sample size required is

$$n = p(1-p)\left[\frac{z}{d}\right]^2.$$

Unless there is a reliable estimate of p available, p is set equal to 0.5 in this expression.

Exercises on Chapter 18

1 A new type of drink dispensing machine is being tested. After it has been set up, 80 drinks are drawn off and the amount of liquid dispensed by the machine measured. This sample is found to have a mean of 150 ml and a standard deviation of 0.2 ml.

    (a) What is the best estimate you can make of the *population* mean amount of liquid dispensed by the machine? In what sense is this 'best'?

    (b) Determine a 98 per cent confidence interval for the population

mean. What does this interval indicate? Why might you doubt
its validity? (Consider the nature of the sample.)

2   A random sample of 500 wage slips shows that the mean weekly
wage of the weekly-paid employees of a certain company is £135.50,
with a standard deviation of £9.30.

(a)   Determine a 95 per cent confidence interval for the mean weekly wage of *all* weekly-paid employees.
(b)   Working to the same confidence, how large a sample would be
needed to determine this population mean accurate to £0.15?

3   As part of an attempt to cost the effects of machine down-time, the
management of a factory asks a member of the finance department
to make random spot-checks on whether a certain machine is running or not. On 800 such occasions, the machine is found *not* to be
running 90 times.

(a)   What is the best estimate the management can make of the
proportion of time the machine is *not* working?
(b)   Determine a 95 per cent confidence interval for this population
proportion. What does this indicate?
(c)   How large a sample would be needed to determine this proportion accurate to 0.015?

4   A mail-order company is analysing a random sample of its computer
records of customers. Among the results are the following distributions:

Size of order	Number of customers	
£	April	September
Less than 1	8	4
1 and less than 5	19	18
5 and less than 10	38	39
10 and less than 15	40	69
15 and less than 20	22	41
20 and less than 30	13	20
30 and over	4	5
Total	144	196

You are required to:

(a)   calculate the arithmetic mean and standard deviation order
size for the *April* sample:
(b)   find 95 per cent confidence limits for the overall mean order
size for the *April* customers and explain their meaning;
(c)   compare the two distributions, given that the arithmetic mean
and standard deviation for the September sample were £13.28
and £7.05 respectively.

ICMA Specimen Paper, published 1986.

5 It is suspected that a certain piece of a company's equipment is used about 25 per cent of the time. In order to check on this, the company management decides to institute a study in which the equipment is observed at random instants of time and note made of the percentage of occasions on which it is being used. How many such observations will be needed to assess the utilization of the equipment within ±2 per cent with 90 per cent confidence?

Part Five

Mathematical Models for Optimization

19 Matrices

Introduction

In this section we leave the study of probability and return to business mathematics, and in particular to *mathematical modelling* and *optimization*. A mathematical model is an abstraction from reality in terms of a set of mathematical expression(s). For example, in an earlier section, we have seen how the profits a company makes in a manufacturing process can be modelled by a single mathematical expression, the profit function. Similarly, a cost function in terms of units of output is a mathematical model of the costs incurred when producing a certain number of an article.

The relevance of this area of study is that, by appropriate mathematical analysis of the model, the business person can determine information about the situation being modelled, and so can obtain useful indications as to what business actions to take. One such type of analysis is that of *optimization*: for example, determining the output of a factory to maximize revenue or to minimize unit costs, and so on.

The first type of modelling we look at here concerns the *matrix* concept. A matrix is an array of numbers viewed as a singular entity; so

$$A = \begin{bmatrix} 1 & 2 \\ 3 & 4 \end{bmatrix} \text{ and } B = \begin{bmatrix} 0 & 0 & 1 \\ 1 & 0 & 0 \\ 0 & 1 & 1 \\ 1 & 1 & 1 \end{bmatrix}$$

are examples of matrices. Further, A has 2 rows and 2 columns and so is known as (2 × 2) ('two by two'). Similarly, B has the *dimensions* (4 × 3) ('four by three'), since it has 4 rows and 3 columns. Before seeing how matrices can be used as business models, we must look at the elements of *matrix algebra*.

Matrix addition, subtraction and scalar multiplication

Provided two matrices X and Y have precisely the same dimensions (in the same row – column order), then operations of *matrix addition* and *matrix subtraction* can be defined. These are simply obtained *elementwise*; that is, the elements in row 1, column 1 are added (or subtracted); elements in row 1, column 2 or position (1, 2) are added, and so on.

Further, *any* matrix can be multiplied by a number elementwise: this is known as *scalar multiplication*.

Example 19.1:

$$\text{If } X = \begin{bmatrix} 1 & 2 \\ 3 & 4 \end{bmatrix}, \ Y = \begin{bmatrix} 1 & 2 \\ 2 & 1 \\ 1 & 1 \end{bmatrix} \text{ and } Z = \begin{bmatrix} 0 & -2 \\ -2 & 0 \\ 1 & 0 \end{bmatrix}$$

determine, where possible: (a) $Y + Z$
(b) $Y - Z$
(c) $X + Y$
(d) $3Z$
(e) $-Y$
(f) $0X$.

(a),(b)   Since Y and Z are both (3×2), these two matrices can be added or subtracted:

$$Y + Z = \begin{bmatrix} 1 & 2 \\ 2 & 1 \\ 1 & 1 \end{bmatrix} + \begin{bmatrix} 0 & -2 \\ -2 & 0 \\ 1 & 0 \end{bmatrix}$$

$$= \begin{bmatrix} 1 + 0 & 2 + (-2) \\ 2 + (-2) & 1 + 0 \\ 1 + 1 & 1 + 0 \end{bmatrix}$$

$$= \begin{bmatrix} 1 & 0 \\ 0 & 1 \\ 2 & 1 \end{bmatrix}$$

$$\text{and } Y - Z = \begin{bmatrix} 1 - 0 & 2 - (-2) \\ 2 - (-2) & 1 - 0 \\ 1 - 1 & 1 - 0 \end{bmatrix} = \begin{bmatrix} 1 & 4 \\ 4 & 1 \\ 0 & 1 \end{bmatrix}$$

(c)   Since X and Y do not have the same dimensions, they cannot be added.

(d) $3Z = 3 \begin{bmatrix} 0 & -2 \\ -2 & 0 \\ 1 & 0 \end{bmatrix}$

$$= \begin{bmatrix} 3 \times 0 & 3 \times -2 \\ 3 \times -2 & 3 \times 0 \\ 3 \times 1 & 3 \times 0 \end{bmatrix}$$

$$= \begin{bmatrix} 0 & -6 \\ -6 & 0 \\ 3 & 0 \end{bmatrix}$$

(e) $-Y = -1 \cdot Y$

$$= \begin{bmatrix} -1 & -2 \\ -2 & -1 \\ -1 & -1 \end{bmatrix}.$$

(f) $0 \cdot X = \begin{bmatrix} 0 & 0 \\ 0 & 0 \end{bmatrix}.$

For obvious reasons, this last matrix is often referred to as the *(2 × 2) zero matrix*, denoted 0_2.

Matrix multiplication. Matrix inversion

In addition to the rather simple operation of scalar multiplication illustrated above, there is an operation of *matrix* multiplication. The definition will appear, at first sight, rather strange and arbitrary, but the later uses will make it seem more natural.

If X is an $(m \times n)$ matrix and Y an $(n \times p)$ matrix, then the product XY is an $(m \times p)$ matrix defined as follows:

the element in position (i,j) in the product is found by multiplying the elements in *row i* of X by the corresponding elements in *column j* of Y, then adding the products.
Symbolically the element in position (i,j) in the product $= x_{i1}\, y_{1j} +$
$x_{i2}\, y_{2j} + \ldots$

where x_{rs} = element in position (r,s) of X, and
$\quad\quad y_{rs}$ = element in position (r,s) of Y.

Some examples will clarify the calculations involved.

Example 19.2:

If $A = \begin{bmatrix} 2 & 1 \\ 3 & 2 \end{bmatrix}$ $B = \begin{bmatrix} 2 & -1 \\ -3 & 2 \end{bmatrix}$ $C = \begin{bmatrix} 1 & 0 \\ 0 & 1 \\ 1 & -1 \end{bmatrix}$ and $D = \begin{bmatrix} 1 & 1 \\ 0 & 1 \end{bmatrix}$

find, where possible (a) *AB*
                    (b) *BA*
                    (c) *AD*
                    (d) *DA*
                    (e) *AC*
                    (f) *CA*
                    (g) A^2

(a)   Since A and B are both (2×2) matrices, the product AB will also have these dimensions. To calculate the values of the four elements in the product:
position $(1, 1)$ arises from row 1 of A and column 1 of B

$$\begin{bmatrix} 2 & 1 \end{bmatrix} \times \begin{bmatrix} 2 \\ -3 \end{bmatrix} = \begin{bmatrix} (2 \times 2) + (1 \times -3) \end{bmatrix}$$

$$= \begin{bmatrix} 1 \end{bmatrix}$$

position (1, 2) arises from row 1 of A and column 2 of B

$$\begin{bmatrix} 2 & 1 \end{bmatrix} \times \begin{bmatrix} -1 \\ 2 \end{bmatrix} = \begin{bmatrix} (2 \times -1) + (1 \times 2) \end{bmatrix}$$

$$= \begin{bmatrix} 0 \end{bmatrix}$$

position (2,1) arises from row 2 of A and column 1 of B
$$(3 \times 2) + (2 \times -3) = 0$$
position (2,2)
$$(3 \times -1) + (2 \times 2) = 1.$$
Hence

$$AB = \begin{bmatrix} 1 & 0 \\ 0 & 1 \end{bmatrix}.$$

(b) $$BA = \begin{bmatrix} 2 & -1 \\ -3 & 2 \end{bmatrix} \begin{bmatrix} 2 & 1 \\ 3 & 2 \end{bmatrix}$$

$$= \begin{bmatrix} (2 \times 2) + (-1 \times 3) \end{bmatrix}$$

$$= \begin{bmatrix} 1 \end{bmatrix}$$

and so on, to give $BA = \begin{bmatrix} 1 & 0 \\ 0 & 1 \end{bmatrix}.$

(c),(d) It is left as an exercise to the reader to show:

$$AD = \begin{bmatrix} 2 & 3 \\ 3 & 5 \end{bmatrix}, \text{ while } DA = \begin{bmatrix} 5 & 3 \\ 3 & 2 \end{bmatrix}.$$

This illustrates that, although

$$AB = BA$$
$$AD \neq DA.$$

We therefore *cannot* assume that matrix multiplication is *commutative*: the order of multiplication *does* matter.

(e),(f) Now, A is (2 × 2) while C is (3 × 2): so *AC does not exist*: their dimensions do not conform to the definition. The product *CA* does, however, conform, and so will be a

$$(3 \times 2) \cdot (2 \times 2) = (3 \times 2) \text{ matrix.}$$

$$CA = \begin{bmatrix} 1 & 0 \\ 0 & 1 \\ 1 & -1 \end{bmatrix} \begin{bmatrix} 2 \\ 3 \end{bmatrix} \begin{bmatrix} 1 \\ 2 \end{bmatrix} = \begin{bmatrix} 1 & 0 \\ 0 & 1 \\ 1 & -1 \end{bmatrix} \begin{bmatrix} 2 \\ 3 \end{bmatrix} \begin{bmatrix} 1 \\ 2 \end{bmatrix}$$

$$= \begin{bmatrix} 2 \\ \end{bmatrix} \qquad = \begin{bmatrix} & 2 \end{bmatrix}$$

and so on:

$$CA = \begin{bmatrix} 2 & 1 \\ 3 & 2 \\ -1 & -1 \end{bmatrix}$$

(g)   The notation A^2 is shorthand for AA; so

$$A^2 = \begin{bmatrix} 2 & 1 \\ 3 & 2 \end{bmatrix} \begin{bmatrix} 2 & 1 \\ 3 & 2 \end{bmatrix}$$

$$= \begin{bmatrix} 7 & 4 \\ 12 & 7 \end{bmatrix}$$

We saw in parts (a) and (b) above that

$$AB = BA = \begin{bmatrix} 1 & 0 \\ 0 & 1 \end{bmatrix}$$

The product matrix in this case is known as the *unit (2 × 2) matrix*, denoted as I_2. This is because, for *any* (2 × 2) matrix, X:

$$XI_2 = I_2X = X.$$

The easy verification of this is left to the reader.
    Further, there is a *square unit* matrix for every dimension $(n \times n)$, I_n:

$$I_n = \begin{bmatrix} 1 & & & \\ & 1 & & 0 \\ 0 & & \ddots & \\ & & & 1 \end{bmatrix} \quad \text{(1's on diagonal, 0's elsewhere)}$$

such that, for every other square $(n \times n)$ matrix, S:

$$SI_n = I_nS = S.$$

    Another associated concept is that of an *inverse* matrix. A square matrix X is said to have an inverse, denoted X^{-1}, if

$$X \cdot X^{-1} = X^{-1} \cdot X = I_n$$

where n = the dimension of X (and of X^{-1}).
Thus, in the above,

$$B = A^{-1}$$
and $A = B^{-1}$.

Example 19.3:

(a)   If $C = \begin{bmatrix} 2 & 1 \\ 1 & 1 \end{bmatrix}$, show that $C^{-1} = \begin{bmatrix} 1 & -1 \\ -1 & 2 \end{bmatrix}$

(b)   Find the inverse matrices of (*i*) $D = \begin{bmatrix} 0 & 1 \\ 1 & 0 \end{bmatrix}$

and (*ii*) $E = \begin{bmatrix} 1 & 1 \\ 1 & 1 \end{bmatrix}$

(a)   To verify that the given matrix is indeed the inverse, we need to compute $C \cdot C^{-1}$ and $C^{-1} \cdot C$:

$$C \cdot C^{-1} = \begin{bmatrix} 2 & 1 \\ 1 & 1 \end{bmatrix} \begin{bmatrix} 1 & -1 \\ -1 & 2 \end{bmatrix}$$

$$= \begin{bmatrix} 2 - 1 & -2 + 2 \\ 1 - 1 & -1 + 2 \end{bmatrix}$$

$$= \begin{bmatrix} 1 & 0 \\ 0 & 1 \end{bmatrix}$$

Similarly, $C^{-1}C = I_2$, which confirms that C^{-1} *is the necessary inverse.*

(b)(i) Suppose $D^{-1} = \begin{bmatrix} a & b \\ c & d \end{bmatrix}$;

then $D \cdot D^{-1} = \begin{bmatrix} 0 & 1 \\ 1 & 0 \end{bmatrix} \begin{bmatrix} a & b \\ c & d \end{bmatrix}$

$$= \begin{bmatrix} c & d \\ a & b \end{bmatrix}.$$

Now, this must equal I_2; so $c = 1$
$$d = 0$$
$$a = 0$$
$$b = 1;$$

thus $D^{-1} = \begin{bmatrix} 0 & 1 \\ 1 & 0 \end{bmatrix}.$

This matrix is thus an example of a matrix which is its own inverse.

(*ii*)   As above, suppose $E^{-1} = \begin{bmatrix} a & b \\ c & d \end{bmatrix}$

$$E \cdot E^{-1} = \begin{bmatrix} 1 & 1 \\ 1 & 1 \end{bmatrix} \begin{bmatrix} a & b \\ c & d \end{bmatrix}$$

$$= \begin{bmatrix} a + c & b + d \\ a + c & b + d \end{bmatrix}$$

As this product must equal I_2: a + c = 1
b + d = 0
a + c = 0
b + d = 1.

These equations are clearly incompatible, showing that *E has no inverse*. Such matrices are known as *singular*, while those that *do* have an inverse (such as C and D in this example) are known as nonsingular.

The above example considers only (2 × 2) matrices. The determination of inverses (*if* they exist) of square matrices with dimensions greater than 2 is a laborious and time-consuming task. We leave the methods involved to more mathematical texts, or, better still, to a computer, and proceed to look at some uses of matrices.

Matrices as models

An example will demonstrate how a commercial situation can be modelled by matrices and how matrix algebra relates to associated financial calculations.

Example 19.4:
A wholesaler sells three major products at the following standard prices:

   product 1: £10/unit
   product 2: £15/unit
   product 3: £20/unit.

In addition, he offers a reduction of 10 per cent on the unit price for any customer who buys 100 or more units of product during a week.

During a certain week customer A buys from the wholesaler 50, 60 and 100 units of products 1, 2 and 3 respectively, while customer B buys 100, 20 and 150 units respectively.

(*a*)   Express the pricing structure of the wholesaler as a (2 × 3) matrix, *P*.
(*b*)   Express the purchasing patterns of the two customers during the week as (3 × 2) matrices, *A* and *B*.
(*c*)   Compute (where possible), the following matrices, and explain what each one represents: (*i*)   U = PA
(*ii*)   V = PB
(*iii*)   W = AP
(*iv*)   X = BP
(*v*)   Y = U + V
(*vi*)   Z = W + X
(*vii*)   N = 1.1P.

(*a*)   As there are three products, and matrix P is to have three columns, we must match products and columns. Similarly, the two unit prices (normal and discount) will have to be matched with the two rows. Hence

$$P = \begin{bmatrix} 10 & 15 & 20 \\ 9 & 13.50 & 18 \end{bmatrix} \quad \begin{matrix} \leftarrow \text{normal prices} \\ \leftarrow \text{discount prices} \end{matrix}$$

↑   ↑   ↑

product 1   product 2   product 3
prices   prices   prices

(b) As in (a), the rows and columns of the matrices must be matched with the purchase patterns. Thus, in matrix A, the three
rows will correspond to the three products, and the two columns to the two price rates:

$$A = \begin{bmatrix} 50 & 0 \\ 60 & 0 \\ 0 & 100 \end{bmatrix} \quad \begin{matrix} \leftarrow \text{numbers of product 1} \\ \leftarrow \text{numbers of product 2} \\ \leftarrow \text{numbers of product 3} \end{matrix}$$

↑   ↑

numbers   numbers
at normal   at discount
price   price

Similarly,

$$B = \begin{bmatrix} 0 & 100 \\ 20 & 0 \\ 0 & 150 \end{bmatrix}.$$

(c)(i) As P is a (2×3) matrix and A is a (3×2), the product PA will
exist and be (2×2). Applying the process of matrix multiplication described earlier,

$$U = PA = \begin{bmatrix} 1400 & 2000 \\ 1260 & 1800 \end{bmatrix}.$$

If we now examine the calculations used to find U, we shall
see a commercial meaning for the elements and an illustration
of why matrices are multiplied in this way. Consider the element in position (1,1):
this arises from row 1 of P and column 1 of A:

(10×50) + (15×60) + (20×0) $= 1400.$

↑   ↑   ↑

50 units of   60 units of   no units
product 1   product 2   of product 3
at normal price   at normal price   at normal price
of £10/unit   of £15/unit

This figure, £*1,400*, thus represents the total amount spent by
customer A on normally priced goods. Similarly, in position
(2,2) of the product:

$(9 \times 0) + (13.50 \times 0) + (18 \times 100) = 1,800.$

Customer A spends *£1,800* on discounted goods.

Position (1,2) of the product arises from row 1 of P, column 2 of A:

$$(10 \times 0) + (15 \times 0) + (20 \times 100) = 2000$$

which thus represents the amount (extra to £1,400) which *would* be spent if discounts were *not* available. Finally, *£1,260* in position (2,1) can be seen to give the amount (extra to £1,800) which *would* be spent if discounts were available on *all* goods.

(*ii*)   This is very similar to part (i):

$$V = PB = \begin{vmatrix} 300 & 4000 \\ 270 & 3600 \end{vmatrix}$$

with interpretations corresponding exactly to those in (i).

(*iii*)   Since A is a (3 × 2) matrix and P is a (2 × 3), AP will exist and be (3 × 3):

$$W = AP = \begin{bmatrix} 500 & 750 & 1000 \\ 600 & 900 & 1200 \\ 900 & 1350 & 1800 \end{bmatrix}$$

Again, by considering how each element arises from the process of matrix multiplication, we shall see a commercial meaning for it:

position (1,1): (50×10) + $(0 \times 9) = 500$

50 units of	no units of
product 1 at	product 1 at
normal £10/unit	discount £9 unit.

Hence customer A spends *£500* on product 1.

Similarly, positions (2,2) and (3,3) show that customer A spends £900 and £1,800 on products 2 and 3 respectively. The other six positions give amounts customer A *would* spend on various amounts of products 1, 2 and 3. As an example:

position (3,1): (0×10) + $(100 \times 9) = 900$;

that is, *£900* would be spent on 100 units of product 1.

(*iv*)   As in (*iii*),

$$X = BP = \begin{bmatrix} 900 & 1350 & 1800 \\ 200 & 300 & 400 \\ 1350 & 2025 & 2700 \end{bmatrix}$$

with interpretations corresponding exactly to those in (iii) above.

(*v*)   Both U and V are (2 × 2) matrices, and so can be added:

$Y = U + V$

$$= \begin{bmatrix} 1700 & 6000 \\ 1530 & 5400 \end{bmatrix}.$$

The values of these elements are clear from the corresponding values in (i) and (ii):

position (1,1):   1400   +   300 = 1700,

and so £1,700 is the *total* amount spent by customers A and B on normally priced goods;

position (1,2):   2000   +   4000 = 6000.

Hence £6,000 is the *total* extra amount (additional to £1,700) which would be spent by both customers if discounts were not available, and so on.

(vi)   As W and X have the same dimensions, they can be added:

$Z = W + X$

$$= \begin{bmatrix} 1400 & 2100 & 2800 \\ 800 & 1200 & 1600 \\ 2250 & 3375 & 4500 \end{bmatrix}$$

Just as in (v), the elements of this matrix represent the *total* amounts spent (or which would be spent) by the two customers, corresponding to the values in (iii) and (iv). As an example:

position (1,1):   500   +   900 = 1400.

The two customers thus spend a total of £1,400 on product 1 in the week under consideration.

(vii) Applying the process of scalar multiplication, we get

$N = 1.1P$

$$= 1.1 \begin{bmatrix} 10 & 15 & 20 \\ 9 & 13.50 & 18 \end{bmatrix}$$

$$= \begin{bmatrix} 11 & 16.50 & 22 \\ 9.90 & 14.85 & 19.80 \end{bmatrix}$$

Now, this matrix N has every element 10 per cent larger than the corresponding one in matrix P. Hence this is a *price* matrix, like P, which represents the price structure which would apply after an overall 10 per cent increase.

Summary

A *matrix* is an array of numbers considered as a single entity. Its *dimensions* are the number of rows (r, say) and the number of columns (c, say), written (r × c). A matrix is *square* if

$r = c.$

Two matrices of the same dimensions can be added or subtracted, elementwise.

Any matrix can be multiplied by a number, by multiplying each element by the number. This is known as *scalar multiplication*.

If X is an $(m \times n)$ matrix with elements x, and Y is an $(n \times p)$ matrix with elements y, then the *matrix product* XY has dimensions $(m \times p)$ such that the element in position (r,s) in the product arises from the sum of the n factors:

$$\Sigma x_{ri} y_{is}.$$

The *inverse* of a square $(n \times n)$ matrix, X, is the matrix X^{-1} such that

$$XX^{-1} = X^{-1}X = I_n$$

where I_n denotes the *unit* $(n \times n)$ matrix

$$I_n = \begin{bmatrix} 1 & & & \\ & 1 & & 0 \\ & & \cdot & \\ & & & \cdot & \\ 0 & & & & 1 \end{bmatrix}.$$

Matrices with inverses are known as *nonsingular*, while those without inverses are *singular*.

Exercises on Chapter 19

1 If $A = \begin{bmatrix} 1 & 0 \\ 1 & 1 \end{bmatrix}$ $B = \begin{bmatrix} 1 & 2 & -1 \\ 0 & 0 & 3 \end{bmatrix}$ $C = \begin{bmatrix} 1 & 2 & 3 \\ 3 & 2 & 1 \\ -1 & 0 & -1 \end{bmatrix}$

evaluate, where possible: (a) $A + I_2$
(b) $C - I_3$
(c) $A + C$
(d) $5B$
(e) $2C + 3I_3$
(f) AB
(g) BA
(h) BC
(i) A^2
(j) B^3
(k) A^{-1}
(l) B^{-1}.

2 If $X = \begin{bmatrix} 2 & 0 \\ 1 & 1 \end{bmatrix}$ and $Y = \begin{bmatrix} -1 & 1 \\ 0 & -1 \end{bmatrix}$

find: (*a*) *XY*
    (*b*) X^{-1}
    (*c*) Y^{-1}
    (*d*) $X^{-1}Y^{-1}$
    (*e*) $Y^{-1}X^{-1}$.

In view of the results of this question, what do you think $(AB)^{-1}$ equals, in general?

3 There are two matrices, *X* and *Y*.

$$X = \begin{bmatrix} 1 \\ 2 \\ 3 \end{bmatrix} \qquad Y = [2 \quad 0 \quad 3].$$

The product *XY* equals:

$$A \begin{bmatrix} 2 & 0 & 3 \\ 4 & 0 & 6 \\ 6 & 0 & 9 \end{bmatrix} \quad B \begin{bmatrix} 2 & 4 & 6 \\ 0 & 0 & 0 \\ 3 & 6 & 9 \end{bmatrix} \quad C\,[2 \quad 0 \quad 9] \quad D\,[1 \quad 1]$$

$$E \text{ None of these.}$$

ICMA Specimen Paper, published 1986.

4 (*a*) A company sells four products *W*, *X*, *Y* and *Z* at unit prices of £4, £6, £8 and £16 respectively. Represent this price structure as a column matrix, *P*.

   (*b*) The orders for these products in the last three trading days (Monday, Tuesday and Wednesday) are given by the matrix *T*:

	W	*X*	*Y*	*Z*	
T =	113	201	118	99	Monday
	128	256	121	108	Tuesday
	131	240	136	103	Wednesday

Only *one* of *PT* and *TP* can be evaluated: find this matrix (to be denoted *R*) and explain its meaning.

   (*c*) The company is considering increasing its selling prices. It is looking in particular at two options:
     (*i*) increase all prices by 10 per cent;
     (*ii*) increase all prices by 10 per cent, *except* Monday trading, which always exhibits low sales, thereby disrupting stock control.

    The matrix *H* is defined so that the product *HR* gives the actual *total* revenue for the three trading days above *and* the total revenues which would have been obtained for both of the options (*i*) and (*ii*). Find *H* and *HR*, under the assumption that the demand pattern would not have been affected by the price increases.

20 Linear programming

Introduction

One of the major roles of mathematical modelling in business is in *optimization*, by which we mean profit maximization, cost minimization or, in general, making the best of the situation facing us. In this chapter we deal with a category of problems of *constrained* optimization; that is, working within finite resources, manpower, and so on.

The model in a *linear programming* example consists of an *objective function*, and a series of *inequalities*, each one representing a constraint such as the maximum amount available of some resource. The objective function is an expression denoting the profit to be maximized, the cost to be minimized, or whatever. The word linear is used because the inequalities can be represented as straight line graphs, while 'programming' in this sense has nothing to do with computers, but is intended to imply a systematic approach to the problem, which is to optimize the objective function, while satisfying the constraints/inequalities.

Setting up a linear programming model

To demonstrate the setting up of a linear programming model, we shall work through an example.

Example 20.1:
A factory produces two products, X and Y. In their manufacture, both products have to be processed for various lengths of time on two machines A and B. The processing times are (in hours):

	product X	*product Y*
machine A	3	2
machine B	1	4

Each machine is available for 60 hours per week. Each unit of X and Y can be sold at a profit of £3,000 and £4,000 respectively. If the objective is to maximize weekly profit, set up a linear programming model to represent this situation.

We begin in a familiar way, by introducing letters to denote the (as yet) unknown numbers of each product produced each week:

let x denote the weekly number of units of X produced,
and y denote the weekly number of units of Y produced.

Now, the constraints on production arise from the limited amount of time available on the two machines. Consider first the time on machine A:

x units of X at 3 hours/unit will use up $3x$ hours
y units of Y at 2 hours/unit will use up $2y$ hours;
thus total time used is $(3x + 2y)$ hours.

This cannot be greater than the maximum weekly time available, namely 60 hours; so

$3x + 2y \leq 60$.

This inequality thus represents the constraint imposed by the limited availability of machine A.

In the same way, by considering time availability on machine B, we arrive at

$x + 4y \leq 60$.

In addition, common sense dictates that the numbers made of each product cannot be negative; that is

$x, y \geq 0$.

Finally, our objective concerns maximizing profit, and so we need an expression for this:

x units of X (per week) at £3,000 profit each: £3000x
y units of Y   at £4,000 profit each: £4000y.
Hence total weekly profit, denoted z, is $3x + 4y$ (£000).

To summarize, the model in this situation is:

maximize $z = 3x + 4y$
subject to: $3x + 2y \leq 60$
                $x + 4y \leq 60$
                $x, y \geq 0$.

Graphical representation of inequalities. Feasible areas

If the inequality signs in the above model are replaced by equal signs, we obtain, for example:

$3x + 2y = 60$.

This can be re-arranged into

$$y = 30 - 1.5x$$

which is of a familiar linear form. This gives a clue to a graphical approach to inequalities, illustrated in the following.

Example 20.2:
Depict the inequalities of example 20.1 graphically.

We have had occasion to plot straight line graphs on a number of previous occasions, but it is worth mentioning a shortcut method when the line has an equation of the form

$$ax + by = c.$$

The approach simply consists of plotting the points where the line cuts the two axes, that is, where x and y have the value zero. In the case of the line

$$3x + 2y = 60$$

these points are

$$x = 0: y = 30$$
$$y = 0: x = 20.$$

The line is shown in Figure 20.1(a).
We are trying, however, to depict the *inequality*

$$3x + 2y \le 60.$$

So consider the two points P and Q shown.
At P, $x = 10$, $y = 10$: so $3x + 2y = 50$, which is less than 60.
At Q, $x = 20$, $y = 20$: so $3x + 2y = 100$, which is more than 60.

This illustrates that points lying *below or on* the line satisfy the 'less than or equal' condition. The area which does satisfy the inequality is thus shown in Figure 20.1(b).
If we now superimpose the graph of the second constraint

$$x + 4y \le 60,$$

we see that, to satisfy both inequalities, a point must lie below *both* lines. Further, since x and y must be positive, we arrive at the shaded area in Figure 20.1(c). This is known as the *feasible area* for the problem, in that any point in the area represents a mix of products X and Y which is feasible; that is, which satisfies all the constraints simultaneously.

The objective function. The optimal solution

Example 20.3:
Depict graphically the objective function of the example under discussion and hence find the number of units of X and Y required to maximize weekly profits.

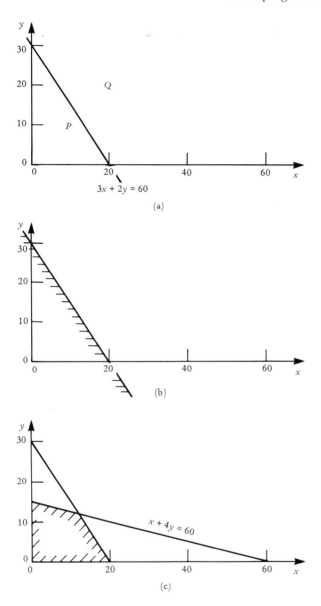

Figure 20.1 *Construction of the feasible area, examples 20.1, 20.2*

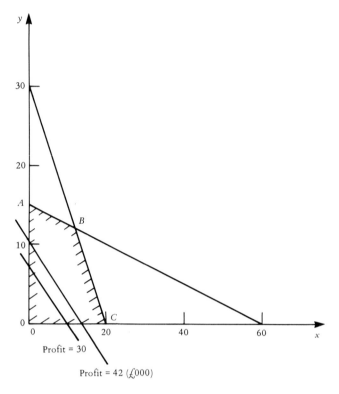

Figure 20.2 *Feasible area and objective function graphs, example 20.3*

Figure 20.2 shows the feasible area found above with the graph of two arbitrarily chosen profit figures superimposed:

(profit) $z = 3x + 4y = 30$ (£000)
and $z = 3x + 4y = 42$.

Any point on these lines, within the feasible area, shows a possible product mix to achieve the stated profit level. Thus

profits of £30,000 can be achieved by many mixes, such as:

$x = 0, y = 7.5$
$x = 4, y = 4.5$, and so on;

profits of £42,000 can be achieved by mixes such as:

$x = 10, y = 3$, etc.

The two lines show how, as weekly profits increase, the line representing the objective function moves parallel to itself, away from the origin. Eventually, a profit level must be reached, beyond which we cannot increase without leaving the feasible region altogether: this level must therefore be the maximum attainable. If we consider the profit line of

Figure 20.2 moving parallel to itself away from the origin, it can be seen that this maximum will be reached in one of two ways:

at one of the *vertices* (or corners) of the feasible area,

or, if the objective function is parallel to a constraint, it could happen that the maximum occurs at *two* vertices and every point on the line between them.

We need only, therefore investigate the values of the objective function at the vertices of the feasible area:

Vertex (x,y):	Profit, $z = 3x + 4y$:
A (0,15)	60
B (12,12)	84
C (20,0)	60

Thus the maximum attainable weekly profit is £84,000, when *12 units of X* and *12 units of Y* are produced per week.

Before leaving this problem, two comments are necessary. If the graph of the objective function is parallel to a constraint line and the optimum occurs at every point between two vertices, this would show up in a table like the above, since there would be two profit figures tying for the maximum. In addition, the co-ordinates of the vertices have to be determined precisely for an accurate answer: in the case of points A and C, this presents no problem as they have been determined in order to plot the lines. This is another advantage of the plotting method mentioned at the start of example 20.2. The point B, however, must either be read off from an accurate graph or, for more precision, obtained by solving the equations of the two lines simultaneously. The reader may wish to refer back to Chapter 4.

To demonstrate the whole process of solving a linear programming problem, and to illustrate how a case of *minimization* can be treated in a similar way to the above, we shall now work through a further example.

Example 20.4:
A chemical company uses three chemicals, L, M and N, in one of its processes. It obtains these by buying in two minerals, E and F. The minimum daily requirements of the chemicals are (tonnes):

L: 24
M: 24
N: 21

The amounts of each chemical present in the two minerals are (percentage by weight):

	E	F
L	8	3
M	6	4
N	3	7.

Determine the optimal daily amount of each mineral which the company should buy if E and F cost £1,200/tonne and £1,500/tonne respectively.

We begin by setting the daily amount bought in

of E = x tonnes
of F = y tonnes.

The constraints here are the *minimum* amounts of each of the three chemicals which must be present. For example, consider chemical L:

x tonnes of E will contribute .08x tonnes of L
y tonnes of F will contribute .03y tonnes of L
total = .08x + .03y tonnes of L.

This must be at least 24 tonnes; so

.08x + .03y ≥ 24.

In the same way, the minimum requirements of M and N give constraints:

.06x + .04y ≥ 24
.03x + .07y ≥ 21.

These, together with the commonsense requirement

$x, y ≥ 0$,

form the complete set of inequalities in the model. Finally, we have the objective function:

minimize cost z = 1200x + 1500y.

The straight lines corresponding to the three constraints are drawn as before. For example, the first:

.08x + .03y = 24
x = 0 gives y = 800
y = 0 gives x = 300

and so these two points are plotted to determine the line. Figure 20.3 shows the three lines: it will be noted that as all the constraints are 'greater than or equal', the feasible area must be on or above all three lines. Since x and y must also be positive, the feasible area is that indicated by the shading.

Now, as we are trying to *minimize* cost, the line representing the objective function must be as *near* as possible to the origin, while still having at least one point in the feasible area. If we imagine the line being moved, parallel to itself, *towards* the origin, we see that, as before, the optimum must occur at a vertex of the feasible area or along one of the boundary lines, between two vertices. Thus, again, we need only investigate the objective function at the vertices:

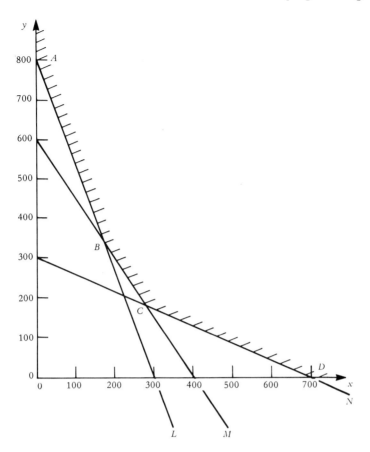

Figure 20.3 *Feasible area, example 20.4*

Vertex (x, y):	Cost, z = 1200x + 1500y
A (0, 800)	1,200,000
B (171.4, 342.9)	720,030
C (280, 180)	606,000
D (700, 0)	840,000.

Hence daily costs can be minimized by buying *280 tonnes of E* and *180 tonnes of F*, the total minimum cost being *£606,000*.

It should be noted that, while the co-ordinates of A and D, and possibly C, can be found from the graph, those of B can only be found accurately by solving the linear equations corresponding to the constraints imposed by the minimum requirements of L and M. This solution is left as an exercise for the reader.

Limitations of this approach

As with all mathematical approaches to problem solving, linear programming has a number of limitations and drawbacks. For example, if we look at the first problem of this chapter, the optimal solution turned out to be in terms of *whole numbers* of units of X and Y: if this had not been the case, we might be advising the manufacturer to make 6.36 tractors and 4.09 ploughs per week (or whatever). This method takes no account of whether the answers should be whole numbers or not.

This same example illustrates another problem: what if we cannot sell 12 units of X and 12 of Y per week (the optimal solution) at the prices stated? Perhaps the most serious critcism of such an application of linear programming is that it ignores any problems of *demand*.

Other limitations relate to assumptions inherently made: the constraints and objective function are linear; there is only one objective to be achieved; the problem is 2-dimensional (that is, only two unknowns, x and y, and so a graphical solution can be found). In real-life problems, any one of these assumptions could be violated, making the solution method illustrated here invalid.

There are a number of variations to the basic linear programming approach which can remedy the above limitations to a greater or lesser extent. We shall not discuss these in this first treatment, but the interested reader may wish to investigate further.

Summary

Linear programming is a technique to *optimize an objective*, subject to *constraints*. This can consist of maximizing profit, subject to limited resources; minimizing cost, subject to satisfying minimum requirements and so on.

The *model* consists of a number of *linear inequalities*, one corresponding to each constraint, and a *linear objective function*. In a 2-dimensional case, the *feasible area* consists of that area on an (x, y)-graph in which all the inequalities are satisfied simultaneously. In order to optimize the objective function, it only needs to be evaluated at the *vertices* of the feasible area.

Exercises on Chapter 20

1   Depict the following inequalities on a graph

$$5x + y \geq 10$$
$$x + y \geq 4$$
$$x + y \leq 6$$

and hence find the feasible area for these inequalities together with

$$x, y \geq 0.$$

Find the optimal values of the following objectives in the above area:

(a) minimize $z = 2x + 3y$;
(b) maximize $z = 2x + 4y$;
(c) maximize $z = 3x + 3y$.

2 A small shop buys in two items, X and Y, at the start of each week, to sell during that week. The shop's storage space for the items is limited to 54 square metres and the owner limits his outlay on the items to £600 per week. Each unit of X and Y occupies 18 square metres and 6 square metres, respectively. Each unit of X can be bought in for £100 and sells for £200. Each unit of Y can be bought in for £100 and sells for £150.
   (a) Set up the linear programming model for this situation, if the owner's objective is to maximize the weekly *net profit* from X and Y. (Hint: inequalities arise from the maximum storage space and from the maximum weekly outlay on X and Y.)
   (b) Determine the feasible area graphically and hence determine the buying-in mix of X and Y which maximizes net profit.
   (c) State why you think the owner might not, in practice, adopt this mix.

3 A catering manager is in the process of replacing the furniture in a canteen. He wishes to determine how many tables of type S (seating 6) and how many of type T (seating 10) to buy. He has to work under the following constraints:

   the canteen must be able to accommodate at least 600 people;
   the available floor space of the canteen is at most 630 square metres.

   He estimates that each type S table needs 7 square metres of floor space, while each type T needs 9.
      Advise the manager on how many of each type to buy if each type S costs £100 and each type T costs £190.

4 A confectionery manufacturer makes two kinds of chocolate bar, A and B, each of which requires three stages of production: mixing, cooking, and boxing. The number of minutes required to complete each process for a box of chocolate bars is as follows:

	Mixing	Cooking	Boxing
A	1.25	0.5	1.5
B	1.2	1.5	0.5

All the production equipment is available for eight hours each day. Accountants have calculated that the contribution on each box of A is £0.50 and on B is £1. The equipment may be used to produce A and B simultaneously. All production may be sold.
   You are required to:

(a)   state the objective function in mathematical terms, assuming the manufacturer wishes to maximize contribution;
(b)   state all the constraints (equations/inequalities) which are relevant to this production problem;
(c)   graph the constraints and determine the optimum production position;
(d)   find the contribution which is generated by this optimum position;
(e)   comment on any assumptions and practical limitations of this method of analysis.

ICMA Specimen Paper, published 1986.

5   A company needs to purchase a number of small printing presses, of which there are two types, X and Y.

Type X costs £4,000, requires two operators, and occupies 20 square metres of floor space. Type Y costs £12,000, also requires two operators, but occupies 30 square metres.

The company has budgeted for a maximum expenditure on these presses of £120,000. The print shop has 480 square metres of available floor space, and work must be provided for at least 24 operators. It is proposed to buy a combination of presses X and Y that will maximize production, given that type X can print 150 sheets per minute and type Y, 300 per minute.

You are required to:
(a)   write down all the equations/inequalities which represent the cost and space conditions. The labour conditions are given by $2X + 2Y \geq 24$;
(b)   draw a graph to represent this problem;
(c)   use the graph to find the numbers of presses X and Y the company should buy to achieve its objective of maximum production;
(d)   state the figure of maximum production and the total cost of the presses in this case.

ICMA, May 1984.

6   A small furniture manufacturer makes two speciality products, tables and chairs. Three stages in the manufacturing process are required – machining, assembling and finishing. The number of minutes required for each unit is shown below:

	Machining	*Assembling*	*Finishing*
Table	4	10	12
Chair	12	5	12

Each day the machining equipment is available for six hours (360 minutes), the assembly shop for six hours and the finishing equipment for eight hours. The contribution is £3 per table and £5 per chair. All equipment can be used for the production of either tables or chairs at all times it is available.

You are required to:
(*a*) state all the equations/inequalities (constraints) which describe the production conditions;
(*b*) graph these constraints;
(*c*) find how many tables and chairs the manufacturer should produce to maximize contribution;
(*d*) calculate this maximum contribution and include any comments or reservations you have about this analysis generally.

ICMA, May 1986.

21 Calculus

Introduction

In this last chapter of the mathematical modelling section, we approach problems of optimization from a different perspective, that of *differential calculus*. Starting from an attempt to generalize the concept of the gradient of a straight line, calculus can be developed into a technique useful for solving problems of profit maximization, cost minimization, and so on.

The differential coefficient

If we look at Figure 21.1, we see that graph A, that of a linear function, has a *constant* slope or gradient. Its value is the same at every point and can be determined by methods discussed in Chapter 2. This is not the case with graph B, however. It is clear that the gradients at the points P and Q are not the same and that, in fact, the gradient has a different value at each point on the graph.

Imagine that the graphs are cross-sections of hills and that we are walking along the hills, left to right. At the point we pass over P, we shall be walking in the direction of the line shown, *the tangent to the curve at the point P*. The gradient of the curve at that point could thus be found by determining the gradient of the tangent, a straight line. Similarly, the gradient of the curve at Q could be determined by drawing in the tangent at that point and measuring the slope of the line produced.

Now, this process would be very time-consuming, since a tangent would have to be drawn at every point of interest. Also, the positioning of the tangent cannot be guaranteed to be accurate, since it has to be judged rather than accurately constructed. Thus, the theory of *differential calculus* is used, since it gives the values of gradients of curves both quickly and accurately.

We will concentrate here on polynomial functions; that is, those of the form

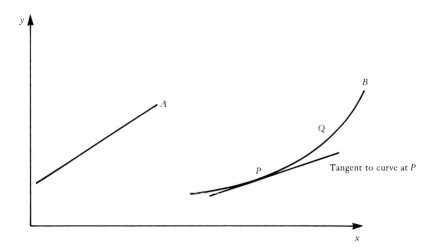

Figure 21.1

$$y = a + bx + cx^2 + dx^3 + \ldots.$$

where $a, b, c, d, \ldots$ are numbers. The theory of calculus shows that if

$$y = ax^n \ (a, n \text{ numbers}),$$

then the gradient of the graph of y is

$$n \cdot ax^{n-1}.$$

In addition, if the function consists of a series of powers of x added together, then the above formula can be applied to each term separately, and the results added, to find the gradient.

The gradient corresponding to y is denoted $\frac{dy}{dx}$ ('*dee-y-by-dee-x*'), the *differential coefficient*. The process of going from y to $\frac{dy}{dx}$ is known as *differentiation*. It should be noted that the differential coefficient is itself a function: that is, it varies. This property is to be expected as we have already pointed out that, in general, the gradient of a curve is different at each point on the curve.

Example 21.1:
Determine the differential coefficients of the following functions:

(a) $y = 3x^2$
(b) $y = 4x^2 + 5x^3$
(c) $y = a$ (a is a number)
(d) $y = a + bx$ (a, b numbers)
(e) $y = 3 + 4x + 5x^2 + x^3 - 2x^4$
(f) $y = 3 + \dfrac{2}{x}$.

(a)   If we compare

$$y = 3x^2$$

with $y = ax^n$

then

$$a = 3, n = 2.$$

The formula now gives

$$\frac{dy}{dx} = nax^{n-1}$$

$$= 2.3x^{2-1}$$

and so $\frac{dy}{dx} = 6x.$

(b)   The formula can be applied to the two parts of the function separately:

$$y = 4x^2 + 5x^3$$

$$\frac{dy}{dx} = 2.4x^{2-1} + 3.5x^{3-1}.$$

That is, $\frac{dy}{dx} = 8x + 15x^2.$

(c)   This example looks different in that there is no 'x' in the function. If, however, we recall that

$$x^0 = 1$$

we have

$$y = a \cdot x^0$$

and so

$$\frac{dy}{dx} = 0 \cdot a^{0-1}$$

$$\frac{dy}{dx} = 0.$$

The graphical interpretation of this result is straightforward. The graph of

$$y = a$$

is a horizontal straight line. While

$$\frac{dy}{dx} = 0$$

tells us that its gradient is zero, a fact we already know.

(d)   Recalling that

$$x = x^1$$

we have

$$y = a + bx^1$$

so $\dfrac{dy}{dx} = 0 + 1 \cdot bx^{1-1}$

$$= bx^0$$

$$\dfrac{dy}{dx} = b.$$

Again there is a graphical meaning to this. The function here is that of a straight line graph (see Chapter 2) and

$$\dfrac{dy}{dx} = b$$

simply tells us that the line's gradient is b.

(e) The results of (c) and (d) above are usually quoted, almost as 'rules', without recourse to the formula. The first two components of this function can thus be differentiated quickly:

$$y = 3 + 4x + 5x^2 \quad + x^3 \quad - 2x^4$$
$$\downarrow \quad \downarrow \quad \downarrow \qquad \downarrow \qquad \downarrow$$
$$\dfrac{dy}{dx} = 0 + 4 \ + 2.5x^1 + 3x^2 - 4.2x^3$$

$$\dfrac{dy}{dx} = 4 + 10x + 3x^2 - 8x^3.$$

(f) The formula cannot be directly applied to this function as all its components are not of the type

$$ax^n.$$

We first ensure that all terms *are* in the required form:

$$y = 3 + \dfrac{2}{x}$$

and so

$$y = 3 + 2x^{-1};$$

hence

$$\dfrac{dy}{dx} = 0 + -1.2x^{-2}$$

$$= -2x^{-2}.$$

Thus

$$\dfrac{dy}{dx} = \dfrac{-2}{x^2}.$$

In case we lose sight of what differentiation is about, we give one further example to emphasize that it concerns the determination of gradients.

Example 21.2:
Find the gradients of the following curves at the points where x is 2.

(a) $y = 4 - 3x^2$.

(b) $y = 1 - 3x + \dfrac{1}{x}$.

(a)   If we recall that $\dfrac{dy}{dx}$ is a function for the gradient, the first step is to

differentiate:

$$y = 4 - 3x^2$$

$$\frac{dy}{dx} = 0 - 2.3x^{2-1}$$

$$= -6x.$$

Hence, when $x = 2$, the gradient of the curve is -12.

(b) $y = 1 - 3x + \dfrac{1}{x}$

$y = 1 - 3x + x^{-1}$ (see (f) in earlier example)

$$\frac{dy}{dx} = 0 - 3 - x^{-2}$$

$$= -3 - \frac{1}{x^2}.$$

Hence, when $x = 2$,

$$\text{the gradient} = -3 - \frac{1}{2^2}$$

$$= -3.25.$$

Maxima and Minima

Optimization often consists of *maximizing* profits, *minimizing* costs, and so on. The connection between these and calculus can be seen from Figure 21.2: the point P is known as a (local) *minimum*, while Q is a (local) *maximum*, the names being self-explanatory. The tangents to the curves at P and Q have been drawn in: they can be seen to have zero gradient, that is

$$\frac{dy}{dx} = 0.$$

A tangent drawn at any other point on the curves (such as the ones shown in Figure 21.1) will have *non zero* slope, and so this property is one which distinguishes maximum and minimum points (or *turning points*) from all others. Thus, if we have a function for the revenue, cost, or whatever, then equating its differential coefficient to zero will enable us to optimize the function.

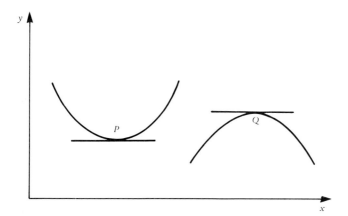

Figure 21.2 *Maximum and minimum points*

Example 21.3:
When a company produces and sells x units of a certain commodity during a day, its profits (£y) are

$y = -100 + 400x - x^2$.

Find the turning point(s) of this function and hence determine the profit-maximizing daily production and the maximum daily profit.
We begin by finding the differential coefficient:

$y = -100 + 400x - x^2$

$\dfrac{dy}{dx} = 400 - 2x$.

Setting this equal to zero:

$\dfrac{dy}{dx} = 0$

$400 - 2x = 0$.

Solving this we get

$x = 200$,

which is thus the position of the only turning point of the profit function.
We now realize a further problem: is this a maximum or a minimum point? In particular, it is to be hoped that this is not a point of profit *minimization*! A further look at Figure 21.2 will resolve this. In the case of the minimum point (P), the gradient is negative to the left and positive to the right, while the sequence is reversed in the case of the maximum point (Q). In other words:

	left of the point	at the point	right of the point
$\dfrac{dy}{dx}$ for minimum:	–	0	+
$\dfrac{dy}{dx}$ for maximum:	+	0	–

Applying this to the current example, we look at the gradient at an x–value either side of 200:

$$x = 100: \frac{dy}{dx} = 400 - 2(100)$$
$$= 200$$
$$x = 300: \frac{dy}{dx} = -200.$$

Thus this point is a *maximum*. To find the corresponding profit figure:

$$y = -100 + 400\,(200) - (200)^2$$
$$= 39{,}900;$$

so the maximum daily profit attainable is *£39,900* if *200 units/day* are produced.

Practical applications

The previous example served to illustrate how differential calculus can be applied to find maxima or minima, but it can be criticized for being impractical.

We are not told how the profit function arose nor on what assumptions it was based. In this section, we shall look at two further applications of the method, one a more plausible cost/revenue example and one involving problem solving.

Example 21.4:
A factory produces only one item. Its weekly fixed costs are £3,200. The variable cost of making one unit of its product is £50. Further, if production is increased beyond a certain point, overtime payments and machine breakdowns cause the variable cost figure to increase. A regression analysis on past results shows that this increase is

$0.5x^2$

where x denotes the weekly production figure.

Derive functions to represent: £C, the weekly cost,
£U, the weekly *unit* cost,
and hence find the factory's most efficient production level. Why might the factory management choose *not* to produce at this level?

The total cost consists of the sum of three elements:

fixed costs $= 3200$
'ordinary' variable costs, £50/unit for x units $= 50x$
'extra' variable costs $= 0.5x^2$;

so

$$C = 3200 + 50x + 0.5x^2.$$

Now, the unit cost (or cost per unit of production) is

$$U = \frac{C}{x}$$

$$U = \frac{3200 + 50x + 0.5x^2}{x}$$

$$U = \frac{3200}{x} + 50 + 0.5x.$$

Any realistic cost function cannot have a local minimum point, since this would imply that, at some point, total costs decrease as production increases. This function, C, is realistic in that it increases as x does: plotting a graph would confirm this. To find the most efficient production level we must therefore consider *unit* costs, trying to find where, if anywhere, they are minimized.

Applying the method of the previous example:

$$U = \frac{3200}{x} + 50 + 0.5x$$

$$\frac{dU}{dx} = -\frac{3200}{x^2} + 0.5.$$

Equating this to zero:

$$-\frac{3200}{x^2} + 0.5 = 0$$

$$x^2 = 6400$$

$$x = \pm 80.$$

Ignoring the impossible production figure of -80, we must now check whether $+80$ represents a maximum or a minimum point.

$$x = 70 \text{ gives } \frac{dU}{dx} = -\frac{3200}{(70)^2} + 0.5$$

$$= -0.153.$$

$$x = 90 \text{ gives } \frac{dU}{dx} = -\frac{3200}{(90)^2} + 0.5$$

$$= +0.105.$$

This is thus a *minimum* point, the corresponding value of the unit cost being

$$U = \frac{3200}{80} + 50 + (0.5)80$$

$$= 130.$$

The most efficient production level is therefore *80 units/week*, with the least unit cost of *£130/unit*.

The main reason this might not be adopted is that it takes no account of how many units can be sold and for how much. The factory management is likely to be interested in revenue and thus profit, as well as efficient production. In general, it is a criticism of profit-maximization and unit cost-minimization applications of calculus that they ignore the market, the revenue-price relationship, by either assuming a fixed price, regardless of the effects on demand, or by not considering it at all, as in this example.

Other questions might be asked about the accuracy of the data used. In particular, how reliable is the '$0.5x^2$' term, which, we are told, has arisen from regression analysis? Such questions were discussed in Chapters 10 and 11, but it is sufficient to note here that the answers can be considered as only approximate.

The final example shows how calculus can be used to solve practical problems other than those involving revenues and costs.

Example 21.5:
A farmer has 800 metres of fencing with which to construct a rectangular enclosure. To save material, he decides to use a long straight hedge as one side of the enclosure. Find the dimensions of the rectangle which maximizes its area, and determine the maximum area.

We begin by denoting the length of each side at right angles to the hedge as x metres. The third, fenced side (parallel to the hedge) must then have length

$$(800 - 2x) \text{ metres,}$$

since the total length of the three sides other than the hedge will then be

$$x + x + (800 - 2x) = 800 \text{ metres,}$$

that is, the available length of fencing.

The area of enclosure, y square metres, is then

$$y = x(800 - 2x)$$
$$y = 800x - 2x^2.$$

To find the turning point(s)

$$\frac{dy}{dx} = 800 - 4x,$$

and so

$$\frac{dy}{dx} = 0$$

gives

$$800 - 4x = 0$$
$$x = 200,$$

with

$$y = 200 (800 - 400)$$
$$y = 80,000.$$

Hence the maximum area which can be enclosed is 80,000 square metres, with two sides of length 200 metres at right angles to the hedge, and one of length 400 metres opposite the hedge.

Summary

If y is a function of x and we draw its graph, then the *differential coefficient*, $\frac{dy}{dx}$, is a function representing the gradient of the curve at every point. Further, if

$$y = ax^n$$

then

$$\frac{dy}{dx} = n \cdot ax^{n-1}.$$

The differential coefficient of a polynomial can be found by differentiating each constituent term separately.

A *turning point* on a curve is a point at which the gradient is zero, that is, where

$$\frac{dy}{dx} = 0.$$

Whether such a point is a *maximum* or a *minimum* can be determined by considering the slope of the graph on either side of the point:

	$\frac{dy}{dx}$ to left	$\frac{dy}{dx}$ at point	$\frac{dy}{dx}$ to right
minimum:	−	0	+
maximum:	+	0	−

Exercises on Chapter 21

1   Find $\frac{dy}{dx}$ for each of the following functions and hence determine the gradient of each function at the point where $x = -1$:
   (a) $y = 2x^5$
   (b) $y = 3x^3 + 6x^6$
   (c) $y = -7 + 4x + 2x^2$
   (d) $y = 5 + 6x$
   (e) $y = x - \dfrac{5}{x}.$

2   A company undertakes a number of analyses of the price-revenue and output-cost relationships for one of its products. From these it is estimated that, if the company produces and sells x units of the product in a month, then the revenue (£R) and cost (£C) attributable to the product during the month are:

$$R = 1100x - x^2$$
$$C = 15000 + 200x + 2x^2.$$

(a) Find a function of x to represent the monthly profit (£P) made from producing and selling the product. Hence use calculus to determine the profit-maximizing production level.

(b) Find a function of x to represent the *unit* cost of production (£U). Hence find the most efficient production level.

(c) Discuss which, if either, of these monthly production figures the company should adopt.

3 A small company manufactures open boxes. It does so by buying in square pieces of material of side 50 cm, cutting out a square of side x cm from each corner, and folding up the four rectangular pieces thus formed, to obtain a box of depth x cms.

(a) Show that the area of the base of such a box is (in square cm)

$$2500 - 200x + 4x^2,$$

and hence find the volume of the box, as a function of x.

(b) Find the value of x which maximizes the volume of the box.

(c) In the process of the above, you should have found a second turning point ($x = 25$) which can be shown to be a minimum. Explain the physical meaning of this value.

4 Regression analysis of the costs incurred in the manufacture and sale of product K has established the relationship

$$C = 31,500 + 6x + 0.07x^2$$

where C = total cost of manufacture and sale,

   x = quantity produced and sold per annum.

The sales department has recently been approached by an overseas agent who has identified a potential market where the selling price per unit (S) is related to the quantity sold by:

$$S = 441 - 0.8q$$

where q = quantity sold in this export market.

If the company decides to sell all its output in this overseas market (that is, $q = x$), find, as functions of x, the annual revenue and profit functions. Hence find the maximum annual profit. At what price would product K be sold in the overseas market, at this point of maximum profit?

ICMA PEI, May 1984.

5 A cost accountant for a bus company estimates that, on a certain route, if the fare is reduced by x per cent, then the number of passengers will increase by 2 per cent. The current revenue on the route is £R.

(a) Show that a reduction in the fare of x per cent will result in the revenue changing to

£R $(1 + 0.01x - 0.0002x^2)$.

(b) Find the percentage fare reduction which will maximize revenue from the route.

ICMA, November 1983.

6 M Limited, as a result of past experience and estimates for the future, has decided that the cost of production of their sole product, P, an advanced process machine, is:

$C = 1064 + 5x + 0.04x^2$

where C = total cost in £000

x = quantity produced (and sold).

The marketing department has estimated that the price of the product is related to the quantity produced and sold by the equation:

$P = 157 - 3x$

where P = price per unit in £000

x = quantity sold.

The government has proposed a tax of £$t'000$ per unit on product P but it is not expected that this will have any effect on the costs incurred in making P or on the demand/price relationship.

You are required to calculate and state:

(a) the price and quantity that will maximize profit when there was no tax;
(b) the price and quantity that will maximize profit if the proposed tax is introduced.

ICMA, PEI, May 1981.

Part Six
Financial Mathematics

22 Interest payments, mortgages and annuities

Introduction

Perhaps the most familiar use of mathematics in finance concerns *interest* calculations and other topics related to investments. In this chapter, we shall see how such calculations are related to the mathematical concept of a *geometric progression*, and then proceed to develop formulae involving such well-known financial areas as interest payments, mortgage repayments and annuity purchases.

Geometric progressions

There is one particular piece of mathematics which will prove very useful in the financial calculations of this chapter. This is concerned with *geometric progressions*, which are series of numbers of the form

$$a, ar, ar^2, ar^3, \ldots$$

where a and r are numbers.

The particular feature which defines a geometric progression is that, after an initial term, a, each term in the progression is a *constant multiple* (r) of the preceding one. We shall need to know the sum of the first n terms of such a series. If we denote this by S:

$$S = a + ar + ar^2 + \ldots + ar^{n-1} \text{(note the nth. term is } ar^{n-1}).$$

If we now multiply this throughout by r:

$$Sr = ar + ar^2 + \ldots + ar^{n-1} + ar^n,$$

and subtracting these two expression gives

$$S - Sr = a \qquad\qquad - ar^n$$

or

$S(1 - r) = a(1 - r^n),$

and so the required expression for S is

$$S = \frac{a(1 - r^n)}{(1 - r)}.$$

We shall not give an abstract example of the use of this formula, but move on to its practical applications in finance.

Interest and depreciation

One of the most basic uses of mathematics in finance concerns calculations of *interest*. Suppose £P is invested at a fixed rate of interest of r per annum and that interest is added at the end of each year; that is, it is *compounded* annually:

after 1 year, the value of the investment will be the initial investment £P, plus the interest accrued, £rP, and so will be

$$P + rP$$
$$= P(1 + r);$$

during the second year, the interest accrued will be r times the amount at the end of the first year, and so will be $r \cdot P(1 + r)$. The value at the end of the second year will be

$$P(1 + r) + r \cdot P(1 + r)$$
$$= P(1 + r)(1 + r)$$
$$= P(1 + r)^2.$$

Proceeding in this way, after n years the value, £V, will be given by

$$V = P(1 + r)^n.$$

This well-known formula is often referred to as the *compound interest formula*.

Example 22.1:
An amount of £5,000 is invested at a fixed rate of 8 per cent per annum. What will be the value of the investment in 5 years' time, if the interest is compounded:

(a) annually;
(b) every 6 months?
What is the *effective* annual rate of interest in the latter case?

(a) The only part of this type of calculation which needs particular care is that concerning the interest rate. The formula assumes that r is a *proportion*, and so, in this case,

$$r = 0.08.$$

In addition, we have

$$P = 5,000$$
$$n = 5$$

So

$$
\begin{aligned}
V &= P(1 + r)^n \\
&= 5000\,(1 + 0.08)^5 \\
&= 5000 \times 1.469328 \\
&= 7346.64.
\end{aligned}
$$

Thus the value of the investment will be *£7,346.64.*

(b) With slight modifications, the basic formula can be made to deal with compounding at intervals other than annually. Since the compounding is done at 6-monthly intervals, 4 per cent (half of 8 per cent) will be added to the value on each occasion. Hence we use

$$r = 0.04.$$

Further, there will be 10 additions of interest during the five years, and so

$$n = 10.$$

The formula now gives

$$
\begin{aligned}
V &= P(1 + r)^n \\
&= 5000\,(1.04)^{10} \\
&= 7401.22.
\end{aligned}
$$

Thus the value in this instance will be *£7401.22.*

Since 4 per cent interest is added after each 6 months, any investment will increase by a factor

$$(1.04)^2 = 1.0816$$

in a year. The effective annual rate is thus 8.16 per cent in this case.

The same basic formula can be used to deal with *depreciation*, in which the value of an item goes *down* at a certain rate. We simply ensure that the rate of 'interest' is negative.

Example 22.2:
A company buys a machine for £20,000. What will its value be after 6 years, if it is assumed to depreciate at a fixed rate of 12 per cent per annum?

We have:

$$P = 20,000$$
$$n = 6$$
$$r = -0.12;$$

hence

$$
\begin{aligned}
V &= P(1 + r)^n \\
&= 20,000\,(1 - 0.12)^6 \\
&= 20,000 \times 0.4644041 \\
&= 9288.08.
\end{aligned}
$$

The machine's value in 6 years' time will therefore be *£9288.08*.

Mortgages

We now look at some of the more complicated financial calculations, beginning with *mortgages*. Most people will be aware that, when a mortgage is taken out on a property over a number of years, there are several ways of repaying the loan. We shall concentrate here on *repayment mortgages*, because they are amongst the most popular, and because they are the only ones which involve complex mathematical calculations.

The features of a repayment morgage are:

a certain amount, £M, is borrowed over n years;
interest (at a rate r) is added to the loan retrospectively at the end of each year;
a constant amount, £P, is paid back each year by the borrower, usually in equal monthly instalments.

(For simplicity, we ignore here any income tax relief and just look at *gross* amounts.)

Consider the value of the amounts paid back:

after one year, P has been paid;
after two years, this initial amount has gained interest at a rate r, and so has value $P(1 + r)$, and a further P has been paid. Thus the value of the amount paid back is $P(1 + r) + P$. After three years, the amount at the end of two years has gained interest at a rate r, and a further P has been paid. Thus the value is

$$[P(1 + r) + P] \cdot (1 + r) + P$$
$$= P(1 + r)^2 + P(1 + r) + P.$$

Proceeding in this way, we see that the value of the repayments after n years is

$$P(1 + r)^{n-1} + P(1 + r)^{n-2} + \ldots + P(1 + r)^2 + P(1 + r) + P.$$

Now, this is a geometric progression with (compare section 22.2):

$$a = P$$
$$'r' = (1 + r)$$
$$'n' = n$$

and so the sum is

$$\frac{P \cdot [1 - (1 + r)^n]}{[1 - (1 + r)]}$$

$$= \frac{P \cdot [1 - (1 + r)^n]}{-r}$$

$$= \frac{P \cdot [(1 + r)^n - 1]}{r}. \quad (*)$$

In the meantime, the initial loan, £M, has accrued compound interest at a rate r for n years, and so, using the compound interest formula, is worth

$M(1 + r)^n$.

Since the amounts repaid must exactly pay off the mortgage in the n-year period, these last two amounts must balance:

$$\frac{P[(1 + r)^n - 1]}{r} = M(1 + r)^n;$$

thus the annual amount to be repaid is

$$P = \frac{Mr (1 + r)^n}{(1 + r)^n - 1}.$$

Example 22.3:

(a) A £30,000 mortgage is taken out on a property at a rate of 12 per cent over 25 years. What will be the gross monthly repayment?

(b) After two years of the mortgage, the interest rate increases to 14 per cent: re-calculate the monthly repayment figure.

(a) We substitute $M = 30,000$
$$r = 0.12$$
$$n = 25$$

into the formula to give

$$P = \frac{Mr (1 + r)^n}{(1 + r)^n - 1}$$
$$= \frac{30,000 \times 0.12 \times 1.12^{25}}{1.12^{25} - 1}$$
$$= \frac{30,000 \times 0.12 \times 17.0001}{16.0001}$$
$$= £3,825.00.$$

As this is an annual figure, we divide by 12 to get the *monthly* repayment figure of *£318.75*.

(b) It is a common feature of house-buying for interest rates to change. To re-calculate P, we first have to find the amount still owing on the loan after 2 years at 12 per cent:

M has increased to $M(1+r)^2$
$$= 30,000 \times 1.12^2$$
$$= £37,632.$$

The value of the repayments is $\dfrac{P [(1 + r)^2 - 1]}{r}$ (see (*) earlier)

$$= \frac{3825 [(1.12)^2 - 1]}{0.12}$$
$$= £8,109$$

and so the amount still owed = 37,632 − 8,109
= £29,523.

It is now as if there is a mortgage for this amount, at 14 per cent to run for the remaining *23* years:

$$P = \frac{Mr(1 + r)^n}{(1 + r)^n - 1}$$

$$= \frac{29523 \times 0.14 \times 1.14^{23}}{1.14^{23} - 1}$$

$$= £4346.70.$$

Dividing this figure by 12 now gives the new *monthly* repayment figure of *£362.22*.

Annuities

An *annuity* is an arrangement by which a person receives a series of constant annual amounts. The length of time during which the annuity is paid can either be until the death of the recipient or for a *guaranteed* minimum term of years, irrespective of whether the annuitant is alive or not. In other types of annuity, the payments are *deferred* until some time in the future, such as the retirement of the annuitant. We do not develop any formulae involving annuity calculations, but give two examples to illustrate how earlier ideas can be applied.

Example 22.4:
A man buys an annuity for £10,000. The annual return from the annuity is £11 per £100 purchased, until death, of which £6 is regarded as capital content and so not taxed. If the man pays income tax at the rate of 30 per cent calculate the net percentage return on the annuity. How does this compare with a building society account paying 5 per cent per annum, net of income tax?
   The gross return is £1,100, of which £600 is capital content,
£500 is taxable.
As income tax is paid at 30 per cent, this will amount to £150.
The *net* return is thus £950.
Expressed as a percentage of the original investment, this is

$$\frac{950}{10,000} \times 100 = 9.5 \text{ per cent.}$$

Thus the net return is *9.5* per cent.
   Although this is considerably higher than the building society rate of 5 per cent, the comparison is far from simple: there are a number of other factors to consider. The building society rate could change. The *gross* amount payable on the annuity is fixed, but if income tax rates change, the *net* annuity rates would vary too. With the annuity, the investor's capital is committed and disappears on his death. In the other case, however, the investor has flexibility and so can arrange to

have some or all of it go to his estate. The comparison is therefore very complicated, and depends largely on the man's judgement or preference between higher returns and flexibility.

Example 22.5:
A woman who has just turned 40 years of age and will retire at 60 can buy a deferred annuity which pays £5,000 per annum on her 60th birthday and on every subsequent birthday until death, with a guaranteed minimum payment of £25,000 if she dies before the age of 64. The annual premium would be £1,000 per annum until retirement, this amount being claimable against income tax.

Alternatively, she could invest the £1,000 per annum (less the tax she would have to pay on this part of her income) at 8 per cent compound interest per annum. Compare these two options at an income tax rate of 30 per cent.

In the second case, the woman would be investing

£700 per annum (after tax)
for 20 years
at 8 per cent.

To calculate how much this investment would be worth at her retirement, we use a formula developed in the section on mortgages:

$$V = \frac{P\left[(1 + r)^n - 1\right]}{r}$$

$$= \frac{700\left[(1.08)^{20} - 1\right]}{.08}$$

$$= £32,033.37.$$

She could now draw out £5,000 per annum from this on each birthday (to match the annuity) and leave the remainder to accrue interest at 8 per cent. The amount of capital left at her death and the amount she would receive from her investment during her retirement would then be:

Age at death	Investment Received(£)	Capital remaining(£)	Annuity Received(£)	Guaranteed(£)
60	5,000	29,196.04	5,000	20,000
61	10,000	26,131.72	10,000	15,000
62	15,000	22,822.26	15,000	10,000
63	20,000	19,248.04	20,000	5,000
64	25,000	15,387.88	25,000	–
65	30,000	11,218.91	30,000	–
66	35,000	6,716.42	35,000	–
67	40,000	1,853.73	40,000	–
68	41,853.73	–	45,000	–
69	41,853.73	–	50,000	–
	etc.		etc.	

(Note that, in the column representing the capital remaining in the investment (year end), £5,000 is taken off, then 8 per cent interest added on, each year.)

It can now be seen that, if the woman's retirement is short, up to 67 years of age, the annuity is the poorer, since the incomes from both options are the same, but the investment has greater capital remaining. For longer retirements, however, the annuity is clearly better as the investment has dried up completely and provides no further income.

Summary

A *geometric progression* is a series of numbers, each one a constant multiple of the one preceding it:

$a, ar, ar^2, ar^3, \ldots$

The sum, S, of the first n terms of such a progression is

$$S = \frac{a(1 - r^n)}{(1 - r)}.$$

The value, £V, of a sum, £P, invested for n years at a compound rate of r per annum is

$$V = P(1 + r)^n.$$

The same formula can be used to calculate the value of *depreciating* quantities by using a negative value of r.

The value, £V, attained in n years by investing £P *per annum* at a compound rate of r per annum (interest calculated at year end) is

$$V = \frac{P\left[(1 + r)^n - 1\right]}{r}$$

The *annual* amount needed, £P, to clear a repayment mortgage, £M, in n years at an interest rate of r per annum is

$$P = \frac{Mr\,(1 + r)^n}{(1 + r)^n - 1}.$$

Exercises on Chapter 22

1 (a) A small company plans to buy a piece of capital equipment costing £6,000 in 3 years' time. It can obtain a fixed rate of interest of 8 per cent annum. What amount would need to be invested at this rate *now*, in order to pay for the equipment, if the interest is compounded:
  (i) yearly, and
  (ii) every 3 months?

(b)   The equipment mentioned in (a) is needed to replace another machine bought by the company 1 year ago for £4,500. If this machine is assumed to depreciate in value at 12 per cent per annum, what will its value be at the time the replacement is bought?

2 (a)   A £25,000 repayment mortgage is taken out on a house at a rate of 11 per cent over 20 years. What will be the gross monthly repayment?

   (b)   After one year of this mortgage, the interest rate decreases to 10 per cent and the house owner borrows a further £3,000 for improvements to the property, this figure being added to the amount owing at that time. If the mortgage is still to be paid off in the *original* 20 years, what is the new gross monthly repayment figure?

3 An insurance company offers annuities at £13 per £100 purchased, until death, £7 of which is tax-free capital content. A building society offers 8 per cent per annum *tax paid*, compounded annually. You are approached, as financial adviser, by someone who pays income tax at 29 per cent and who has £20,000 to invest.

   (a)   What is the net percentage return on the annuity?

   (b)   Complete the following table up to 15 years, and hence comment on the comparative merits of the two investments.

	Building Society		Annuity
Death after (years):	Received during year(£):	Amount remaining (£)	Received during year(£):
1	2252	19,167.84	2252
2	2252	18,269.11	2252
.	.	.	.
.	.	.	.
.	.	.	.

(Assume that the investor draws out sufficient capital from the Building Society *at the start* of each year, to match the income of the annuity, and then the interest is added on at the end.)

4 A finance director estimates that his company will have to spend £0.25 million on new machinery in two years from now. Two alternative methods of providing the money are being considered, both assuming an annual rate of interest of 10 per cent:

   (a)   a single sum of money, £A, to be set aside and invested now, with interest compounded every six months. How much should this single sum be, and what is the effective annual rate of interest?

   (b)   £B to be put into a reserve fund every six months, starting now. If interest is compounded every six months, what should £B be, in order that the £0.25 million will be available in two years from now?

ICMA, May 1984.

5 In three years' time a considerable amount of the plant and machinery in your company's factory will need replacing. You estimate that a sum of £280,000 will be required for this.

(a) If you were to set aside sufficient funds now to be invested at 12 per cent per annum compounded quarterly (i.e. every three months),
  (i) what sum of money would you need, and
  (ii) what is the effective annual rate of interest?

(b) If, again assuming that investments made during the three years will be at 12 per cent per annum compounded quarterly, you decide instead to invest £4,000 at the end of every quarter, what additional sum needs to be set aside now in order to provide £280,000 at the end of the three years?

ICMA, May 1981.

6 (a) A company borrows £100,000 on the last day of the year and agrees to repay it by four equal amounts, the repayments being made at the end of each of the following four years. Compound interest at 12 per cent per annum is payable. What is the amount of each repayment?

(b) A new machine will cost £50,000 and has an expected life of five years. Scrap value at the end of the fifth year will be £1,000. Annual depreciation is to be calculated as a fixed percentage of its current book value. What should the percentage be?

(c) £1,000 is invested at 12 per cent per annum, with interest added every quarter-end. How long will it take for the investment to amount to £3,000?

ICMA, May 1982.

23 Discounting

Introduction

Accountants can often assist in business decision-making by providing detailed financial information on the various options. For example, when deciding between a number of competing tenders for supplying machinery, the exact amounts of money to be paid at certain times in the future will be known for each option. Similarly, investors will often be able to estimate the future annual payoffs to be obtained from a range of possible investments. One important factor which these, and similar, decisions have in common is that the financial inflows and/or outflows do not occur all at the same time, but are staggered. As we shall see, this complicates the decision analysis to some extent.

The reason for this complication can be seen thus: would you prefer to have £100 now or £100 in one year's time? The sensible answer to this would be to have the money *now*, since it could be invested at some interest rate, so that its value would be more than £100 after one year. If you consider that inflows/outflows can occur at many points in the future, it can be seen that the analysis cannot consist merely of totalling future amounts of money. Indeed, the concepts of *present value* and *net present value* are needed.

Present values

The *present value* of a sum of money to be paid or received in the future is its value *at present*, in the sense that it is the sum of money which could be invested *now* (at a certain rate of interest) to reach the required value at the subsequent specified time. Some examples will make this clearer and illustrate two ways of calculating present values.

Example 23.1:
Find the present value of

254

(a) £200 payable in 2 years' time, assuming an investment rate of 7 per cent per annum, compounded annually, is available;

(b) £350 receivable in 3 years' time, assuming an annually compounded investment rate of 6 per cent per annum is available.

(a) From the definition, we need to find that sum of money which would have to be invested at 7 per cent per annum and have value £200 in 2 years' time. Suppose this is £X, then the compound interest formula of Chapter 22 gives:

$$V = P(1 + r)^n.$$

Thus $200 = X (1 + 0.7)^2$

giving $X = \dfrac{200}{1.1449}$

$= 174.69.$

Thus the present value is £*174.69*: that is, with an interest rate of 7 per cent, there is no difference between paying £174.69 now and paying £200 in 2 years' time.

(b) Using the compound interest formula again:

$$350 = X (1 + 0.6)^3$$

$X = \dfrac{350}{1.191016}$

$= 293.87.$

The present value is thus £*293.87*.

This method of calculation is said to be *from first principles*. Alternatively, the present value tables in Appendix 1 give a present value factor of 0.87 for $n = 2$ years at $r = 7$ per cent. This means that the present value of £1 for this combination is £0.87: hence the present value (PV) of £200 is

$200 \times 0.87 = £174.$

Similarly, the PV factor for $n = 3$ and $4 = 6$ per cent is 0.84; so the PV of £350 is

$350 \times 0.84 = £294.$

Before leaving the PV tables, we note that they simply give the approximate values of

$$\frac{1}{(1 + r)^n}$$

thereby simplifying the calculations considerably.

It can be seen that use of the tables loses some accuracy. When there are many such calculations, however, their use is considerably faster, and so tables are generally preferred. However, their use is not always possible, since you will note there are 'gaps' in the tables. For instance, the combination $n = 2\frac{1}{2}$ years and $r = 4.5$ per cent does not appear in the tables, and so first principles would have to be used in an example involving these values.

Net present values. Practical examples

In many situations, there are a number of financial inflows and outflows involved, at a variety of times. In such cases, *the net present value* (NPV) is the total of the individual present values, after *discounting* each, as above.

Example 23.2:
A company can purchase a machine now for £10,000. The company accountant estimates that the machine will contribute £2,500 per annum to profits for five years, after which time it will have to be scrapped for £500. Find the NPV of the machine if the interest rate for the period is assumed to be 5 per cent. (Assume, for simplicity, that all inflows occur at year ends.)

We set out the calculations in a systematic, tabular form:

After year	Total inflow (£)	Discount factor (from tables, Appendix 1)	PV
0	−10,000	1	−10,000
1	2,500	0.95	2,375
2	2,500	0.91	2,275
3	2,500	0.86	2,150
4	2,500	0.82	2,050
5	3,000	0.78	2.340
			1,190

Hence the NPV is *£1,190*. The *cumulative* present value table in Appendix 1 makes the calculation of the *total* PV arising from an inflow of £2,500 at a constant interest rate of 5 per cent for *each* of four years. The factor is 3.55, and so the total PV is

2500 × 3.55 = 8875,

which agrees (approximately) with the middle four entries of the above table.

The idea of NPV enables us to compare two or more options, as illustrated below.

Example 23.3:
An investor is considering three options, only one of which she can afford. All three have the same initial outlay, but there are different income patterns available from each. Investment A pays £2,000 each year at the end of the next five years. Investment B pays £1,000 at the end of the first year, £1,500 at the end of the second year, and so on until the final payment of £3,000 at the end of the fifth year. Investment C pays £4000 at the end of the first year, £3,000 at the end of the second year, and £2,000 at the end of the third.

The investor estimates a constant rate of interest of 10 per cent throughout the next five years: which investment should she choose?

The cumulative present value factor for a constant inflow at 10 per cent for five years is 3.79; hence the NPV of investment A is

$2000 \times 3.79 = £7580.$

The other two investments do not involve constant inflows and so the PVs for individual years have to be summed:

Year (end)	PV factor	Investment B		Investment C	
		Inflow	PV	Inflow	PV
1	0.91	1000	910	4000	3640
2	0.83	1500	1245	3000	2490
3	0.75	2000	1500	2000	1500
4	0.68	2500	1700	–	–
5	0.62	3000	1860	–	–
			£7215		£7630

In summary, the NPVs of investments A, B and C are £7580, £7215 and £7630 respectively. As the outlay for each is the same, the investor should choose C.

Problems when using NPV in practice

One of the major difficulties with present values is the estimation of the 'interest rates' used in the calculations. Clearly, the appropriate rate(s) at the start of the time period under consideration will be known, but future values can be only estimates. As the point in time moves farther and farther into the future, the rates become more and more speculative. For this reason, the NPVs of investments A and C in example 23.3 are so close as to be indistinguishable, practically speaking.

Many situations in which NPV might be involved are concerned with capital investments, with the capital needing to be raised from the market. For this reason, the 'interest rate(s)' are referred to as *the cost of capital*, since they reflect the rate(s) at which the capital market is willing to provide the necessary money.

Partly because of the uncertainties concerning future interest rates and partly because business people often wish to see a quick return on investments, the criterion of choosing the option with the highest NPV is not always adopted in practice. Another popular criterion is *payback*. The calculations here simply consist of estimating how long each option will take to pay back the initial investment. The choice criterion is then to pick the option with the quickest payback, or, in questions of whether to undertake a project or not, to take on projects with payback periods of less than some specified maximum, such as 18 months. This criterion can be criticized because it ignores the cost of capital, but, as the periods of time involved are usually short, this may not be important. Potentially more critical is the way payback ignores any income *after* the project breakeven point has been reached.

Finally, we mention that there are other criteria and problems relating to investment appraisal, but these are more appropriate in management accounting texts and the reader is left to consult these further.

Summary

The *present value* (PV) of a sum of money payable/receivable in the future is that sum which would have to be invested *now* (at a given rate of interest) to reach the target sum at the required future point in time. The PV can be calculated from the appropriate table in Appendix 1, or from first principles, using the compound interest formula:

$$V = P (1 + r)^n$$

giving the PV of X as

$$PV = \frac{X}{(1 + r)^n}$$

The *net present value* (NPV) of an investment is the total of the present values of all the inflows and outflows involved in the investment. The NPV can be calculated from the appropriate table in Appendix 1, provided all the inflows are the same, or by summing all the individual PVs, calculated as above.

Exercises on Chapter 23

1 Calculate the present values of the following sums of money, both from first principles and, where possible, using the table of present value factors:

    (a) £500 in 3 years' time, at an interest rate of 8%;
    (b) £7,000 in 5 years' time, at an interest rate of 2%;
    (c) £4,000 in 6 years' time, at an interest rate of 5.4%;
    (d) £500 in 3 years' time, at an interest rate of 2% *per quarter*.

2 A company wishes to buy a machine to perform a certain task. It has received tenders from two manufacturers, both of whose machines are technically indistinguishable. Manufacturer X requires an immediate payment on delivery of £10,000 and further payments of £2,500 each after 1, 2, 3 and 4 years. Manufacturer Y requires £5,000 on delivery and payments of £5,000 each after 1, 2 and 3 years. The current cost of capital is 4 per cent.

    (a) Calculate the NPV of the two payment methods, assuming the cost of capital does not change, and hence advise the company on which offer to choose.
    (b) Suggest reasons why the company may not take your advice.

(c) Repeat the calculations in (a), assuming that interest compounding takes place every 6 months (at a rate of 2 per cent per half year).

3 An investor has £10,000 to invest in long-term investments. The details of three possible offers are given below:

Income:	Offer 1 (initial outlay £8,000)	Offer 2 (initial outlay £9,000)	Offer 3 (initial outlay £9,000)
after 1 year	£2,500	£3,000	£2,000
after 2 years	£2,500	£3,000	£2,500
after 3 years	£2,500	£2,500	£3,000
after 4 years	£2,500	£2,500	£4,000

Advise the investor on the relative merits of the three offers, if interest rates are currently running at 7 per cent per annum.

4 A company wishes to acquire a machine for the next five years and considers the following methods of paying for it:

(a) Outright purchase for £400,000 with a maintenance contract of £20,000 payable annually in advance. The machine would have a second-hand resale value after five years of £50,000.
(b) Rent the machine for five years at £110,000 per annum, payable annually in advance, inclusive of all maintenance.
(c) Hire-purchase of a down payment of £200,000 followed by four annual payments of £95,000, inclusive of all maintenance, after which time the company owns the machine. The machine would have a second-hand resale value after five years of £50,000.

Assuming the cost of capital to be 12 per cent, use the criterion of net present value (NPV) to find which method is the most economical. Comment briefly on your answer.

ICMA, November 1983.

5 Several projects are being evaluated by an accountant. The year-end cash flows are shown below, with outflows shown in brackets. All cash flows are in thousands:

	1985	1986	1987	1988	1989	1990	1991
Project A:	(200)	(100)	50	100	200	100	50
Project B:	(100)	(200)	0	50	150	250	50

(a) Find the net present value of both A and B assuming a rate of interest of 12 per cent.
(b) Project C has the same cash outflows as A in 1985 and 1986, and over the next five years the cash inflows show the same pattern. What would the minimum cash inflows have to be, 1987–1991, to make C worthwhile?

ICMA, November 1985.

6 A company has to choose between three mutually exclusive investments, A, B and C, each of which has a life of four years. A, B and C
cost respectively £30,000, £40,000 and £35,000. The year-end cash
flows would be as follows:

	Investment A	Investment B	Investment C
	Year-end cash flows (£000)		
Year 1	15	17	20
Year 2	15	20	18
Year 3	10	13	8
Year 4	5	10	4

The cost of capital is 14 per cent.
    Using the criterion of net present value, which one represents: (*a*)
the best investment, (*b*) the worst investment?

ICMA, November 1982.

24 Stock control

Introduction

An important aspect of running many businesses is the control of *stock*. It is clearly desirable to have a sufficient stock of goods to supply customers without delay, as and when required. This aim could be achieved simply by having a stock which is large when compared to the demand, but the expense of the capital so tied up and of the storage space needed usually precludes such a solution. On the other hand, a very small stock could be kept, and very frequent, small replenishments made. The drawback then is that the high capital and storage costs are replaced by high delivery and other replenishment costs. The problem thus comes down to finding a compromise between these two extremes of high and low stock levels, so as to minimize costs while maintaining customer service.

The basic economic order model

We begin by developing a very simple, basic model for the replenishment of and drain on stock. This model assumes that there is a constant demand for the goods concerned, so that the stock level is reducing at a constant rate. Further, we assume that stock is replenished by a constant amount (X units) at regular intervals (T) and that these amounts are put into stock just as supplies run out. The graph of the number of units in stock against time is therefore the 'saw-tooth' shape shown in Figure 24.1.

We now consider the costs associated with this model. The *order costs* (delivery and administrative costs of each order) are denoted C_o, while the capital and storage costs (the *holding costs*) are denoted C_h per unit per annum. If the annual demand is D, then, as X units are ordered each

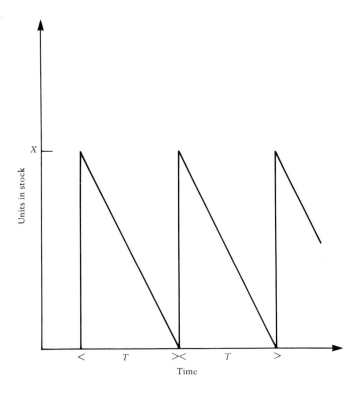

Figure 24.1 *Stock levels, basic economic order model*

time, the annual number of orders to be made will be D/X and the total ordering costs will be

$$\frac{D}{X} \cdot C_o.$$

Consider one of the triangular 'saw-tooths' shown in Figure 24.1. During the time period represented by this part of the graph, the average amount in stock at any point in time is half the height of the triangle, namely $X/2$. As this pattern repeats itself constantly, this also gives the average stock held over *all* time. The total holding costs are thus

$$\frac{X}{2} \cdot C_h.$$

Adding these two costs gives the *total stock cost, C*:

C = total ordering costs + total holding costs

$$C = \frac{DC_o}{X} + \frac{XC_h}{2}.$$

This is a function of X, all other factors being assumed constant. This reflects the aspect we referred to earlier, that the two components of cost, and thus the total, depend on the number ordered. We can now use differential calculus (Chapter 21) to minimize C:

$$\frac{dC}{dX} = -\frac{DC_o}{X^2} + \frac{C_h}{2}$$

and so

$$\frac{dC}{dX} = 0$$

gives

$$-\frac{DC_o}{X^2} + \frac{C_h}{2} = 0$$

$$\frac{C_h}{2} = \frac{DC_o}{X^2}$$

$$X^2 = \frac{2DC_o}{C_h}$$

$$X = \sqrt{\frac{2DC_o}{C_h}}.$$

This figure is known as the *economic order quantity* (EOQ) and this model as the *basic EOQ model*. We illustrate their use in an example.

Example 24.1:
A retail company estimates that the demand for one of its products is running at approximately 10,000 units per year. The product retails at £5 per unit. The company accountant estimates that administrative delivery costs for each order of the product amount to £125. Further, she determines that the capital and storage costs of keeping one unit in store for a year is 5 per cent of retail price. How often should the store order replenishment stock of the product and what is the associated stock cost?

As the company is apparently adopting the policy of ordering a constant amount at regular intervals, we will adopt the basic EOQ model. We are given

$$D = 10,000 \text{ units per annum,}$$

$$C_h = 5 \text{ per cent of £5}$$
$$= £0.25 \text{ per unit per annum}$$

and $C_o = £125$ per order.

The EOQ formula now gives

$$X = \sqrt{\frac{2DC_o}{C_h}}$$

$$= \sqrt{\frac{2 \times 10,000 \times 125}{0.25}}$$

$$= 3162.3 \; units.$$

Thus, to obtain 10,000 units each year, the company must order

$$\frac{10,000}{3162.3} = 3.16 \; times \; each \; year$$

$$\left(or \; \frac{D}{X}\right).$$

These two answers, of course, are impractical as they stand, partly because it is contrary to common sense to speak of '3.16 orders' per year and partly due to the assumptions made. In particular, we have assumed that demand for the product arrives at a constant rate. It is more realistic to suggest that the company should order *3000 units at a time*, so that (on average) 3⅓ orders are made per year, or an order is made *slightly more often than once every 4 months*, on average. The associated costs are:

$$total \; ordering \; costs = \frac{DC_o}{X}$$

$$= \frac{10,000 \times £125}{3,000}$$

$$= £416.67;$$

$$total \; holding \; costs = \frac{XC_h}{2}$$

$$= \frac{3,000 \times 0.25}{2}$$

$$= £375.$$

Hence the total stock cost for this product would be, on average, approximately *£790 per year* with this order pattern.

The economic batch quantity model

The *economic batch quantity (EBQ) model* is a variation on the basic EOQ model, which caters for situations in which stock is replenished *gradually*, rather than at discrete points in time. In this model, we assume that orders are placed as soon as stock runs out, and that replenishments start arriving immediately at a rate of R units per annum until the order is completed; then no further stock is delivered until the next stockout. The total amount ordered is still denoted X and all the remaining notation is as above.

The rate of replenishment must clearly be greater than that of demand, so that stocks begin to rise until the whole order of X units has arrived. The stocks will then fall steadily to zero, at which point

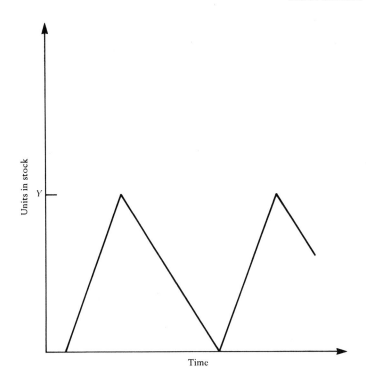

Figure 24.2 *Stock levels, economic batch quantity model*

another order is placed and the cycle begins again. The graph of the number of units in stock against time will therefore be as shown in Figure 24.2.

It is now important to find the value of the maximum stock level, denoted Y in the figure. If there are N working days per year, then, during the replenishment part of the cycle,

$\dfrac{R}{N}$ units are put into stock per day,

$\dfrac{D}{N}$ units are taken out of stock per day, and so

stock increases at a rate $\dfrac{R}{N} - \dfrac{D}{N}$ units per day.

Further, since a total of X units are ordered, and they arrive at a rate $\dfrac{R}{N}$ per day, the order takes

$$\dfrac{X}{R/N}$$

$$= \dfrac{NX}{R} \text{ days to arrive.}$$

Thus

$$Y = \left[\frac{R}{N} - \frac{D}{N} \right] \frac{NX}{R} \text{ units}$$

$$Y = \left[1 - \frac{D}{R} \right] X \text{ units.}$$

We can now consider the costs connected with this model. As before, $\frac{D}{X}$ orders will be made at a cost of C_o, so ordering costs will be

$$\frac{D}{X} \cdot C_o$$

Figure 24.2 shows that, during each cycle, the average amount of stock is $\frac{1}{2}Y$, which, at a holding cost of C_h/unit/annum, gives a holding cost of

$$\frac{Y}{2} \cdot C_h$$

$$= \frac{1}{2} \left[1 - \frac{D}{R} \right] X C_h.$$

The total cost is thus

$$C = \frac{DC_o}{X} + \frac{X C_h (1 - D/R)}{2}.$$

It will be noted that this is the same as for the EOQ model, but for the constant factor $(1 - D/R)$. The calculus will therefore be the same as before, except for the inclusion of this term. The reader is left to verify that the value of X to minimize C is

$$X = \sqrt{\frac{2C_o D}{C_h (1 - D/R)}}.$$

This value is known as the *economic batch quantity* (EBQ) and the model as the *economic batch model*.

Example 24.2:
If, in example 24.1, the company trades for 300 days per year and delivery of stock, rather than being instantaneous can be made at a rate of 200 units per day, determine the optimal order pattern and costs.
    As before,

$$D = 10,000 \text{ units per annum}$$
$$C_h = \text{£0.25 per unit per annum}$$
$$C_o = \text{£125 per order.}$$

We also need R, the *annual* rate at which stock is replenished, during the relevant part of the stock cycle. This is

$$R = 300 \times 200 = 60,000 \text{ units per annum.}$$

The EBQ formula now gives

$$X = \sqrt{\frac{2 \times 125 \times 10,000}{0.25 \ (1 \ - \ 10,000/60,000)}}$$

$$= 3,464 \ units.$$

Thus, to obtain 10,000 units each year, the company must order

$$\frac{D}{X} = \frac{10,000}{3,464}$$

$$= 2.89 \ times \ each \ year.$$

As before, we round this to a sensible order figure, of *3,500 units at a time*, so that (on average) *just under three orders are made per year*. The associated costs are:

$$\text{ordering costs} = \frac{DC_o}{X}$$

$$= \frac{10,000 \times £125}{3,500}$$

$$= £357.14;$$

$$\text{holding costs} = \frac{XC_h(1 \ - \ D/R)}{2}$$

$$= \frac{3,500 \times 0.25(1 \ - \ 10,000/60,000)}{2}$$

$$= £364.58.$$

Hence the total stock cost for this product would be, on average, approximately £720 per year with this order pattern.

Limitations of these models in practice

It is clear that an assumption of gradual replenishment is more realistic than one of instantaneous replenishment, and so the EBQ model is more generally applicable than the EOQ model. Even this model, however, depends on the assumption that the drain on stock is *constant* over time. There are two major reasons why this condition may not obtain: seasonality and random fluctuations. Many products are highly seasonal in their demand: for example suntan lotion sells in greater quantity during the warmer months than during the colder months of the year. In such cases, provided the pattern of seasonal variation is fairly constant and predictable, then some systematic approach to stock control may be possible, but not by using these constant demand models.

Even with non-seasonal products there will be fluctuations within any constant demand patterns. If they are generally small, they will have little effect on the results of these models, which can therefore be relied on to some extent. If, however, the fluctuations are large, the predictions of the models are unreliable. There are modifications to the approach which take account of variations and uncertainties in the figures: the interested reader is advised to investigate such models elsewhere.

There are other reasons why the results of the model may not be absolutely accurate: delays in delivery, changing costs of capital and ordering, and so on. All in all, then, the results of the models under consideration here can be considered only approximate. However, provided the assumptions of the models are more or less applicable, the formulae can provide reasonable guidelines for the stock manager and the accountant.

Summary

If the demand for a product is a constant D units per year,

the delivery and other costs of an order for the product is C_o, and
the capital and storage costs of one unit of the product is C_h per year,

then the *Economic Order Quantity* (EOQ) is

$$X = \sqrt{\frac{2DC_o}{C_h}}.$$

This model assumes instantaneous stock replenishment as stocks run out.

If, instead, stock is gradually replenished at a constant rate of R units per year until the order is complete, and then the stocks are allowed to dwindle to zero before another order starts arriving, the *Economic Batch Quantity* (EBQ) is

$$X = \sqrt{\frac{2C_o D}{C_h(1 - D/R)}}$$

and the maximum stock level attained is

$$Y = (1 - D/R) X.$$

Exercises on Chapter 24

1   A warehouse manager is reviewing the stocking policy of her company, beginning with product P, the bulkiest item stored. It is the current practice to order P in batches of 250, and these are timed to arrive just as stock runs out. Past information suggests that the whole order arrives more or less together and that demand for P runs at a fairly steady rate of 50 units per day. Furthermore, the company accountant has estimated that storing P costs £2 per unit per annum, while the cost of each order is £20.

Assuming that the company operates for 250 days per year, find the economic order quantity and calculate the annual savings in total costs this would give compared to current practice.

2   The manager in exercise 1 now turns her attention to product Q, the highest priced item stored in the warehouse. Demand for Q is a fairly steady 20 units per day and the cost of storing Q is £5 per unit per annum. Ordering costs are the same as those for product P. The production pattern for Q, however, is such that any replenishment order does not arrive in the warehouse all at once, but at a steady rate of 50 units per day until the complete order has arrived. Current practice is to order 1000 units of Q in one batch, timed so that they begin to arrive just as stocks run out.

  Find the economic batch quantity for product Q and calculate the savings this would represent, compared to current practice.

  Comment on the validity of the models used in exercises 1 and 2.

3   Your organization uses 1,000 packets of paper each year (48 working weeks). The variable costs of placing an order, progressing delivery and payment have been estimated at £12 per order.

  Storage and interest costs have been estimated at £0.50 per packet per annum based on the average annual stock.

  The supplier requires four weeks between order and delivery.

  Assume certainty of demand, lead time* and costs.

  You are required to:

  (a)   calculate the EOQ;
  (b)   calculate the stock level at which the orders will be placed;
  (c)   calculate the total minimum cost.

(* Lead time = time lapse between placing the order and receiving delivery.)

ICMA PEI, May 1986.

4   You are determining the stock policy for Part K and have the following data:

Cost of placing an order and receiving delivery	£50.00
Holding cost per unit of stock for one year	£2.40
Annual demand (certain and regular)	48,000 units
Estimated purchase cost per unit	£1.00
Delivery rate (until order completed)	2000/week.

  You are required to:

  (a)   calculate the total cost of placing orders and holding stock if 20, 40, 60, 80 or 100 orders are placed during the year;
  (b)   determine the minimum cost using a simple EBQ model.

ICMA PEI, November 1984.

5   Some practitioners have challenged the reliability and relevance of the economic order quantity (EOQ) inventory (stock) model which all cost and management textbooks have for so long advocated.

You are required to:

(*a*)   state and explain the deficiencies of the traditional EOQ model;

(*b*)   discuss the extent to which the EBQ model overcomes these deficiencies.

ICMA PEI, May 1985.

25 Project planning

Introduction

In this concluding chapter, we consider an approach to optimal resource allocation and other aspects of project planning. The basic requirements for the method are:

the project can be subdivided into a number of distinct *activities*;
the length of time each activity will take to complete can be estimated;
for each activity, a complete list of *predecessors* can be determined. (A
predecessor is an activity which must be finished before another can
begin.)

Under these conditions, a pictorial representation or *network* can be
drawn and a number of analyses undertaken. The most fundamental
factors which can be determined are the minimum project completion
time and a list of those activities which need most careful management,
in order to avoid delay.

Network construction

A network consists of a series of circles joined by lines. The lines denote
the activities, and the circles, or *nodes*, denote *events*, or points at which
one set of activities ends and another begins. Furthermore, the nodes
are numbered, for ease of reference, and the activity lines are arrowed
to show the order of the activities through the project. We mention two
more basic conventions in network construction before giving an
example:

the network should begin at a single node and end at a single node;
the nodes should be numbered so that arrows proceed from lower to
higher numbers.

Example 25.1:
A project can be simply analysed as the following series of activities:

A: planning; when this is finished,
B: hire the workforce, and, simultaneously with this,
C: order the materials.
When the workforce and the materials are both ready,
D: proceed to construct.
Finally, when the construction has been completed,
E: inspect the finished job.

The network for this simplistic analysis is shown in Figure 25.1. It will be noted that the only slight complications, that activities B and C can start and run concurrently, once activity A has finished, and that *both* B and C must finish before D can start, are incorporated by using a *dummy activity*. Without this, we should be implying that construction could begin without waiting for the materials to be ready, which is clearly illogical. Any number of dummies can, and should, be incorporated in a network, to cater for situations where an activity has more than one predecessor. Care should be taken, however, not to create spurious predecessors by the careless use of dummies: for example a dummy from node 3 to node 5 would imply that ordering the materials came *immediately* before the final inspection, which is not the case.

Finally, we note that dummies are denoted by dotted lines (with arrows) and that the numbering of the nodes shown is not the only possible one. In fact, *any* numbers could be used, provided the convention that arrows proceed from lower to higher numbers is obeyed.

Example 25.2:
A project is analysed as follows:

Activity:	Immediate predecessor(s):
A	–
B	A
C	B
D	C
E	C
F	D,E
G	E
H	F
J	G
K	H,J

Construct a network to represent this project.

At the outset we note that there are two activities, F and K, with two immediate predecessors each, and so we expect that a dummy activity will have to be incorporated at these two points. The network is shown in Figure 25.2(a). This is not the only way it could be drawn, since activity K could be drawn coming off the node at which H finishes. In this case, the dummy on the arrow would have to be reversed (to ensure

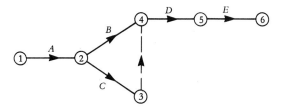

Figure 25.1 *Network, example 25.1*

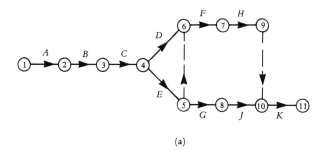

(a)

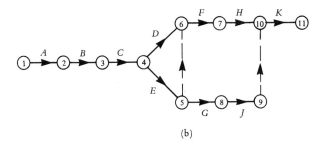

(b)

Figure 25.2 *Networks, example 25.2*

that J is an immediate predecessor of K) and the numbering of the nodes towards the end would have to be amended, to fit in with the convention of arrows going from lower to higher nodes: see Figure 25.2(b). We shall see later how two apparently different networks can be compared to see whether they represent the same project.

Finally, to illustrate the care needed when using dummies, consider the dummy activity 5–6. It might seem possible to have F emanating from node 5, with the arrow on the dummy 5–6 reversed. The position here, however, is complicated by activity G *also* emanating from node 5: the dummy as described would imply that D was an immediate predecessor of G. Particular attention is therefore needed with dummies when more than one activity emerges from a single node.

Network analysis

We now proceed to analyse networks in terms of time. In particular, we now consider examples in which the time taken to complete each activity is known.

Example 25.3:

If, in the project of example 25.2, the times needed to complete each activity are as below, find how long it will take to complete the project, provided there are no delays and each activity can begin immediately after its predecessors have finished. Also discuss the management of the project, in order to achieve its completion in minimum time:

activity:	time to complete (days):
A	5
B	5
C	5
D	5
E	3
F	2
G	4
H	6
J	3
K	2

If we look at either Figure 25.2(a) or (b), we can see that there are the following *paths* (or routes from the first to the last node) through the network:

(i) A–B–C–D–F–H–K (omitting the implied dummy between H and K)

(ii) A–B–C–E–F–H–K (omitting the two implied dummies)

(iii) A–B–C–E–G–J–K

This list is the same for both versions: compiling a list such as this is one way of comparing two networks to see whether they represent the same project.

Alternatively, the paths can be denoted by the node numbers, and, further, the *lengths* of the paths (in days) can be determined by adding the lengths of the activities within each path, to give:

(i)   1–2–3–4–6–7–9–10–11: length = 30 days

(ii) 1–2–3–4–5–6–7–9–10–11: length = 28 days

(iii)   1–2–3–4–5–8–10–11: length = 27 days.

It will be noted that, again, dummies are not explicitly included in a path and that dummies have length *zero*, since they have been introduced by us, only as an aid to drawing the network, and do not exist as activities in reality.

We now address the question of project duration. It may be tempting to think that this is the shortest path, but this cannot be so since it would leave the longer paths unfinished. *All* activities (and therefore paths) must be finished before the project can be considered complete, and so it is the *longest* path which determines the project time. The minimum time to complete this project is thus *30 days*.

The longest path is known as the *critical path* and the activities on it are known as *critical activities*. They are important because no delay can be allowed on them, without delaying the whole project; whereas, on non-critical activities, a certain amount of flexibility or delay can be tolerated. Critical activities, therefore, have to be monitored most closely in order to minimize project completion times.

The question now arises as to how much delay or leeway can be allowed on non-critical activities, without causing overall delays. This amount of 'leeway' is termed *float*. More precisely, *total* float is the amount of time an activity can be delayed without delaying the whole project; *free* float is the amount an activity can be delayed without delaying a subsequent activity: alternatively, this latter form of float can be viewed as the delay possible without using up any float on an activity which follows.

Example 25.4:
Determine the floats associated with example 25.3.
To calculate the floats, we build up the following table:

| | | Earliest | | Latest | | Float | |
Activity	Duration	Start	Finish	Start	Finish	Total	Free
1–2	5	0	5	0	5	0	0
2–3	5	5	10	5	10	0	0
3–4	5	10	15	10	15	0	0
4–5	3	15	18	17	20	2	0
4–6	5	15	20	15	20	0	0
5–6	0	18	18	20	20	2	2
5–8	4	18	22	21	25	3	0
6–7	2	20	22	20	22	0	0
7–9	6	22	28	22	28	0	0
8–10	3	22	25	25	28	3	3
9–10	0	28	28	28	28	0	0
10–11	2	28	30	28	30	0	0

The first two columns of the table, reading from the left, are simply repetitions of the basic information on the project's activities and durations. The next two columns show the earliest times each activity can start and finish if the project is to be completed within the minimum 30 days. They are calculated as follows:

activity 1–2 can start immediately (time 0), and so this is its earliest start; add on the duration and we get its earliest finish, namely after 5 days;

activity 2–3 can start immediately 1–2 finishes (time 5); adding the duration gives the earliest finish of 10.

Proceeding in this way, we can move down the table, completing the two columns. Slight complications occur with activities like 6–7 which begin at a node (number 6) with more than one node leading into it. In such a case, the argument goes as follows:

before 6–7 can begin, *both* 4–6 *and* 5–6 must have finished; thus 6–7 cannot begin until time *20*. Add on the duration time (2 days) and we get the earliest finish time of 22 for this activity.

Activity 10–11 also has two immediate predecessors: the reader should check the earliest start and finish times in this case.

We now consider the *latest* start and finish times, shown in columns 5 and 6. Here we start at the *bottom* of the table, working *upwards* through the activities in *reverse* numerical order of the *ending* nodes. This will be seen to be the reverse of the process for determining earliest times:

activity 10–11 must finish by time 30 (in order to avoid delay): *subtract* the duration time to get the latest start time of 28 days. *Both* activities 8–10 and 9–10 must finish by this time (to avoid delay), and so these two both have a latest finish time of 28; subtract the appropriate duration times to get latest starts. Next we look at activity(-ies) ending in node 9, and so on.

Again, there is a slight complication with nodes such as 4 and 5 which have more than one activity leading from them:

any activities leading into node 5 must finish in time for *both* 5–6 *and* 5–8 to start on time; the latest finish time of 4–5 is thus *20* (*not* 21).

The reader should now check the corresponding entry for activity 3–4.

It is now a straightforward matter to determine *total float*: this is the maximum delay permissible on each activity, and so is

latest start time – earliest start time; or, equivalently,
latest finish time – earliest finish time.

The entries in the seventh column of the table are now clear.

To determine the *free float* of each activity, its earliest finish time must be compared to the earliest start times of *all immediate* successors. Consider, as examples:

activity 5–6: earliest finish time = 18,
   only one successor (6–7), earliest start time = 20:
   thus free float = 2;
activity 4–5: earliest finish time = 18,
   two successors (5–6 and 5–8), both with earliest start time = 18:
   thus free float = 0.

It will be noted that critical activities have zero float: the definition of criticality demands this. The values of the floats on non-critical activities are very useful to project managers. For instance, a delay of one day on activity 8–10 would not be too important, as both total and free floats are three days. A delay of one day on activity 4–5, however, would be of interest to management: the project could still be completed on time (total float = two days), but the zero free float shows there would be a 'knock-on' effect, using up one day's float on later activity(-ies).

We give another, partially worked, example to illustrate further the process of evaluating floats.

Example 25.5:
Find the minimum project duration, the critical path, and the total and free floats for the project:

Activity	Duration (weeks)
1–2	3
1–3	1
1–5	3
2–4	4
2–5	4
3–5	5
4–6	6
5–7	5
6–7	0
7–8	4

It will be noted that the network has effectively already been drawn here; otherwise the node numbers could not have been specified. It is a relatively simple matter now to verify the following paths and lengths:

1–2–4–6–7–8: 17 weeks
1–2–5–7–8:   16 weeks
1–3–5–7–8:   15 weeks
1–5–7–8:   12 weeks.

The critical activities are thus *1–2, 2–4, 4–6 and 7–8* and the minimum project duration time is *17 weeks*. The activity 6–7 is not included in this list because it is a *dummy*, rather than a real activity.

The earliest and latest times table is:

Activity	Duration	Earliest Start	Earliest Finish	Latest Start	Latest Finish	Float Total	Float Free
1–2	3	0	3	0	3	0	0
1–3	1	0	1	2	3	2	0
1–5	3	0	3	5	8	5	4
2–4	4	3	7	3	7	0	0
2–5	4	3	7	4	8	1	0
3–5	5	1	6	3	8	2	1
4–6	6	7	13	7	13	0	0
5–7	5	7	12	8	13	1	1
6–7	0	13	13	13	13	0	0
7–8	4	13	17	13	17	0	0

We illustrate some of the entries in the table:

earliest start, 5–7: this activity cannot start until *both* 2–5 and 3–5
have finished; hence the earliest start is 7 weeks
(*not* 6);

latest finish, 1–2: this activity must finish in time to avoid delaying
both 2–4 and 2–5; hence the latest finish is 3 weeks
(*not* 4);

free float, 3–5: earliest finish time = 6,
subsequent activity (5–7) has earliest start time =
7,
thus free float = 1 week.

The remaining entries in the table can be found by working *down* the
table through the earliest start time column, and then by working *up*
the table through the latest finish times.

Limitations and extensions

One of the problems with network analysis is that it assumes a project
can be subdivided into distinct, definable 'activities'. In practice, the
distinction may not be clear-cut, since there will tend to be overlaps
and 'blurred edges' to the activities. Another problem encountered in
practice is that real projects can have many constituent elements, thus
leading to highly complex networks. As one of the objects of the exercise
of drawing a network is to simplify matters, thereby aiding project
management, this can be a major drawback.

Computerization does not help overcome these two limitations to
any great extent. It can, however, remedy another criticism of the
elementary analysis above, namely that it is very static. Practical projects are dynamic, in that delays occur in the middle of an activity,
estimated durations of future activities are often revised in mid-project,
and so on. For instance, in example 25.5 above, if there were a 3-week
delay in the middle of activity 1–3, there would be a new critical path,
the project length would increase to 18 weeks and all the floats would
change. Although the interested reader might wish to work through the
example again with this revised information, it would be a very simple
matter to change this one piece of data, already stored in a computer,
and re-run the program.

Another way in which network analysis can be dynamic is that estimates of activity durations may have some degree of variation built
into them:

4 ± 1 weeks, rather than
4 weeks.

A technique called Project Evaluation and Review Technique (PERT)
is a variation on basic network analysis. Other extensions deal with
aspects of resource distribution and management, and cost management: the reader is referred to more advanced texts.

Summary

A *network* is a diagram to represent the component activities of a project and their sequence. The network consists of arrow lines (depicting the activities) connecting *nodes*, and *dummy* activities when an activity has more than one immediate predecessor. The nodes in a network must be numbered so that arrows proceed from lower to higher numbers.

The *critical path* in a network is that sequence of activities, from the start node to the end one, which takes the longest time. It is this which determines the minimum project duration time.

By constructing a table of earliest and latest start and finish times for each activity, *total float* and *free float* can be found for each one:

total float = latest start time − earliest start time
free float = earliest start time amongst *all* succeeding activities − earliest finish time.

Exercises on Chapter 25

1 Draw a network to represent the following project and hence determine the critical path and the minimum project completion time:

Activity	*Immediate Predecessors*	*Duration (days)*
A	NONE	5
B	NONE	4
C	A	3
D	B	2
E	C	2
F	C,D	4
G	E	1
H	F	2

2 An Operational Research Project consists of the following activities:

	Activities	*Duration (days)*
A	Preliminary meeting	1
B	Problem formulation	8
C	Plant visits	5
D	Data collection	14
E	Data analysis	10
F	Supplementary data	14
G	Preliminary notes	15
H	Model construction	11
J	Solution	5
K	Discussions	3
L	Devise operating rules	6
M	Draft report	18
N	Final report	12

Construct a network incorporating just the following sequence restrictions:

B to follow A	F to follow E	K to follow F and J
C to follow B	G to follow B	L to follow K
D to follow B	H to follow C and E	M to follow C, E and G
E to follow D	J to follow H	N to follow L and M

What is the critical path through the network? Give the least time to project completion.

3   A small building project consists of nine activities. The duration of each activity is shown in the table below:

Activity	Duration (days)
1– 2	8
1– 3	10
1–11	20
2– 8	5
3– 7	6
3– 8	8
7– 8	1
7–11	10
8–11	12

(a)   Draw a network for the project.
(b)   What are the critical activities and the minimum project completion time?
(c)   Draw up a table showing, for each activity:
   (i)   The earliest and latest start and finish times
   (ii)   The total and free float.

(d)   Considering each part (i–iv) separately, what would be the effect on the project completion time of:
   (i)   Activity 3–8 taking 11 days to complete instead of the estimated 8.
   (ii)   Activity 7–11 taking 15 days to complete instead of the estimated 10.
   (iii)   The start of activity 2–8 being delayed until day 12.
   (iv)   Activity 8–11 unexpectedly being completed by day 25.

4   Consider the following activities in a construction project with associated times and preceding activities:

Activity	Preceding Activities	Time in Days
A	–	7
B	–	10
C	–	5
D	A,B	8
E	B,C	9
F	C,D	12
G	D,E	14
H	F,G	6

What is the minimum time needed to complete this project? Why might the project in fact *not* take this time to complete?

ICMA, PEI, November 1982.

5 A production manager analyses one of the projects under his control as follows:

Activity	Immediate Predecessor(s)	Estimated Duration (weeks)
A	–	3
B	–	3
C	A	2
D	B	4
E	D	2
F	C,D	1
G	F	2
H	E,G	1
J	H	4
K	J	3
L	J	4
M	K,L	2

(a) Construct a network to represent this project and hence estimate the minimum time to complete the project.

(b) Explain the terms 'critical path' and 'dummy' in relation to *this* project. Why is it important to know the critical path?

(c) Explore ways in which the manager could use the network to help manage the project.

Solutions to numerical exercises

Chapter 2

1 (a) The line has equation $y = -3 + 2x$.

4 (a) C.
   (b) C.

6 (a) The equation is $y = 7.2 - 0.00033x$. (The gradient of the line, estimated from a graph, will only be approximately equal to -0.00033.)
   (b) The revenue function is

   $$\text{revenue} = 7.2x - 0.00033x^2.$$

Chapter 3

1 Accurate solutions from formulae:
   (a) $x = -1.5$.
   (b) $x = +1$ (the 'two' solutions coincide here).
   (c) no solutions (the graph does not cross the x-axis; the formula involves the square root of a negative number).

2 Revenue $= 80x - x^2$.
   Profit $= -200 + 60x - 1.1x^2$.
   The breakeven points are daily production of 4 units (price £76) and 51 units (price £29): the factory should aim its production/prices between the two limits.

3 £1.50.
   If the delivery charge was £25, the unit price would be £1.30.

4 (b) Revenue $= 35X - \dfrac{1}{20}X^2$.

(c)   Total Cost = 2000 + 10X.

(d)   Profit = − 2000 + 25X − $\frac{1}{20}X^2$.

Breakeven points are 100 units (price £30) and 400 units (price £15).

5   Profit = − 500 + 20x − 0.1x²
Breakeven points : x = 29 units and x = 171 units.

Profit = − 500 + 150x − x²
Breakeven points : x = 3 tons and x = 147 tons.

Profit = − 15000 + 5.4x − 0.000666x²
Breakeven points : x = 3561 units and x = 12641 units. (These answers are approximate since the revenue function, and therefore the profit function, arise from an approximate answer: see answer to exercise 6, Chapter 2.)

Chapter 4

1   (a) x = 3, y = 4.
    (b) x = 6, y = 4.
    (c) x = 3.5, y = 1 and x = − 4.5, y = 25.
    (d) x = 2.5, y = 8.75 (The 'two' solutions coincide in this case.)

2   100 units of X, 400 units of Y.

3   Each unit of X costs 63p, each unit of Y 82p.

4   A.

5   (a) The numbers are 7 and 12.
    (b) 25 metres by 32 metres.

6   250 units of A, 900 units of B.

Chapter 6

2   (d) The figure of £7,500 is exceeded 66 per cent of the time (approximation from ogive). The raw data would give a different answer because grouping into classes to draw the ogive loses precision. Also the graphical construction assumes the data are evenly spread throughout each class: this may not be the case.

3   (c) (i)   £30,000 to under £40,000 is the most popular range (the highest point on the histogram)
         (ii) 49 per cent sell for over £50,000
         (iii) The 20 per cent least expensive houses sell for less than

£33,000. (The last two answers are approximations from the ogive.)

5 (a)   15.2 per cent earn less than £5,000 p.a.
  (b)   46 men earn less than £5,000 p.a.

6 (b)   The highest 25 per cent salaries lie over £3,700.
      The highest 50 per cent salaries lie over £4,100.
      The highest 75 per cent salaries lie over £4,400.
      (All approximations from the ogive.)

Chapter 7

1 (a)   This continuous variable has no extreme values (little evidence of skewness and no open-ended classes), and so the mean is the most appropriate measure.
  (b)   Mean = 0.265.
  (c)   The mid-point has been taken as the most representative value in each class. To be a valid comparison, the sample of 100 should be representative of the sector of the economy.

2 (a)   To evaluate the mean, the open-ended classes have to be closed. The assumed closing values will affect the mean value, but not the median.
  (b)   Median turnover = £227,000. This value arises from a construction from an ogive, which assumes that the values are equally distributed throughout their respective classes.

3 (a)   Mean = 2.03 accidents reported per week, median = mode = 1 accident reported per week.
  (b)   The mean is the only measure which uses all the distribution: it is the long-term average weekly number of accidents. Average weekly cost = £1624.
  (c)   The median value of one accident is an appropriate representative figure, because of the extreme skewness in the distribution.

4 (i)   Mean = £13,510; median = £944
  (ii) Mean = £18,103; median = £3727. (All answers to nearest £.)

The mean in both cases has used the 'value of losses' as 'Σ fx' in the formula for the mean.

5 (i)   1.07 per unit
  (ii) 1.07 per unit. (Both answers to nearest .01.)

6 (i)   The mean is the most valid measure for use in further calculations
  (ii) Mean monthly value of orders = £330,000.

Chapter 8

1 (*a*) Factory F: mean = 2.03 accidents/week;
                  mean absolute deviation = 1.38 accidents/week.
       Factory G: mean = 2.04 accidents/week;
                  mean absolute deviation = 1.60 accidents/week.
   (*b*) Factory F: standard deviation = 1.73 accidents/week.
       Factory G: standard deviation = 2.03 accidents/week.

2 (*a*) Inter-quartile range = £18,000 (nearest £100).

3 (*a*) Mean = 37.325 minutes; standard deviation = 52.73 minutes;
       coefficient of variation = 141.3 per cent.

4 (*a*) The mean order size = £11.92, standard deviation = £8.07.
       (These values depend on the assumed closing value for the
       upper class.)
   (*b*) The coefficients of variation are April 67.7 per cent
                                          September 53.1 per cent.

Thus the average order size has increased from April to September,
while the amount of spread has decreased.

5 (*a*)   (i) Median earnings = £54.85
        (*ii*) Coefficient of variation = 24.2 per cent.

6   (*i*)   £150,000
     (*ii*)   £140,000
    (*iii*)   £140,000
     (*iv*)   £120,000
      (*v*)   £145,000
     (*vi*)   £12,500
    (*vii*)   £51,575
   (*viii*)   £30,000

Chapter 9

1   (*i*)   114.9
    (*ii*)   106.4
   (*iii*)   106.5.

2   (*i*)   58.2%
    (*ii*)   47.3%
   (*iii*)   122.3%.

3 (*a*) Real profits, at January 1973 prices:

	(*£ million equivalent*)
1983	65.0
1984	68.4
1985	72.0

   (*b*) £12.78.

4 (*b*)   134.

5 (*b*)   (*i*)   116.9
          (*ii*) 128.4.

6 (*c*)   16.1%.
  (*d*)   £1.704 million.
          £1.781 million.

Chapter 10

1 (*b*) $r = -0.964$.

2 (*a*) $r = +0.977$.

3 (*a*) $r' = +0.899$.

4 (*b*)   Pearson's $r = -0.871$.

6 Spearman's $r' = +0.821$.

Chapter 11

1 (*c*) $y = 1.14 + 1.96x$.

2 (*a*) y = revenue (£), x = number of salespersons:

          $y = 5856 + 1309x$.

          (*i*)   £25,500
          (*ii*) £18,900 (to nearest £100).

  (*b*)   (*i*)   £9,000
          (*ii*) £7,900.

3 y = % understrength items, x = % of element E:

          $y = 1.015 - 2.168x$.

   The forecast is that batch number 140 will produce 0.91% under-strength items.

4 (*c*)   Provided the cost-mileage relationship is similar in the new region, type L should be chosen, as the cost/extra mile is lower.
  (*d*)   The 'average' car will travel 12,000 miles (50 per cent higher than 8,000) and so $X = 12$

          substituted in $Y = 5.585 + 0.4697X$
          gives $Y = £1120$ (nearest £10).

   Thus, for five cars, the running costs will be £5600.

5 (*b*) $Y = 14.536 + 2.122X$.
  (*c*)   £14,500 (to nearest £100).
  (*d*)   £67,600.

6 (b) y = manufacturing costs, x = quantity produced

$y = 4.622 + 0.4796x$.

(c) £9,400 (to nearest £100).
(d) 3000 books (to nearest 100).

Chapter 12

1 (a) Answers rounded to nearest £000:

Forecast sales, period 55: £286,000
period 56: £251,000
period 57: £226,000
period 58: £219,000
period 59: £204,000
period 60: £189,000
period 61: £194,000
period 62: £208,000
period 63: £217,000
period 64: £230,000
period 65: £238,000
period 66: £287,000.

2 Forecasts, rounded to nearest £000: 1989 Q1: £58,000
Q2: £58,000
Q3: £72,000
Q4: £54,000

Values of I:

	Q1	Q2	Q3	Q4
1985	0.9928	0.9605	0.9820	0.9715
1986	0.9724	1.0300	1.0572	1.0535
1987	1.0348	1.0095	0.9607	0.9748

3 (a) $T = 7.65 + 0.609t$ (000 units).

(b) Values of S: Q1: 1.130
Q2: 0.879
Q3: 0.988
Q4: 1.004.

(c) To nearest 100 units: 1989 Q1: 23,100 units
Q2: 18,500 units
Q3: 21,400 units
Q4: 22,400 units
1990 Q1: 25,800 units
Q2: 20,600 units
Q3: 23,800 units
Q4: 24,800 units.

4 (b),(c)   Forecast *sales* : 1985. Q1: £288,000
                         Q2: £407,000
                         Q3: £532,000
                         Q4: £273,000.

5 (a) $T = 125.58 + 3.168t$ (1980 Q2: t = 1, etc.)

  (b)   Values of S: Q1: 0.939
                  Q2: 0.951
                  Q3: 0.967
                  Q4: 1.144

Forecast index, 1983 Q4: 198.

6 (a)   Values of seasonal component: Q1: 0.9342
                              Q2: 1.0612
                              Q3: 1.0389
                              Q4: 0.9485

  (b)   Forecast sales, to nearest £000: 1986 Q1: £516,000
                                    Q2: £597,000
                                    Q3: £596,000
                                    Q4: £555,000.

  (c)   Deseasonalized sales (nearest £000):

	Q1	Q2	Q3	Q4
1983	£428,000	£405,000	£472,000	£464,000
1984	£450,000	£504,000	£472,000	£485,000
1985	£514,000	£518,000	£510,000.	

Chapter 13

1 (a) $\dfrac{70}{88}$.

  (b) $\dfrac{39}{88}$.

  (c) $\dfrac{3}{88}$.

  (d) $\dfrac{74}{88}$.

  (e)   (i) $\dfrac{11}{39}$.

        (ii) $\dfrac{11}{18}$.

2 (b)   0.78.
  (c)   If it is dry *and* a profit is still not made. Probability = 0.08.

3 (b)   0.72.

4   (*i*) $\dfrac{800}{2200}$

    (*ii*) $\dfrac{500}{2200}$

    (*iii*) $\dfrac{1100}{2200}$.

5   (*i*)   0.496
    (*ii*)   0.398.

6   (*a*)   (*i*)   0.941192
         (*ii*)   0.000392
         (*iii*)   0.019208.

    (*b*)   0.683.

Chapter 14

1   (*b*)   0.28 rejects per batch.
    (*c*)   £2100.

2   (*b*)   (*i*)   A
         (*ii*)   C
         (*iii*)   B, with expected payoff of £2250.

3   (*b*)   Quote £2.60 per component. (If this is accepted, hire the new machinery.)

4   £1,250.

5

		Probability	0	100	200	300	400
	0	0.05	0	−10	−20	−30	−40
Daily	100	0.3	0	20	10	0	−10
demand	200	0.3	0	20	40	30	20
(loaves)	300	0.25	0	20	40	60	50
	400	0.1	0	20	40	60	80
Expected daily profit			0	£18.50	£28	£28.50	£21.50

Daily number of loaves produced

The bakery should produce 300 loaves per day.

6   15 cases (expected profit £10,500).

Chapter 15

1   (*b*)   (*i*)   0.027
         (*ii*)   0.189
         (*iii*)   0.441
         (*iv*)   0.343.

    (*c*) $\mu = 2.1$ contracts, $\sigma = 0.794$ contracts.

2 (*a*)   (*i*)   0.3660
          (*ii*)   0.3697
          (*iii*) 0.1849.
   (*b*)   0.0794.
   (*c*)   £59,550.

3 (*a*)   μ = 8 graduates, σ = 2.191 graduates.
   (*b*)   0.0160.

4 (*a*)   *p* (0 sixes) = 0.5787
          p (1 six)   = 0.3472
          p (2 sixes) = 0.0694
          p (3 sixes) = 0.0046.
   (*b*)   0.33696.

5 (*a*)   0.6778 (Note that this includes the possibility of nine or ten
          booked passengers arriving for the flight.)
   (*b*)   0.1209.

6 (*a*)   0.0086.

Chapter 16

1 (*a*)   *Number of ships arriving per day*   *p*
          0   0.3012
          1   0.3614
          2   0.2169
          3   0.0867
          4   0.0261
          5 or more   0.0077

   (*b*)   μ = 1.2 ships/day, σ = 1.095 ships/day.

2 (*a*)   0.6065.
   (*b*)   0.0821.
   (*c*)   0.0000, to 4 decimal places.
          54.38 per cent of weeks.
          If the rate reduces to 2.2 reported accidents/week, this value
          will increase to 62.27 per cent of weeks.

3 (*a*)   binomial: 0.3677
          Poisson: 0.3679.
   (*b*)   binomial: 0.0802
          Poisson: 0.0803.

4 (*a*) 0.2231.
   (*b*)   0.1912.
   (*c*)   0.1991.

5 (*a*)   0.6050.
   (*b*)   0.6065.

6   (*a*)   0.3679.
    (*b*)   0.2642.

Chapter 17

1   (*a*)   0.1056.
    (*b*)   £7,920.
    (*c*)   Probability increases to 0.413. Annual bonus payout increases to £30,100.

2   (*a*)   98.76%.
    (*b*)   0.00182 cm.

3   (*a*)   0.0475.
    (*b*)   1.00115 kg.
    (*c*)   1.15 kg (on average).

4   p (rope from A having breaking strength over 750 kg) = 0.9938,
    p (rope from B having breaking strength over 750 kg) = 0.9996.
    Choose supplier B.

5   (*a*)   46.9 hours.
    (*b*)   26%.

6   0.1056.

Chapter 18

1   (*a*)   150 ml.
    (*b*)   Between 149.95 ml and 150.05 ml.

2   (*a*)   Between £134.60 and £136.40.
    (*b*)   18,102 wage slips.

3   (*a*)   0.1125.
    (*b*)   Between 0.0906 and 0.1344.
    (*c*)   1705 such spot-checks. (This uses the earlier value of p, which has been found from a presumably reliable random sample).

4   (*a*) $\bar{x}$ = £11.92, s = £8.07.
    (*b*)   Between £10.60 and £13.24.

5   Assuming the 'suspected' proportion of 0.25 is reliable, 1,261 observations would be needed. Otherwise, 1,681 observations are needed. (Note that these answers arise from the z–value 1.64. Equally, a z–value of 1.65 could be used, giving answers of 1277 and 1702 respectively.)

Chapter 19

1 (c), (g), (j) and (l) cannot be found.

(a) $\begin{bmatrix} 2 & 0 \\ 1 & 2 \end{bmatrix}$ (b) $\begin{bmatrix} 0 & 2 & 3 \\ 3 & 1 & 1 \\ -1 & 0 & -2 \end{bmatrix}$ (d) $\begin{bmatrix} 5 & 10 & -5 \\ 0 & 0 & 15 \end{bmatrix}$

(e) $\begin{bmatrix} 5 & 4 & 6 \\ 6 & 7 & 2 \\ -2 & 0 & 1 \end{bmatrix}$ (f) $\begin{bmatrix} 1 & 2 & -1 \\ 1 & 2 & 2 \end{bmatrix}$

(h) $\begin{bmatrix} 8 & 6 & 10 \\ -3 & 0 & -3 \end{bmatrix}$ (i) $\begin{bmatrix} 1 & 0 \\ 2 & 1 \end{bmatrix}$ (k) $\begin{bmatrix} 1 & 0 \\ -1 & 1 \end{bmatrix}$

2 (a) $\begin{bmatrix} -2 & 2 \\ -1 & 0 \end{bmatrix}$ (b) $\begin{bmatrix} ½ & 0 \\ -½ & 1 \end{bmatrix}$ (c) $\begin{bmatrix} -1 & -1 \\ 0 & -1 \end{bmatrix}$

(d) $\begin{bmatrix} -½ & -½ \\ ½ & -½ \end{bmatrix}$ (e) $\begin{bmatrix} 0 & -1 \\ ½ & -1 \end{bmatrix}$

3 A.

4 (a) $P = \begin{bmatrix} 4 \\ 6 \\ 8 \\ 12 \end{bmatrix}$ (b) $R = TP = \begin{bmatrix} 4186 \\ 4744 \\ 4700 \end{bmatrix}$

(c) $H = \begin{bmatrix} 1 & 1 & 1 \\ 1.1 & 1.1 & 1.1 \\ 1 & 1.1 & 1.1 \end{bmatrix}$ $HR = \begin{bmatrix} 13630 \\ 14993 \\ 1457.4 \end{bmatrix}$

Chapter 20

1 (a) Minimum $z = 8$, at the point $(4,0)$.
   (b) Maximum $z = 22$, at the point $(1,5)$.
   (c) Maximum $z = 18$, at the points $(1,5)$ and $(6,0)$ and *all points between*.

2 (a) If x and y are the numbers of X and Y respectively:

$$18x + 6y \leq 54$$
$$100x + 100y \leq 600$$
$$x, y \geq 0.$$

Maximize $z = 100x + 50y$.
   (b) Buy in 1.5 units of X and 4.5 units of Y, giving a maximum net profit of £375. This solution, involving '0.5 units' is impractical: the owner would have to buy in some combination such as 1 unit of X, 5 units of Y, giving a profit of £350.

3 The graphical solution is to buy 56.25 type S tables and 26.25 type T tables. In practice, he would have to buy a combination such as 56 of type S and 26 of type T, at a total cost of £10,540.

4 $(c),(d)$ The maximum daily profit £338.50, obtained by producing 113 boxes of A and 282 boxes of B per day.

5 $(c),(d)$ Maximum production is 3900 sheets per minute, if 18 type X

and 4 type Y presses are bought.

6 $(c),(d)$ The maximum contribution is £170 per day, obtained by producing 15 tables and 25 chairs per day.

Chapter 21

1     $\dfrac{dy}{dx}$:   gradient at $x = -1$:

   (a) $10x^4$ 10.
   (b) $9x^2 + 36x^5$ $-27.$
   (c) $4 + 4x$ 0.
   (d) 6   6.
   (e) $1 + \dfrac{5}{x^2}$ 6.

2 (a) $P = -15,000 + 900x - 3x^2$.
       This is maximized at $x = 150$ units.

   (b) $U = \dfrac{15,000}{x} + 200 + 2x$.

       This is minimized at $x = 87$ units.

3 (b) $x = 8.33$ cm.

4   Annual revenue $= 441x - 0.8x^2$.
   Annual profit $= -31,500 + 435x - 0.87x^2$.
   Maximum annual profit $= £22,875$ when $x = 250$ units, at which point the unit selling price is £241.

5 (b) $x = 25\%$.

6 (a) $x = 25$ units at price £82/unit
   (b) $x = 25 - \dfrac{t}{6.08}$ units at price £$(82 + \dfrac{3t}{6.08})$/unit.

Chapter 22

1 (a) (i) £4,763 (to nearest £)
        (ii) £4,731.

   (b)   £2,699.

2 (a)   £261.62.
   (b)   £275.06.

3 (a)   11.26%.

Death after (years)	Building Society Received during Year (£):	Building Society Amount remaining (£):	Annuity Received during year (£):
1	2,252	19,167.84	2,252
2	2,252	18,269.11	2,252
3	2,252	17,298.48	2,252
4	2,252	16,250.19	2,252
5	2,252	15,118.05	2,252
6	2,252	13,895.33	2,252
7	2,252	12,574.80	2,252
8	2,252	11,148.62	2,252
9	2,252	9,608.35	2,252
10	2,252	7,944.86	2,252
11	2,252	6,148.29	2,252
12	2,252	4,207.99	2,252
13	2,252	2,112.47	2,252
14	2,112.47	–	2,252
15	–	–	2,252

4 (a) A = £205.676 (nearest £).
         Effective annual rate = 10.25%.
   (b) B = £45,244.

5 (a)   (i)   £196,386
         (ii) 12.551%.

   (b)   £156,570.

6 (a)   £32,923.44.
   (b)   54.27%.
   (c)   38 quarters (9½ years).

Chapter 23

1 From first principles: (a)   £396.92.
                          (b)   £6,340.11.
                          (c)   £2,917.54.
                          (d)   £394.25.

2 (a)   NPV (X) = £19,100
         NPV (Y) = £18,950.
   (c)   NPV (X) = £19,000
         NPV (Y) = £18,750.

3   NPV (offer 1) = £475
    NPV (offer 2) = £350
    NPV (offer 3) = £535.

4   Option (b) is most economical, with NPV (cost) = £444,400.

5   (a)   NPV (A) = £32,500
          NPV (B) = £21,500.
    (b)   The minimum inflows, following the pattern of A, for C to be
          preferable to B are (£000):

Year:	1987	1988	1989	1990	1991
Inflow:	48.3	96.6	193.2	96.6	48.3

6   (a)   B is best, with NPV = £5,100.
    (b)   C is worst, with NPV = £4,260.

Chapter 24

1   EOQ = 500 units, giving an annual saving of £125.

2   EBQ = 258.2, say 250 units. Annual saving = £825.

3   (a)   EOQ = 219.1, say 200 packets.
    (b)   When 4 weeks' supply (i.e. 83 packets) are left in stock.
    (c)   £110.

4   EBQ = 2000 units (24 orders/annum):

Number of orders	X	Y	Order cost (£)	Holding cost (£)	Total (£)
20	2400	1200	1000	1440	2440
24	2000	1000	1200	1200	2400
40	1200	600	2000	720	2720
60	800	400	3000	480	3480
80	600	300	4000	360	4360
100	480	240	5000	288	5288

(Based on an assumption of 48 weeks/year.)

Chapter 25

1   Critical path: ACFH
    Minimum project duration time = 14 days.

2   Critical path: ABDEHJKLN
    Minimum project duration time = 70 days.

3

Activity	Duration	Earliest		Latest		Float	
		Start	Finish	Start	Finish	Total	Free
1– 2	8	0	8	5	13	5	0
1– 3	10	0	10	0	10	0	0
1–11	20	0	20	10	30	10	10
2– 8	5	8	13	13	18	5	5
3– 7	6	10	16	11	17	1	0
3– 8	8	10	18	10	18	0	0
7– 8	1	16	17	17	18	1	1
7–11	10	16	26	20	30	4	4
8–11	12	18	30	18	30	0	0

Critical path: 1–3, 3–8, 8–11.
Minimum project completion time = 30 days.

(d)   (i)   Project completion time increases by 1 day
      (ii) Project completion time increases by 1 day; new critical
            path
      (iii) No effect at all
      (iv) Project completion time decreases by 4 days; new critical
            path.

4   Minimum time = 39 days.

5   (a)   Minimum time to complete = 23 days.

Appendix 1

Area under the normal curve

This table gives the area under the normal curve between the mean and a point x standard deviation above the mean. The corresponding area for deviations below the mean can be found by symmetry.

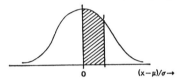

$\dfrac{x-\mu}{\sigma}$	0.00	0.01	0.02	0.03	0.04	0.05	0.06	0.07	0.08	0.09
0.0	.0000	.0040	.0080	.0120	.0159	.0199	.0239	.0279	.0319	0389
0.1	.0398	.0438	.0478	.0517	.0557	.0596	.0636	.0675	.0714	0753
0.2	.0793	.0832	.0871	.0910	.0948	.0987	.1026	.1064	.1103	1141
0.3	.1179	.1217	.1255	.1293	.1331	.1368	.1406	.1443	.1480	1517
0.4	.1554	.1591	.1628	.1664	.1700	.1736	.1772	.1808	.1844	1879
0.5	.1915	.1950	.1985	.2019	.2054	.2088	.2123	.2157	.2190	2224
0.6	.2257	.2291	.2324	.2357	.2389	.2422	.2454	.2486	.2618	2549
0.7	.2580	.2611	.2642	.2673	.2704	.2734	.2764	.2794	.2823	2852
0.8	.2881	.2910	.2939	.2967	.2995	.3023	.3051	.3078	.3106	3133
0.9	.3159	.3186	.3212	.3238	.3264	.3289	.3315	.3340	.3365	3389
1.0	.3413	.3438	.3461	.3485	.3508	.3531	.3554	.3577	.3599	3621
1.1	.3643	.3665	.3686	.3708	.3729	.3749	.3770	.3790	.3810	3830
1.2	.3849	.3869	.3888	.3907	.3925	.3944	.3962	.3980	.3997	4015
1.3	.4032	.4049	.4066	.4082	.4099	.4115	.4131	.4147	.4162	4197
1.4	.4192	.4207	.4222	.4236	.4251	.4265	.4279	.4292	.4306	4319
1.5	.4332	.4345	.4357	.4370	.4382	.4394	.4406	.4418	.4430	4441
1.6	.4452	.4463	.4474	.4485	.4495	.4505	.4515	.4525	.4535	4545
1.7	.4554	.4564	.4573	.4582	.4591	.4599	.4608	.4616	.4625	4633
1.8	.4641	.4649	.4656	.4664	.4671	.4678	.4686	.4693	.4699	4706
1.9	.4713	.4719	.4726	.4732	.4738	.4744	.4750	.4756	.4762	4767
2.0	.4772	.4778	.4783	.4788	.4793	.4798	.4803	.4808	.4812	4817
2.1	.4821	.4826	.4830	.4834	.4838	.4842	.4846	.4850	.4854	4857
2.2	.4861	.4865	.4868	.4871	.4875	.4878	.4881	.4884	.4887	4890
2.3	.4893	.4896	.4898	.4901	.4904	.4906	.4909	.4911	.4913	4916
2.4	.4918	.4920	.4922	.4925	.4927	.4929	.4931	.4932	.4934	4936
2.5	.4938	.4940	.4941	.4943	.4945	.4946	.4948	.4949	.4951	4952
2.6	.4953	.4955	.4956	.4957	.4959	.4960	.4961	.4962	.4963	4964
2.7	.4965	.4966	.4967	.4968	.4969	.4970	.4971	.4972	.4973	4974
2.8	.4974	.4975	.4976	.4977	.4977	.4978	.4979	.4980	.4980	4981
2.9	.4981	.4982	.4983	.4983	.4984	.4984	.4985	.4985	.4986	4986
3.0	.49865	.4987	.4987	.4988	.4988	.4989	.4989	.4989	.4990	4990
3.1	.49903	.4991	.4991	.4991	.4992	.4992	.4992	.4992	.4993	4993
3.2	.49931	.4993	.4994	.4994	.4994	.4994	.4994	.4995	.4995	4995
3.3	.49952	.4995	.4995	.4996	.4996	.4996	.4996	.4996	.4996	4997
3.4	.49966	.4997	.4997	.4997	.4997	.4997	.4997	.4997	.4997	4998
3.5	.49977									

The Poisson distribution

χ	*m* 0.1	0.2	0.3	0.4	0.5	0.6	0.7	0.8	0.9	1.0
0	.9048	.8187	.7408	.6703	.6065	.5488	.4966	.4493	.4066	.3679
1	.0905	.1637	.2222	.2681	.3033	.3293	.3476	.3595	.3659	.3679
2	.0045	.0164	.0333	.0536	.0758	.0988	.1217	.1438	.1647	.1839
3	.0002	.0011	.0033	.0072	.0126	.0198	.0284	.0383	.0494	.0613
4	.0000	.0001	.0002	.0007	.0016	.0030	.0050	.0077	.0111	.0153
5	.0000	.0000	.0000	.0001	.0002	.0004	.0007	.0012	.0020	.0031
6	.0000	.0000	.0000	.0000	.0000	.0000	.0001	.0002	.0003	.0005
7	.0000	.0000	.0000	.0000	.0000	.0000	.0000	.0000	.0000	.0001

χ	*m* 1.1	1.2	1.3	1.4	1.5	1.6	1.7	1.8	1.9	2.0
0	.3329	.3012	.2725	.2466	2231	.2019	.1827	.1653	.1496	.1353
1	.3662	.3614	.3543	.3452	.3347	.3230	.3106	.2975	.2842	.2707
2	.2014	.2169	.2303	.2417	.2510	.2584	.2640	.2678	.2700	.2707
3	.0738	.0867	.0998	.1128	.1255	.1378	.1496	.1607	.1710	.1804
4	.0203	.0260	.0324	.0395	.0471	.0551	.0636	.0723	.0812	.0902
5	.0045	.0062	.0084	.0111	.0141	.0176	.0216	.0260	.0309	.0361
6	.0008	.0012	.0018	.0026	.0035	.0047	.0061	.0078	.0098	.0120
7	.0001	.0002	.0003	.0005	.0008	.0011	.0015	.0020	.0027	.0034
8	.0000	.0000	.0001	.0001	.0001	.0002	.0003	.0005	.0006	.0009
9	.0000	.0000	.0000	.0000	.0000	.0000	.0001	.0001	.0001	0002

χ	*m* 2.1	2.2	2.3	2.4	2.5	2.6	2.7	2.8	2.9	3.0
0	.1225	.1108	.1003	.0907	.0821	.0743	.0672	.0608	.0550	.0498
1	.2572	.2438	.2306	.2177	.2052	.1931	.1815	.1703	.1596	.1494
2	.2700	.2681	.2652	.2613	.2565	.2510	.2450	.2384	.2314	.2240
3	.1890	.1966	.2033	.2090	.2138	.2176	.2205	.2225	.2237	.2240
4	.0992	.1082	.1169	.1254	.1336	.1414	.1488	.1557	.1622	.1680
5	.0417	.0476	.0538	.0602	.0668	.0735	.0804	.0872	.0940	.1008
6	.0146	.0174	.0206	.0241	.0278	.0319	.0362	.0407	.0455	.0504
7	.0044	.0055	.0068	.0083	.0099	.0118	.0139	.0163	.0188	.0216
8	.0011	.0015	.0019	.0025	.0031	.0038	.0047	.0057	.0068	.0081
9	.0003	.0004	.0005	.0007	.0009	.0011	.0014	.0018	.0022	.0027
10	.0001	.0001	.0001	.0002	.0002	.0003	.0004	.0005	.0006	.0008
11	.0000	.0000	.0000	.0000	.0000	.0001	.0001	.0001	.0002	.0002
12	.0000	.0000	.0000	.0000	.0000	.0000	.0000	.0000	.0000	.0001

					m					
χ	3.1	3.2	3.3	3.4	3.5	3.6	3.7	3.8	3.9	4.0
0	.0450	.0408	.0369	.0334	.0302	.0273	.0247	.0224	.0202	.0183
1	.1397	.1304	.1217	.1135	.1057	.0984	.0915	.0850	.0789	.0733
2	.2165	.2087	.2008	.1929	.1850	.1771	.1692	.1615	.1539	.1465
3	.2237	.2226	.2209	.2186	.2158	.2125	.2087	.2046	.2001	.1954
4	.1734	.1781	.1823	.1858	.1888	.1912	.1931	.1944	.1951	.1954
5	.1075	.1140	.1203	.1264	.1322	.1377	.1429	.1477	.1522	.1563
6	.0555	.0608	.0662	.0716	.0771	.0826	.0881	.0936	.0989	.1042
7	.0246	.0278	.0312	.0348	.0385	.0425	.0466	.0508	.0551	.0595
8	.0095	.0111	.0129	.0148	.0169	.0191	.0215	.0241	.0269	.0298
9	.0033	.0040	.0047	.0056	.0066	.0076	.0089	.0102	.0116	.0132
10	.0010	.0013	.0016	.0019	.0023	.0028	.0033	.0039	.0045	.0053
11	.0003	.0004	.0005	.0006	.0007	.0009	.0011	.0013	.0016	.0019
12	.0001	.0001	.0001	.0002	.0002	.0003	.0003	.0004	.0005	.0006
13	.0000	.0000	.0000	.0000	.0001	.0001	.0001	.0001	.0002	.0002
14	.0000	.0000	.0000	.0000	.0000	.0000	.0000	.0000	.0000	.0001

					m					
χ	4.1	4.2	4.3	4.4	4.5	4.6	4.7	4.8	4.9	5.0
0	.0166	.0150	.00136	.0123	.0111	.0101	.0091	.0082	.0074	.0067
1	.0679	.0630	.0583	.0540	.0500	.0462	.0427	.0395	.0365	.0337
2	.1393	.1323	.1254	.1188	.1125	.1063	.1005	.0948	.0894	.0842
3	.1904	.1852	.1798	.1743	.1687	.1631	.1574	.1517	.1460	.1404
4	.1951	.1944	.1933	.1917	.1898	.1875	.1849	.1820	.1789	.1755
5	.1600	.1633	.1662	.1687	.1708	.1725	.1738	.1747	.1753	.1755
6	.1093	.1143	.1191	.1237	.1281	.1323	.1362	.1398	.1432	.1462
7	.0640	.0686	.0732	.0778	.0824	.0869	.0914	.0959	.1002	.1044
8	.0328	.0360	.0393	.0428	.0463	.0500	.0537	.0575	.0614	.0653
9	.0150	.0168	.0188	.0209	.0232	.0255	.0280	.0307	.0334	.0363
10	.0061	.0071	.0081	.0092	.0104	.0118	.0132	.0147	.0164	.0181
11	.0023	.0027	.0032	.0037	.0043	.0049	.0056	.0064	.0073	.0082
12	.0008	.0009	.0011	.0014	.0016	.0019	.0022	.0026	.0030	.0034
13	.0002	.0003	.0004	.0005	.0006	.0007	.0008	.0009	.0011	.0013
14	.0001	.0001	.0001	.0001	.0002	.0002	.0003	.0003	.0004	.0005
15	.0000	.0000	.0000	.0000	.0001	.0001	.0001	.0001	.0001	.0002

χ	5.1	5.2	5.3	5.4	*m* 5.5	5.6	5.7	5.8	5.9	6.0
0	.0061	.0055	.0050	.0045	.0041	.0037	.0033	.0030	.0027	.0025
1	.0311	.0287	.0265	.0244	.0225	.0207	.0191	.0176	.0162	.0149
2	.0793	.0746	.0701	.0659	.0618	.0580	.0544	.0509	.0477	.0446
3	.1348	.1293	.1239	.1185	.1133	.1082	.1033	.0985	.0938	.0892
4	.1719	.1681	.1641	.1600	.1558	.1515	.1472	.1428	.1383	.1339
5	.1753	.1748	.1740	.1728	.1714	.1697	.1678	.1656	.1632	.1606
6	.1490	.1515	.1537	.1555	.1571	.1584	.1594	.1601	.1605	.1606
7	.1086	.1125	.1163	.1200	.1234	.1267	.1298	.1326	.1353	.1377
8	.0692	.0731	.0771	.0810	.0849	.0887	.0925	.0962	.0998	.1033
9	.0392	.0423	.0454	.0486	.0519	.0552	.0586	.0620	.0654	.0688
10	.0200	.0220	.0241	.0262	.0285	.0309	.0334	.0359	.0386	.0413
11	.0093	.0104	.0116	.0129	.0143	.0157	.0173	.0190	.0207	.0225
12	.0039	.0045	.0051	.0058	.0065	.0073	.0082	.0092	.0102	.0113
13	.0015	.0018	.0021	.0024	.0028	.0032	.0036	.0041	.0046	.0052
14	.0006	.0007	.0008	.0009	.0011	.0013	.0015	.0017	.0019	.0022
15	.0002	.0002	.0003	.0003	.0004	.0005	.0006	.0007	.0008	.0009
16	.0001	.0001	.0001	.0001	.0001	.0002	.0002	.0002	.0003	.0003
17	.0000	.0000	.0000	.0000	.0000	.0001	.0001	.0001	.0001	.0001

χ	6.1	6.2	6.3	6.4	*m* 6.5	6.6	6.7	6.8	6.9	7.0
0	.0022	.0020	.0018	.0017	.0015	.0014	.0012	.0011	.0010	.0009
1	.0137	.0126	.0116	.0106	.0098	.0090	.0082	.0076	.0070	.0064
2	.0417	.0390	.0364	.0340	.0318	.0296	.0276	.0258	.0240	.0223
3	.0848	.0806	.0765	.0726	.0688	.0652	.0617	.0584	.0552	.0521
4	.1294	.1249	.1205	.1162	.1118	.1076	.1034	.0992	.0952	.0912
5	.1579	.1549	.1519	.1487	.1454	.1420	.1385	.1349	.1314	.1277
6	.1605	.1601	.1595	.1586	.1575	.1562	.1546	.1529	.1511	.1490
7	.1399	.1418	.1435	.1450	.1462	.1472	.1480	.1486	.1489	.1490
8	.1066	.1099	.1130	.1160	.1188	.1215	.1240	.1263	.1284	.1304
9	.0723	.0757	.0791	.0825	.0858	.0891	.0923	.0954	.0985	.1014
10	.0441	.0469	.0498	.0528	.0558	.0588	.0618	.0649	.0679	.0710
11	.0245	.0265	.0285	.0307	.0330	.0353	.0377	.0401	.0426	.0452
12	.0124	.0137	.0150	.0164	.0179	.0194	.0210	.0227	.0245	.0264
13	.0058	.0065	.0073	.0081	.0089	.0098	.0108	.0119	.0130	.0142
14	.0025	.0029	.0033	.0037	.0041	.0046	.0052	.0058	.0064	.0071
15	.0010	.0012	.0014	.0016	.0018	.0020	.0023	.0026	.0029	.0033
16	.0004	.0005	.0005	.0006	.0007	.0008	.0010	.0011	.0013	.0014
17	.0001	.0002	.0002	.0002	.0003	.0003	.0004	.0004	.0005	.0006
18	.0000	.0001	.0001	.0001	.0001	.0001	.0001	.0002	.0002	.0002
19	.0000	.0000	.0000	.0000	.0000	.0000	.0000	.0001	.0001	.0001

χ	7.1	7.2	7.3	7.4	*m* 7.5	7.6	7.7	7.8	7.9	8.0
0	.0008	.0007	.0007	.0006	.0006	.0005	.0005	.0004	.0004	.0003
1	.0059	.0054	.0049	.0045	.0041	.0038	.0035	.0032	.0029	.0027
2	.0208	.0194	.0180	.0167	.0156	.0145	.0134	.0125	.0116	.0107
3	.0492	.0464	.0438	.0413	.0389	.0366	.0345	.0324	.0305	.0286
4	.0874	.0836	.0799	.0764	.0729	.0696	.0663	.0632	.0602	.0573
5	.1241	.1204	.1167	.1130	.1094	.1057	.1021	.0986	.0951	.0916
6	.1468	.1445	.1420	.1394	.1367	.1339	.1311	.1282	.1252	.1221
7	.1489	.1486	.1481	.1474	.1465	.1454	.1442	.1428	.1413	.1396
8	.1321	.1337	.1351	.1363	.1373	.1382	.1388	.1392	.1395	.1396
9	.1042	.1070	.1096	.1121	.1144	.1167	.1187	.1207	.1224	.1241
10	.0740	.0770	.0800	.0829	.0858	.0887	.0914	.0941	.0967	.0993
11	.0478	.0504	.0531	.0558	.0585	.0613	.0640	.0667	.0695	.0722
12	.0283	.0303	.0323	.0344	.0366	.0388	.0411	.0434	.0457	0.481
13	.0154	.0168	.0181	.0196	.0211	.0227	.0243	.0260	.0278	.0296
14	.0078	.0086	.0095	.0104	.0113	.0123	.0134	.0145	.0157	.0169
15	.0037	.0041	.0046	.0051	.0057	.0062	.0069	.0075	.0083	.0090
16	.0016	.0019	.0021	.0024	.0026	.0030	.0033	.0037	.0041	.0045
17	.0007	.0008	.0009	.0010	.0012	.0013	.0015	.0017	.0019	.0021
18	.0003	.0003	.0004	.0004	.0005	.0006	.0006	.0007	.0008	.0009
19	.0001	.0001	.0001	.0002	.0002	.0002	.0003	.0003	.0003	.0004
20	.0000	.0000	.0001	.0001	.0001	.0001	.0001	.0001	.0001	.0002
21	.0000	.0000	.0000	.0000	.0000	.0000	.0000	.0000	.0001	.0001

χ	8.1	8.2	8.3	8.4	*m* 8.5	8.6	8.7	8.8	8.9	9.0
0	.0003	.0003	.0002	.0002	.0002	.0002	.0002	.0002	.0001	.0001
1	.0025	.0023	.0021	.0019	.0017	.0016	.0014	.0013	.0012	.0011
2	.0100	.0092	.0086	.0079	.0074	.0068	.0063	.0058	.0054	.0050
3	.0269	.0252	.0237	.0222	.0208	.0195	.0183	.0171	.0160	.0150
4	.0544	.0517	.0491	.0466	.0443	.0420	.0398	.0377	.0357	.0337
5	.0882	.0849	.0816	.0784	.0752	.0722	.0692	.0663	.0635	.0607
6	.1191	.1160	.1128	.1097	.1066	.1034	.1003	.0972	.0941	.0911
7	.1378	.1358	.1338	.1317	.1294	.1271	.1247	.1222	.1197	.1171
8	.1395	.1392	.1388	.1382	.1375	.1366	.1356	.1344	.1332	.1318
9	.1256	.1269	.1280	.1290	.1299	.1306	.1311	.1315	.1317	.1318
10	.1017	.1040	.1063	.1084	.1104	.1123	.1140	.1157	.1172	.1186
11	.0749	.0776	.0802	.0828	.0853	.0878	.0902	.0925	.0948	.0970
12	.0505	.0530	.0555	.0579	.0604	.0629	.0654	.0679	.0703	.0728
13	.0315	.0334	.0354	.0374	.0395	.0416	.0438	.0459	.0481	.0504
14	.0182	.0196	.0210	.0225	.0240	.0256	.0272	.0289	.0306	.0324

χ	8.1	8.2	8.3	8.4	*m* 8.5	8.6	8.7	8.8	8.9	9.0
15	.0098	.0107	.0116	.0126	.0136	.0147	.0158	.0169	.0182	.0194
16	.0050	.0055	.0060	.0066	.0072	.0079	.0086	.0093	.0101	.0109
17	.0024	.0026	.0029	.0033	.0036	.0040	.0044	.0048	.0053	.0058
18	.0011	.0012	.0014	.0015	.0017	.0019	.0021	.0024	.0026	.0029
19	.0005	.0005	.0006	.0007	.0008	.0009	.0010	.0011	.0012	.0014
20	.0002	.0002	.0002	.0003	.0003	.0004	.0004	.0005	.0005	.0006
21	.0001	.0001	.0001	.0001	.0001	.0002	.0002	.0002	.0002	.0003
22	.0000	.0000	.0000	.0000	.0001	.0001	.0001	.0001	.0001	.0001

χ	9.1	9.2	9.3	9.4	*m* 9.5	9.6	9.7	9.8	9.9	10
0	.0001	.0001	.0001	.0001	.0001	.0001	.0001	.0001	.0001	.0000
1	.0010	.0009	.0009	.0008	.0007	.0007	.0006	.0005	.0005	.0005
2	.0046	.0043	.0040	.0037	.0034	.0031	.0029	.0027	.0025	.0023
3	.0140	.0131	.0123	.0115	.0107	.0100	.0093	.0087	.0081	.0076
4	.0319	.0302	.0285	.0269	.0254	.0240	.0226	.0213	.0201	.0189
5	.0581	.0555	.0530	.0506	.0483	.0460	.0439	.0418	.0398	.0378
6	.0881	.0851	.0822	.0793	.0764	.0736	.0709	.0682	.0656	.0631
7	.1145	.1118	.1091	.1064	.1037	.1010	.0982	.0955	.0928	.0901
8	.1302	.1286	.1269	.1251	.1232	.1212	.1191	.1170	.1148	.1126
9	.1317	.1315	.1311	.1306	.1300	.1293	.1284	.1274	.1263	.1251
10	.1198	.1210	.1219	.1228	.1235	.1241	.1245	.1249	.1250	.1251
11	.0991	.1012	.1031	.1049	.1067	.1083	.1098	.1112	.1125	.1137
12	.0752	.0776	.0799	.0822	.0844	.0866	.0888	.0908	.0928	.0948
13	.0526	.0549	.0572	.0594	.0617	.0640	.0662	.0685	.0707	.0729
14	.0342	.0361	.0380	.0399	.0419	.0439	.0459	.0479	.0500	.0521
15	.0208	.0221	.0235	.0250	.0265	.0281	.0297	.0313	.0330	.0347
16	.0118	.0127	.0137	.0147	.0157	.0168	.0180	.0192	.0204	.0217
17	.0063	.0069	.0075	.0081	.0088	.0095	.0103	.0111	.0119	.0128
18	.0032	.0035	.0039	.0042	.0046	.0051	.0055	.0060	.0065	.0071
19	.0015	.0017	.0019	.0021	.0023	.0026	.0028	.0031	.0034	.0037
20	.0007	.0008	.0009	.0010	.0011	.0012	.0014	.0015	.0017	.0019
21	.0003	.0003	.0004	.0004	.0005	.0006	.0006	.0007	.0008	.0009
22	.0001	.0001	.0002	.0002	.0002	.0002	.0003	.0003	.0004	.0004
23	.0000	.0001	.0001	.0001	.0001	.0001	.0001	.0001	.0002	.0002
24	.0000	.0000	.0000	.0000	.0000	.0000	.0000	.0001	.0001	.0001

χ	11	12	13	14	m 15	16	17	18	19	20
0	.0000	.0000	.0000	.0000	.0000	.0000	.0000	.0000	.0000	.0000
1	.0002	.0001	.0000	.0000	.0000	.0000	.0000	.0000	.0000	.0000
2	.0010	.0004	.0002	.0001	.0000	.0000	.0000	.0000	.0000	.0000
3	.0037	.0018	.0008	.0004	.0002	.0001	.0000	.0000	.0000	.0000
4	.0102	.0053	.0027	.0013	.0006	.0003	.0001	.0001	.0000	.0000
5	.0224	.0127	.0070	.0037	.0019	.0010	.0005	.0002	.0001	.0001
6	.0411	.0255	.0152	.0087	.0048	.0026	.0014	.0007	.0004	.0002
7	.0646	.0437	.0281	.0174	.0104	.0060	.0034	.0018	.0010	.0005
8	.0888	.0655	.0457	.0304	.0194	.0120	.0072	.0042	.0024	.0013
9	.1085	.0874	.0661	.0473	.0324	.0213	.0135	.0083	.0050	.0029
10	.1194	.1048	.0859	.0663	.0486	.0341	.0230	.0150	.0095	.0058
11	.1194	.1144	.1015	.0844	.0663	.0496	.0355	.0245	.0164	.0106
12	.1094	.1144	.1099	.0984	.0829	.0661	.0504	.0368	.0259	.0176
13	.0926	.1056	.1099	.1060	.0956	.0814	.0658	.0509	.0378	.0271
14	.0728	.0905	.1021	.1060	.1024	.0930	.0800	.0655	.0514	.0387
15	.0534	.0724	.0885	.0989	.1024	.0992	.0906	.0786	.0650	.0516
16	.0367	.0543	.0719	.0866	.0960	.0992	.0963	.0884	.0772	.0646
17	.0237	.0383	.0550	.0713	.0847	.0934	.0963	.0936	.0863	.0760
18	.0145	.0256	.0397	.0554	.0706	.0830	.0909	.0936	.0911	.0844
19	.0084	.0161	.0272	.0409	.0557	.0699	.0814	.0887	.0911	.0888
20	.0046	.0097	.0177	.0286	.0418	.0559	.0692	.0798	.0866	.0888
21	.0024	.0055	.0109	.0191	.0299	.0426	.0560	.0684	.0783	.0846
22	.0012	.0030	.0065	.0121	.0204	.0310	.0433	.0560	.0676	.0769
23	.0006	.0016	.0037	.0074	.0133	.0216	.0320	.0438	.0559	.0669
24	.0003	.0008	.0020	.0043	.0083	.0144	.0226	.0328	.0442	.0557
25	.0001	.0004	.0010	.0024	.0050	.0092	.0154	.0237	.0336	.0446
26	.0000	.0002	.0005	.0013	.0029	.0057	.0101	.0164	.0246	.0343
27	.0000	.0001	.0002	.0007	.0016	.0034	.0063	.0109	.0173	.0254
28	.0000	.0000	.0001	.0003	.0009	.0019	.0038	.0070	.0117	.0181
29	.0000	.0000	.0001	.0002	.0004	.0011	.0023	.0044	.0077	.0125
30	.0000	.0000	.0000	.0001	.0002	.0006	.0013	.0026	.0049	.0083
31	.0000	.0000	.0000	.0000	.0001	.0003	.0007	.0015	.0030	.0054
32	.0000	.0000	.0000	.0000	.0001	.0001	.0004	.0009	.0018	.0034
33	.0000	.0000	.0000	.0000	.0000	.0001	.0002	.0005	.0010	.0020
34	.0000	.0000	.0000	.0000	.0000	.0000	.0001	.0002	.0006	.0012
35	.0000	.0000	.0000	.0000	.0000	.0000	.0000	.0001	.0003	.0007
36	.0000	.0000	.0000	.0000	.0000	.0000	.0000	.0001	.0002	.0004
37	.0000	.0000	.0000	.0000	.0000	.0000	.0000	.0000	.0001	.0002
38	.0000	.0000	.0000	.0000	.0000	.0000	.0000	.0000	.0000	.0001
39	.0000	.0000	.0000	.0000	.0000	.0000	.0000	.0000	.0000	.0001

Entries in the table give the probabilities that an event will occur χ times when the average number of occurrences is m.

Binomial coefficients

r:	0	1	2	3	4	5	6	7	8	9	10
n=1	1	1									
2	1	2	1								
3	1	3	3	1							
4	1	4	6	4	1						
5	1	5	10	10	5	1					
6	1	6	15	20	15	6	1				
7	1	7	21	35	35	21	7	1			
8	1	8	28	56	70	56	28	8	1		
9	1	9	36	84	126	126	84	36	9	1	
10	1	10	45	120	210	252	210	120	45	10	1
11	1	11	55	165	330	462	462	330	165	55	11
12	1	12	66	220	495	792	924	792	495	220	66
13	1	13	78	286	715	1287	1716	1716	1287	715	286
14	1	14	91	364	1001	2002	3003	3432	3003	2002	1001
15	1	15	105	455	1365	3003	5005	6435	6435	5005	3003
16	1	16	120	560	1820	4368	8008	11440	12870	11440	8008
17	1	17	136	680	2380	6188	12376	19448	24310	24310	19448
18	1	18	153	816	3060	8568	18564	31824	43758	48620	43758
19	1	19	171	969	3876	11628	27132	50388	75582	92378	92378
20	1	20	190	1140	4845	15504	38760	77520	125970	167960	184756

Example: $(a + b)^4 = a^4 + 4a^3b + 6a^2b^2 + 4ab^3 + b^4$

Present value of £1

The table shows the value today of £1 to be received or paid after a given number of years $Vn \cdot r = (1 + r)^{-n}$

At rate r / After n years	1%	2%	3%	4%	5%	6%	7%	8%	9%	10%	11%	12%
1	.99	.98	.97	.96	.95	.94	.93	.93	.92	.91	.90	.89
2	.98	.96	.94	.92	.91	.89	.87	.86	.84	.83	.81	.80
3	.97	.94	.92	.89	.86	.84	.82	.79	.77	.75	.73	.71
4	.96	.92	.89	.85	.82	.79	.76	.74	.71	.68	.66	.64
5	.95	.91	.86	.82	.78	.75	.71	.68	.65	.62	.59	.57
6	.94	.89	.84	.79	.75	.70	.67	.63	.60	.56	.53	.51
7	.93	.87	.81	.76	.71	.67	.62	.58	.55	.51	.48	.45
8	.92	.85	.79	.73	.68	.63	.58	.54	.50	.47	.43	.40
9	.91	.84	.77	.70	.64	.59	.54	.50	.46	.42	.39	.36
10	.91	.82	.74	.68	.61	.56	.51	.46	.42	.39	.35	.32
11	.90	.80	.72	.65	.58	.53	.48	.43	.39	.35	.32	.29
12	.89	.79	.70	.62	.56	.50	.44	.40	.36	.32	.29	.26
13	.88	.77	.68	.60	.53	.47	.41	.37	.33	.29	.26	.23
14	.87	.76	.66	.58	.51	.44	.39	.34	.30	.26	.23	.20
15	.86	.74	.64	.56	.48	.42	.36	.32	.27	.24	.21	.18

At rate r After n years	13%	14%	15%	16%	17%	18%	19%	20%	30%	40%	50%
1	.88	.88	.87	.86	.85	.85	.84	.83	.77	.71	.67
2	.78	.77	.76	.74	.73	.72	.71	.69	.59	.51	.44
3	.69	.67	.66	.64	.62	.61	.59	.58	.46	.36	.30
4	.61	.59	.57	.55	.53	.52	.50	.48	.35	.26	.20
5	.54	.52	.50	.48	.46	.44	.42	.40	.27	.19	.13
6	.48	.46	.43	.41	.39	.37	.35	.33	.21	.13	.09
7	.43	.40	.38	.35	.33	.31	.30	.28	.16	.09	.06
8	.38	.35	.33	.31	.28	.27	.25	.23	.12	.07	.04
9	.33	.31	.28	.26	.24	.23	.21	.19	.09	.05	.03
10	.29	.27	.25	.23	.21	.19	.18	.16	.07	.03	.02
11	.26	.24	.21	.20	.18	.16	.15	.13	.06	.02	.01
12	.23	.21	.19	.17	.15	.14	.12	.11	.04	.02	.008
13	.20	.18	.16	.15	.13	.12	.10	.09	.03	.013	.005
14	.18	.16	.14	.13	.11	.10	.09	.08	.03	.009	.003
15	.16	.14	.12	.11	.09	.08	.07	.06	.02	.006	.002

Cumulative present value of £1

Years	1%	2%	3%	4%	5%	6%	7%	8%	9%	10%	11%	12%
1	.99	.98	.97	.96	.95	.94	.94	.93	.92	.91	.90	.89
2	1.97	1.94	1.91	1.89	1.86	1.83	1.81	1.78	1.76	1.74	1.71	1.69
3	2.94	2.88	2.83	2.78	2.72	2.67	2.62	2.58	2.53	2.49	2.44	2.40
4	3.90	3.81	3.72	3.63	3.55	3.47	3.39	3.31	3.24	3.17	3.10	3.04
5	4.85	4.71	4.58	4.45	4.33	4.21	4.10	3.99	3.89	3.79	3.70	3.61
6	5.80	5.60	5.42	5.24	5.08	4.92	4.77	4.62	4.49	4.36	4.23	4.11
7	6.73	6.47	6.23	6.00	5.79	5.58	5.39	5.21	5.03	4.87	4.71	4.56
8	7.65	7.33	7.02	6.73	6.46	6.21	5.97	5.75	5.54	5.34	5.15	4.97
9	8.57	8.16	7.79	7.44	7.11	6.80	6.52	6.25	6.00	5.76	5.54	5.33
10	9.47	8.98	8.53	8.11	7.72	7.36	7.02	6.71	6.42	6.15	5.89	5.65
11	10.37	9.79	9.25	8.76	8.31	7.89	7.50	7.14	6.81	6.50	5.21	5.94
12	11.26	10.58	9.95	9.39	8.86	8.38	7.94	7.54	7.16	6.81	5.49	6.19
13	12.13	11.35	10.64	9.99	9.39	8.85	8.36	7.90	7.49	7.10	6.80	6.42
14	13.00	12.11	11.30	10.56	9.90	9.30	8.75	8.24	7.79	7.37	6.98	6.63
15	13.87	12.85	11.94	11.12	10.38	9.71	9.11	8.56	8.06	7.61	7.19	6.81

Years	Net rate of interest assumed										
	13%	14%	15%	16%	17%	18%	19%	20%	30%	40%	50%
1	.89	.88	.87	.86	.85	.85	.84	.83	.77	.71	.67
2	1.67	1.65	1.63	1.61	1.59	1.57	1.55	1.53	1.36	1.22	1.11
3	2.36	2.32	2.28	2.25	2.21	2.17	2.14	2.11	1.81	1.59	1.41
4	2.97	2.91	2.86	2.80	2.74	2.69	2.64	2.59	2.17	1.85	1.61
5	3.52	3.43	3.35	3.27	3.20	3.13	3.06	2.99	2.44	2.04	1.74
6	4.00	3.89	3.78	3.69	3.59	3.50	3.41	3.33	2.64	2.17	1.82
7	4.42	4.29	4.16	4.04	3.92	3.81	3.71	3.61	2.80	2.26	1.88
8	4.80	4.64	4.49	4.34	4.21	4.08	3.95	3.84	2.93	2.33	1.92
9	5.13	4.95	4.77	4.61	4.45	4.30	4.16	4.03	3.02	2.38	1.95
10	5.43	5.22	5.02	4.83	4.66	4.49	4.34	4.19	3.09	2.41	1.97
11	5.69	5.45	5.23	5.03	4.83	4.66	4.49	4.33	3.15	2.44	1.98
12	5.92	5.66	5.42	5.20	4.99	4.79	4.61	4.44	3.19	2.46	1.99
13	6.12	5.84	5.58	5.34	5.12	4.91	4.71	4.53	3.22	2.47	1.99
14	6.30	6.00	5.72	5.47	5.23	5.01	4.80	4.61	3.25	2.48	1.99
15	6.46	6.14	5.85	5.58	5.32	5.09	4.88	4.68	3.27	2.48	2.00

Random numbers

03 47 43 73 86	36 96 47 36 61	46 98 63 71 62	33 26 16 80 45	60 11 14 10 95
97 74 24 67 62	42 81 14 57 20	42 53 32 37 32	27 07 36 07 51	24 51 79 89 73
16 76 62 27 66	56 50 26 71 07	32 90 79 78 53	13 55 38 58 59	88 97 54 14 10
12 56 85 99 26	96 96 68 27 31	05 03 72 93 15	57 12 10 14 21	99 26 49 81 76
55 59 56 35 64	38 54 82 46 22	31 62 43 09 90	06 18 44 32 53	23 83 01 30 30
16 22 77 94 39	49 54 43 54 82	17 37 93 23 78	87 35 20 96 43	84 26 34 91 64
84 42 17 53 31	57 24 55 06 88	77 04 74 47 67	21 76 33 50 25	83 92 12 06 76
63 01 63 78 59	16 95 55 67 19	98 10 50 71 75	12 86 73 58 07	44 39 52 38 79
33 21 12 34 29	78 64 58 07 82	52 42 07 44 38	15 51 00 13 42	99 66 02 79 54
57 60 86 32 44	09 47 27 96 54	49 17 46 09 62	90 52 84 77 27	08 02 73 43 28
18 18 07 92 46	44 17 16 58 09	79 83 86 19 62	06 76 50 03 10	55 23 64 05 05
26 62 38 97 75	84 16 07 44 99	83 11 46 32 24	20 14 85 88 45	10 93 72 88 71
23 42 40 64 74	82 97 77 77 81	07 45 32 14 08	32 98 94 07 72	93 85 79 10 75
52 36 28 19 95	50 92 26 11 97	00 56 76 31 38	80 22 02 53 53	86 60 42 04 53
37 85 94 35 12	83 39 50 08 30	42 34 07 96 88	54 42 06 87 98	35 85 29 48 39
70 29 17 12 13	40 33 20 38 26	13 89 51 03 74	17 76 37 13 04	07 74 21 19 30
56 62 18 37 35	96 83 50 87 75	97 12 25 93 47	70 33 24 03 54	97 77 46 44 80
99 49 57 22 77	88 42 95 45 72	16 64 36 16 00	04 43 18 66 79	94 77 24 21 90
16 08 15 04 72	33 27 14 34 09	45 59 34 68 49	12 72 07 34 45	99 27 72 95 14
31 16 93 32 43	50 27 89 87 19	20 15 37 00 49	52 85 66 60 44	38 68 88 11 80
68 34 30 13 70	55 74 30 77 40	44 22 78 84 26	04 33 46 09 52	68 07 97 06 57
74 57 25 65 76	59 29 97 68 60	71 91 38 67 54	13 58 18 24 76	15 54 65 95 52
27 42 37 86 53	48 55 90 65 72	96 57 69 36 10	96 46 92 42 45	97 60 49 04 91
00 39 68 29 61	66 37 32 20 30	77 84 57 03 29	10 45 65 04 26	11 04 96 67 24
29 94 98 94 24	68 49 69 10 82	53 75 91 93 30	34 25 20 57 27	40 48 73 51 92
16 90 82 66 59	83 62 64 11 12	67 19 00 71 74	60 47 21 29 68	02 02 37 03 31
11 27 94 75 06	06 09 19 74 66	02 94 37 34 02	76 70 90 30 86	38 45 94 30 38
35 24 10 16 20	33 32 51 26 38	79 78 45 04 91	16 92 53 56 16	02 75 50 95 98
38 23 16 86 38	42 38 97 01 50	87 75 66 81 41	40 01 74 91 62	48 51 84 08 32
31 96 25 91 47	96 44 33 49 13	34 86 82 53 91	00 52 43 48 85	27 55 26 89 62
66 67 40 67 14	64 05 71 95 86	11 05 65 09 68	76 83 20 37 90	57 16 00 11 66
14 90 84 45 11	75 73 88 05 90	52 27 41 14 86	22 98 12 22 08	07 52 74 95 80
68 05 51 18 00	33 96 02 75 19	07 60 62 93 55	59 33 82 43 90	49 37 38 44 59
20 46 78 73 90	97 51 40 14 02	04 02 33 31 08	39 54 16 49 36	47 95 93 13 30
64 19 58 97 79	15 06 15 93 20	01 90 10 75 06	40 78 78 89 62	02 67 74 17 33
05 26 93 70 60	22 35 85 15 13	92 03 51 59 77	59 56 78 06 83	52 91 05 70 74
47 97 10 88 23	09 98 42 99 64	61 71 62 99 15	06 51 29 16 93	58 05 77 09 51
68 71 86 85 85	54 87 66 47 54	73 32 08 11 12	44 95 92 63 16	29 56 24 29 48
26 99 61 65 53	58 37 78 80 70	42 10 50 67 42	32 17 55 85 74	94 44 67 16 94
14 65 52 68 75	87 59 36 22 41	26 78 63 06 55	13 08 27 01 50	15 29 39 39 43
17 53 77 58 71	71 41 61 50 72	12 41 94 96 26	44 95 27 36 99	02 96 74 30 83
90 26 59 21 19	23 52 23 33 12	96 93 02 18 39	07 02 18 36 07	25 99 32 70 23
41 23 52 55 99	31 04 49 69 96	10 47 48 45 88	13 41 43 89 20	97 17 14 49 17
60 20 50 81 69	31 99 73 68 68	35 81 33 03 76	24 30 12 48 60	18 99 10 72 34
91 25 38 60 90	94 58 28 41 36	45 37 59 03 09	90 35 57 29 12	82 62 54 65 60
34 50 57 74 37	98 80 33 00 91	09 77 93 19 82	74 94 80 04 04	45 07 31 66 49
85 22 04 39 43	73 81 53 94 79	33 62 46 86 28	08 31 54 46 31	53 94 13 38 47
09 79 13 77 48	73 82 97 22 21	05 03 27 24 83	72 89 44 05 60	35 80 39 94 88
88 75 80 18 14	22 95 75 42 49	39 32 82 22 49	02 48 07 70 37	16 04 61 67 87
90 96 23 70 00	39 00 03 06 90	55 85 78 38 36	94 37 30 69 32	90 89 00 76 33

Index